DISS & DISTRICT

THROUGH TIME

Elizabeth Walne

AMBERLEY PUBLISHING

First published 2012

Amberley Publishing
The Hill, Stroud, Gloucestershire, GL5 4EP
www.amberley-books.com

ISBN 978 1 4456 1143 3 (print)
ISBN 978 1 4456 1167 9 (ebook)

British Library Cataloguing in Publication Data.
A catalogue record for this book is available from the British Library.

Typesetting by Amberley Publishing.
Printed in Great Britain.

Introduction

'Diss, which gives name to this hundred, is a small but pleasant and well-built market town, on the acclivities of a deep lake, or mere, on the north side of the vale of the River Waveney, which divides it from Suffolk, 22 miles SSW of Norwich, 23 miles N by W of Ipswich, and 91 miles NE by N of London.'

And so begins *White's Directory* of 1845's introduction to the market town of Diss, now labelled the 'Gateway to the Waveney Valley'.

Having grown up in Badingham, gone to Thomas Mills High School in Framlingham, studied at UEA in Norwich and lived in Wymondham, I would describe myself as a local girl. I've been visiting Diss since I was little, when I regularly went along to market days on a Friday with my Mum and Dad. Diss has strong connections with my 'home town' of Framlingham, the Town Estate there generating an income for Diss from the days of Elizabeth I. Going backwards, I can trace much of my ancestry to the area (the Walnes for instance once being local landowners) and currently, I also write a column for a local newspaper on researching family history. For all these reasons, I jumped at the chance to put together this book. Hopefully it will be the first of many local publications combining my loves of genealogy, social history and photography.

The oft-quoted Sir John Betjeman knew little of Diss but 'a lonely railway station' and 'the headquarters of the British Goat Society' before he got to know it better and decided it was, as he hoped, the 'perfect English country town' (*Diss Town Guide*, 1975/76). Asking around as I planned this book, I tried to find out what local people liked best about the place. The answers were varied, and included the following: the Market Place; the Mere; antiques' shopping; the sales; the countryside; local pubs; and most of all – the community.

Going back to 1845, *White's* was perhaps not quite so complimentary, stating that 'the early annals of Diss are barren of all that is momentous; but we find that the plague raged here in the year 1579'!

I enjoyed visiting Diss and District this summer immensely, and took photographs on seven different visits, occasionally accompanied by my husband and friends. This work includes the parish of Diss and ancient bordering parishes of Roydon, Bressingham, Shelfanger, Winfarthing, Tibenham, Gissing, Burston, Thelveton and Scole, not all of which are today civil or ecclesiastical parishes in their own right.

For the 'old' images, I reviewed well over 1,000 photographs, prints, maps, pamphlets, drawings and paintings dating from the 1700s through to the early days of photography in the mid-nineteenth century and right through to the 1990s. Obviously not all of them appear here, but I have tried to include a variety of dates and collections. Inside, we get a sneak peek at the Victorian Diss and District that our great grandparents might remember, as well as images from living memory for some – the 1940s, 1960s and even 1980s. I cannot claim to be one that remembers even the 1980s views, but I have found the process fascinating nonetheless, and hope others of my age will also enjoy looking at the areas in a different way.

The rich pictorial archives represented in this volume hopefully provide something of interest for everyone with a connection to Diss. The town is many things to many people, and while it would prove impossible to include a picture of every building in Diss and surrounding parishes, I hope I have included images that capture the spirit of both the people and the surroundings in this part of South Norfolk.

I hope you enjoy it, Elizabeth.

Acknowledgements

Norfolk as a whole has an incredible pictorial archive, and I have made much use of the resources at the Norfolk Heritage Centre (see Picture Norfolk, www.picture.norfolk.gov.uk) and the Norfolk Record Office to find inspiration for this volume, as well as contacting local groups and organisations.

The Norfolk Heritage Centre is home to the Norfolk local studies collection and is situated in the Norfolk and Norwich Millennium Library. The Norfolk Record Office is at the Archive Centre on Martineau Lane. Their references take the form 'NRO, catalogue reference' and their catalogue can be searched at www.archives.norfolk.gov.uk.

My grateful thanks go to my colleagues at both the Norfolk Record Office and Norfolk Heritage Centre for their support. Particular thanks go to Clare Everitt for all her advice and patience when I spoke of nothing but Diss images in the Picture Norfolk collections for half a year. The Picture Norfolk images were provided courtesy of the Norfolk County Council Library and Information Service. Also to Gordon, Val and Janice for their photograph-dating abilities and everybody else who allowed me to outstay my welcome and set up home in both search rooms for many more voluntary hours a week than I'm actually contracted to be there normally! Completing my thanks to Norfolk County Council staff, my grateful appreciation to Alison Yardy of the Norfolk Historic Environment Service for her help with local aerial photographs, and for going the extra mile to assist me.

I am also very grateful to the Cleer S Alger Trust and trustee Stephen Govier for identifying images found in Norfolk Record Office deposits (MS 10824 and MS 10825) as Alger photographs, and their permission for me to reproduce nine of them here in all their glory. Thanks too to Jonathan Plunkett for his generous permission for me to use his father's outstanding Norfolk images in this book (see www.georgeplunkett.co.uk for more of his incredible photographs).

Thanks too to the Francis Frith Collection, Archant, English Heritage (for National Buildings Record) and Fielden and Mason for their permission to reproduce their images. Also a special mention to Claire Bolster and her family for allowing me to use a family wedding photograph taken at Burston, and to John Hutton at Diss Town Football Club for a modern team image and help identifying faces in the older image.

Of course I cannot forget the kind responses from others I contacted during this process, including Diss Museum, the Mary Evans Picture Collection and followers of my twitter account (@yrlocalhistory) and Facebook page.

Not all the images in the book have been traced, having been donated to Norfolk County Council over a period of many years. Having taken reasonable steps to identify copyright and reproduction rights, I apologise if I have unintentionally left the owner of a particular image unidentified and would ask you to contact me if you have further information.

Any mistakes are my own, and again I apologise if anything contained is found to be incorrect.

I thank my family and friends for their patience, proofreading and car-identifying skills (the latter two mean you, Dad!) and their occasional appearance in photographs to create modern-day parallels to older images.

Last but not least, I thank you, the reader, for taking the time to glance through this book. I very much hope you enjoy it, and I dearly hope some of you will decide to do some of your own local research and make use of our fantastic local archives and collections in so doing.

Until next time, Elizabeth.

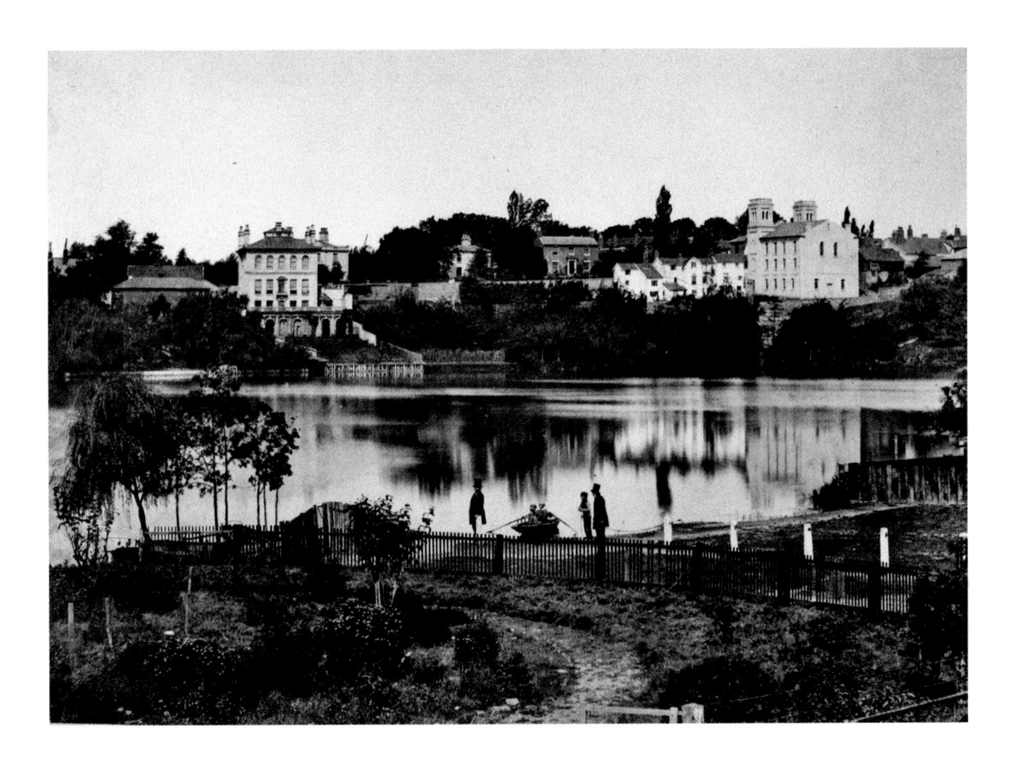

The Mere

Diss came to be because of the Mere, making this the perfect place to start. *White's Directory* of 1845 tells us that the water was once 'considered to be of unfathomable depth, and supposed by some to have been the crater of a volcano'. On accurate measurement in 1835 however, it was found to cover just over 5 acres, at an average depth of just over 17 feet. The Victorian image above was taken a couple of decades later, and makes a wonderful juxtaposition to the newer view. (Cleer S Alger Trust; NRO, MS 10824)

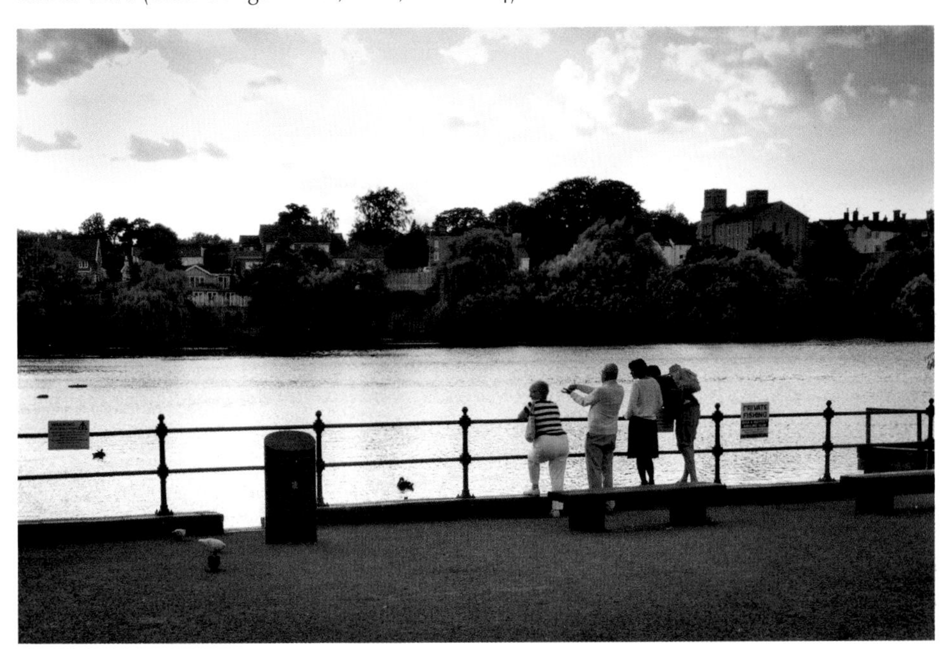

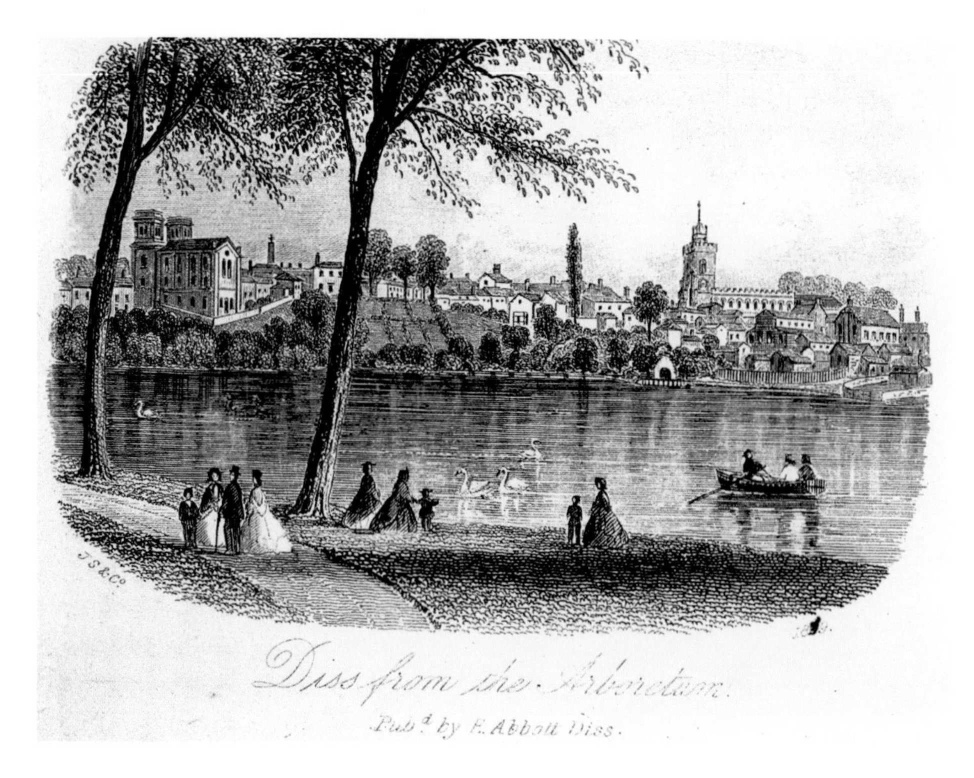

'From the Arboretum'

This image, entitled 'Diss from the Arboretum', shows our Victorian ancestors enjoying the Park Field and Mere from what were once ornamental gardens, 'a delightful contrast with the expansive sheet of water below'. The new image was taken from a slightly different angle, but the Baptist chapel and St Mary the Virgin church are still very much focal points when looking across from this spot on the modern path around the Mere, which now includes viewing/fishing platforms. (NRO, MS 10825)

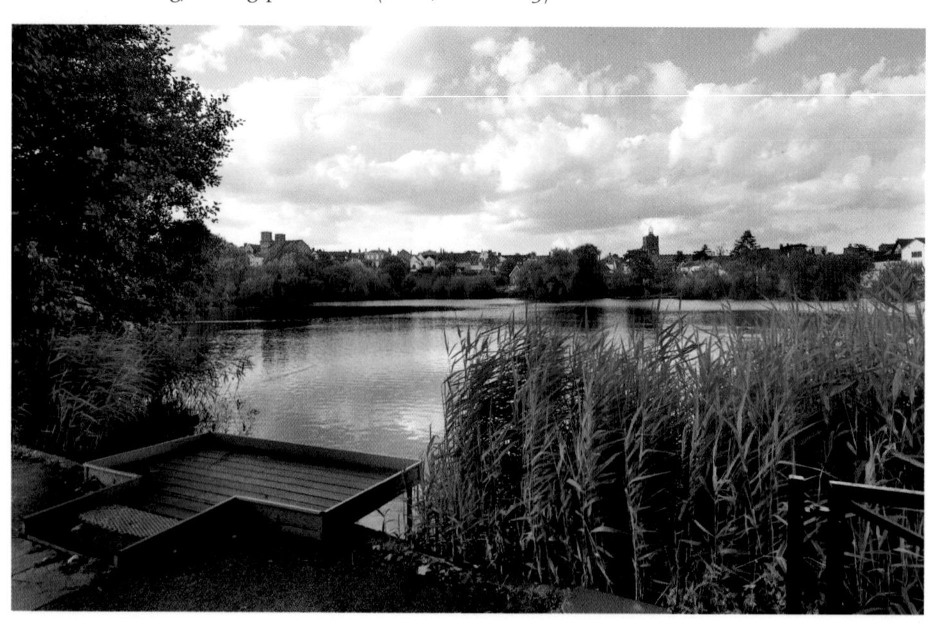

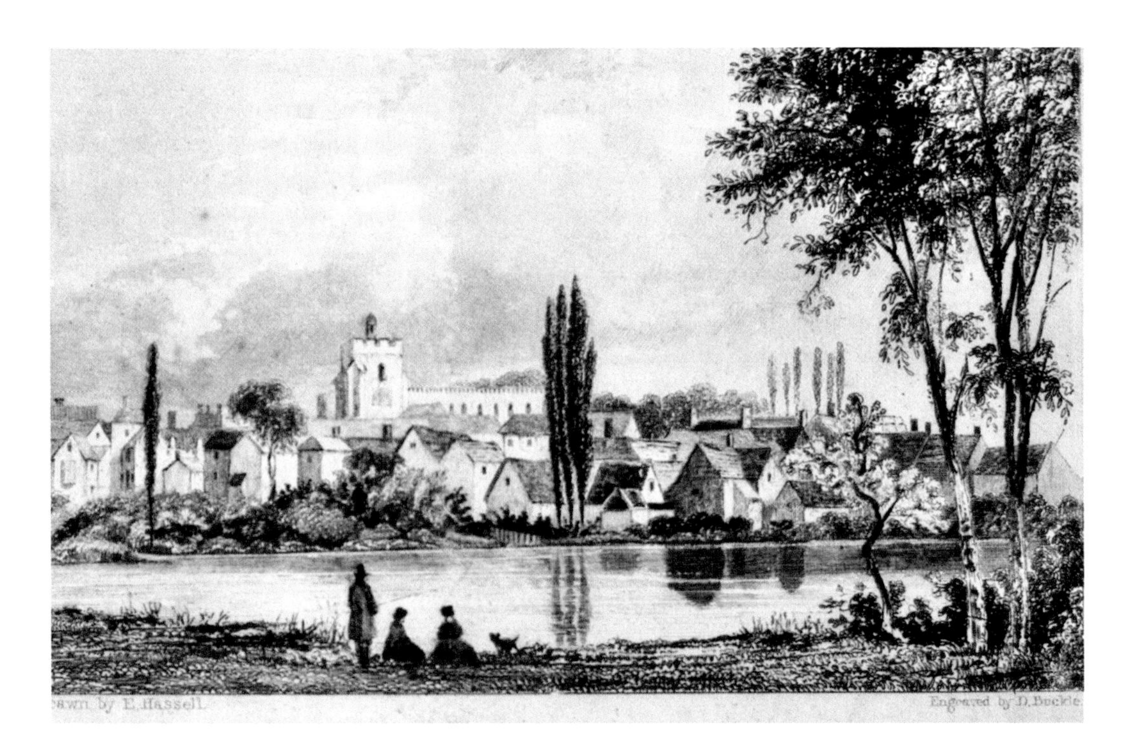

Mere Engraving
This drawing, by E. Hassell, engraved by D. Buckle, shows a peaceful scene across the Mere. In 1845, it was described as having a 'muddy bottom well stored with eels, and a rare fish called chasers'. Until 1912, when the waterworks were built, most of Diss' sewers flowed into here and water for 'culinary purposes' had to come from wells. Now much cleaner, a fountain is often seen playing in the centre, funded by the Diss and District Rotary Club in 2005. (NRO, MS 10824)

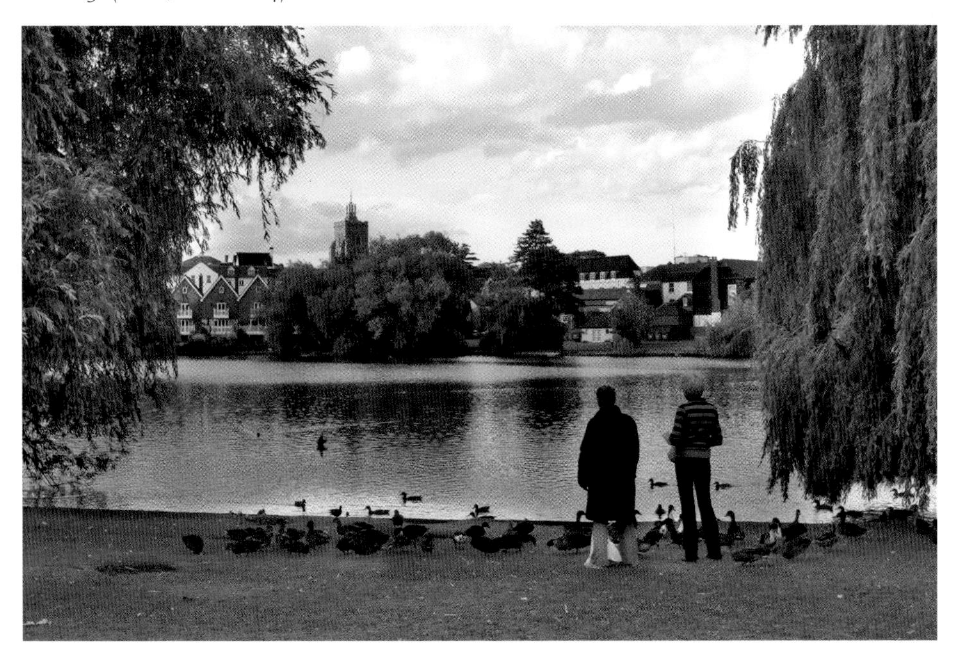

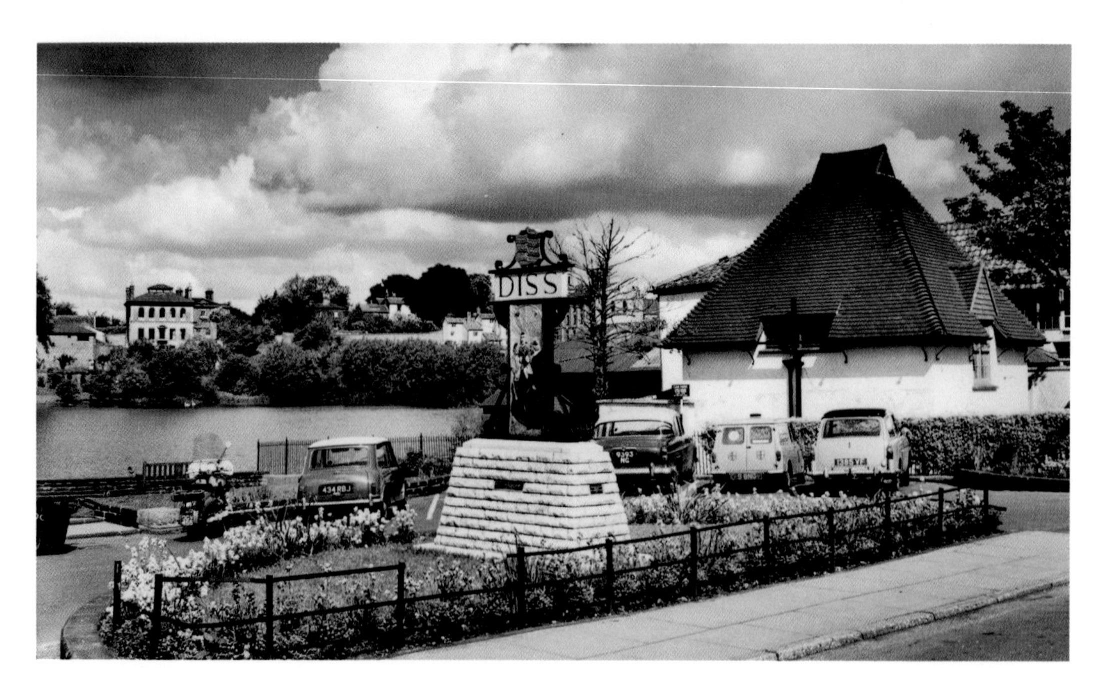

Mere's Mouth

At first glance, this scene has changed little. Look closer though, and the prominent form of Grassmere House, built in the 1850s, has all but gone, its arches alone remaining. A long-time meeting place for locals and tourists alike, on the south side of the Mere, as early as 1864, *White's Directory* describes 'a plot of land tastefully laid out ... containing a number of seats ... TL Taylor Esq. permits the townspeople to use it as a promenade'. (The Francis Frith Collection)

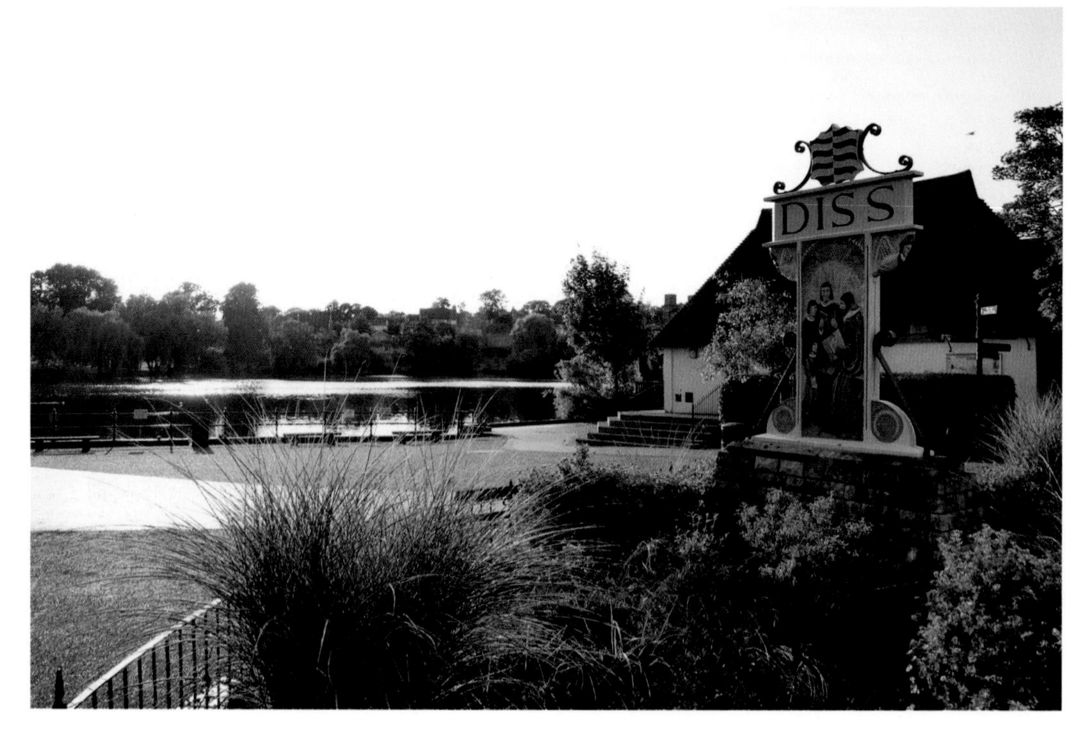

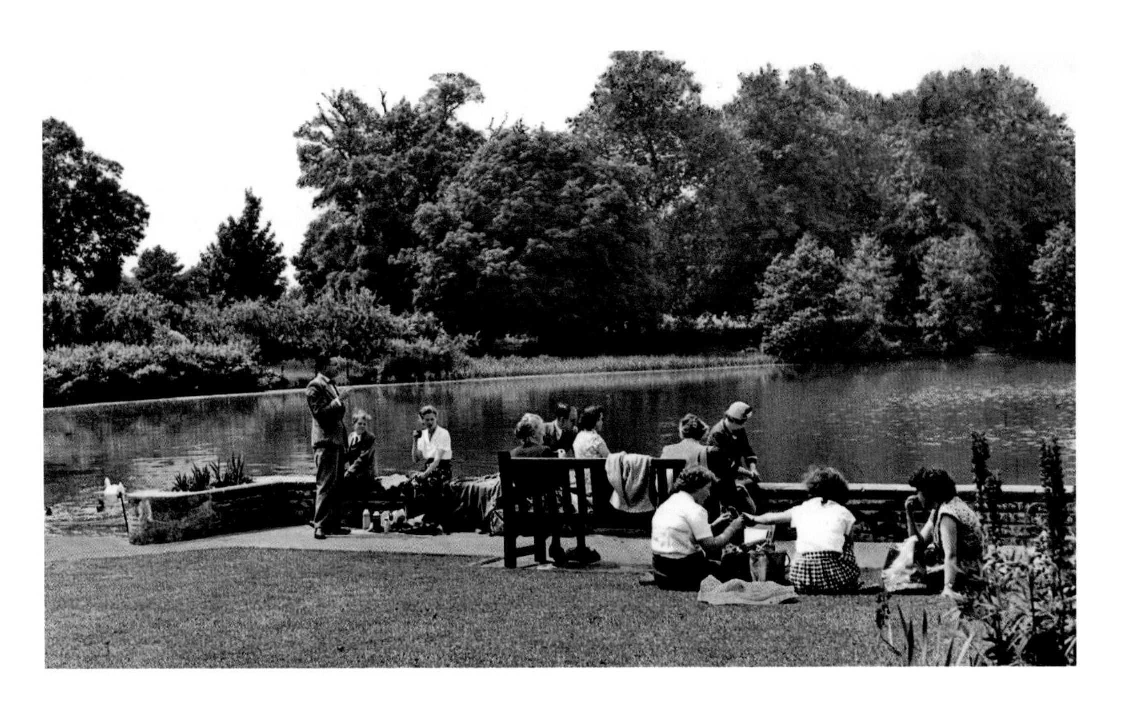

Picnickers

The Mere has been used for many things over the centuries: a place to water animals on the way to market, a place to source water to quench fires (as was the case during a terrible fire in 1640), and particularly in the last 200 years, a place for leisure. There are more than sixty years between these images. The railings and the conversation topics might be new, but this is a place that still draws great numbers of people for a picnic and a chat. (The Francis Frith Collection)

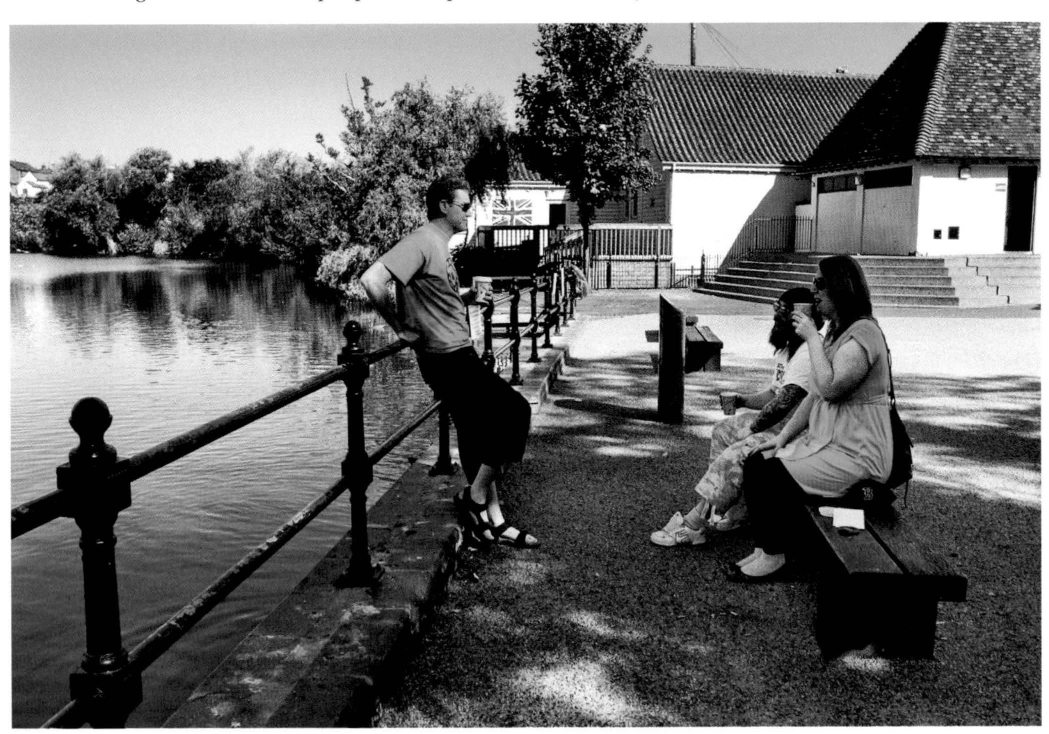

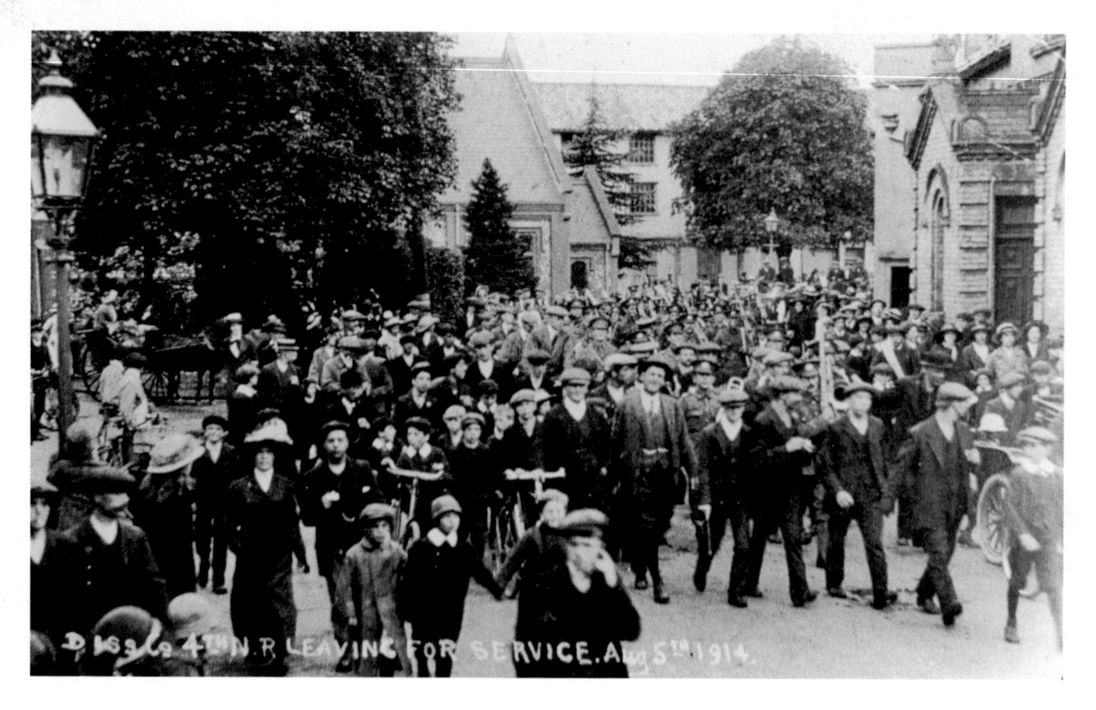

Leaving for the Great War

Moving onto Mere Street, this image shows the Diss Company, 4th Volunteer Battalion of the Norfolk Regiment, leaving for service on 5 August 1914. Sadly, we know over 100 Diss men would not return. Of the buildings shown, the church hall (behind them) and the Methodist chapel (to their right) have been lost to history. The building between them, too, has gone, replaced with a relatively modern supermarket development. (Untraced; part of image collection donated to NCC)

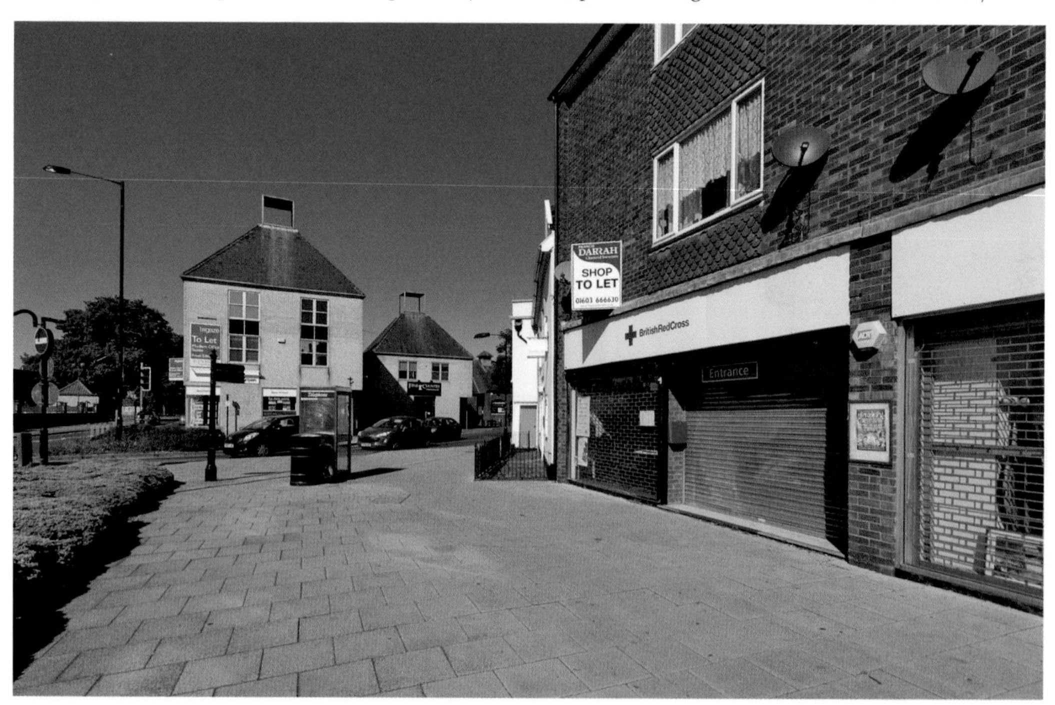

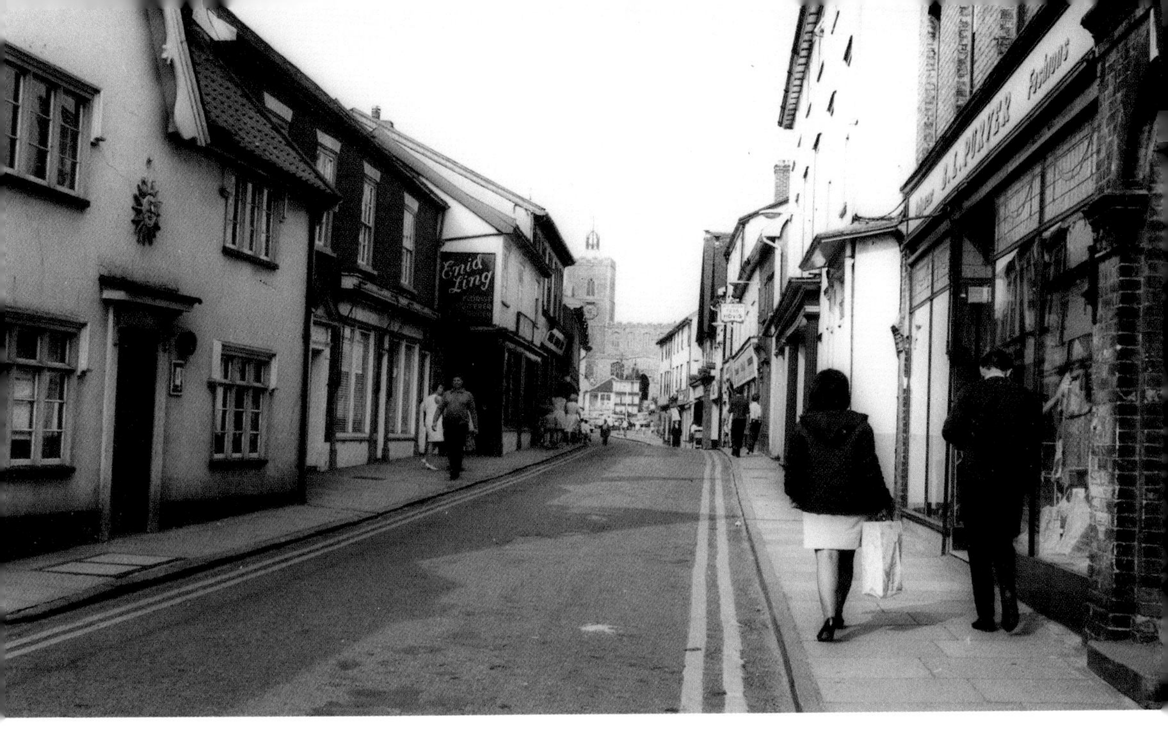

Mere Street

Further on, we come to what was formally known as the Sun or Rising Sun (see above the door in the older image). The Waterfront Inn, with a lovely mere view, is one of several old pubs which survive in today's Diss. This particular Inn dates back as far as the seventeenth century. We also see, beyond the pub in the older image, Enid Ling's (florist, fruiterer and greengrocer) and across the road, B. L. Purver fashions. (The Francis Frith Collection)

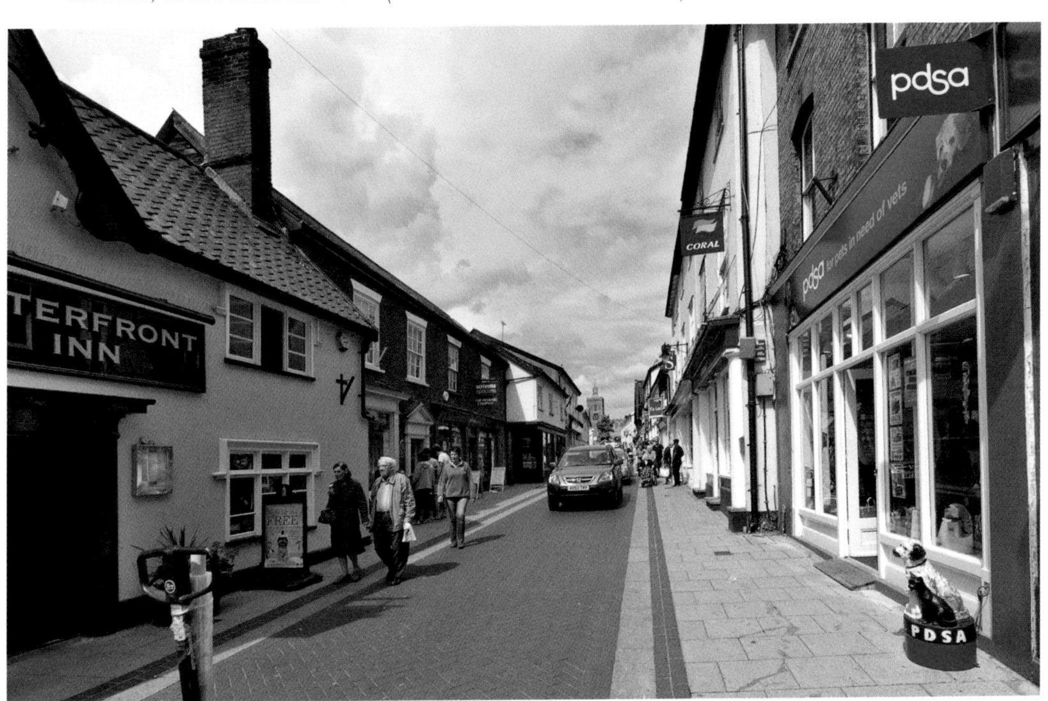

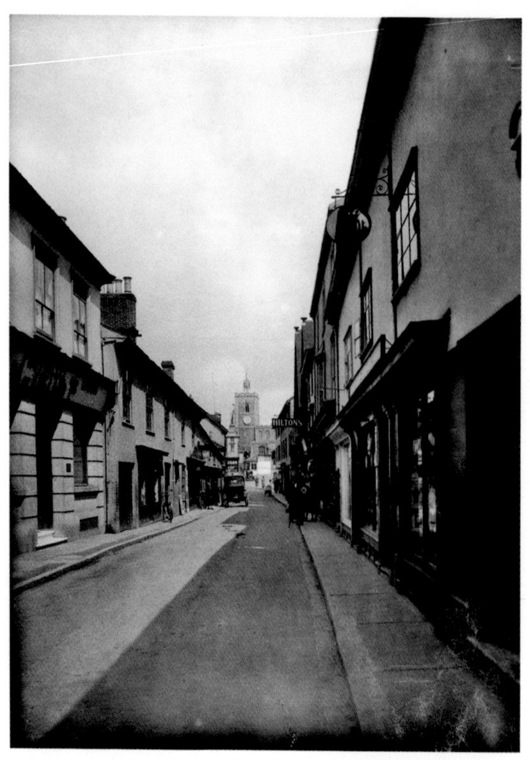

1920s Shopping
In some ways, the 1925 image we see here is not so far removed from the modern-day scene. Although the shop fronts have changed a little and new stores have moved in – often chain stores replacing older independent ones – the buildings themselves have largely survived in this part of Mere Street. Most are still recognisable as those that formerly sold all sorts of different goods – from boots by Hilton's to gramophones by His Master's Voice. (The Francis Frith Collection)

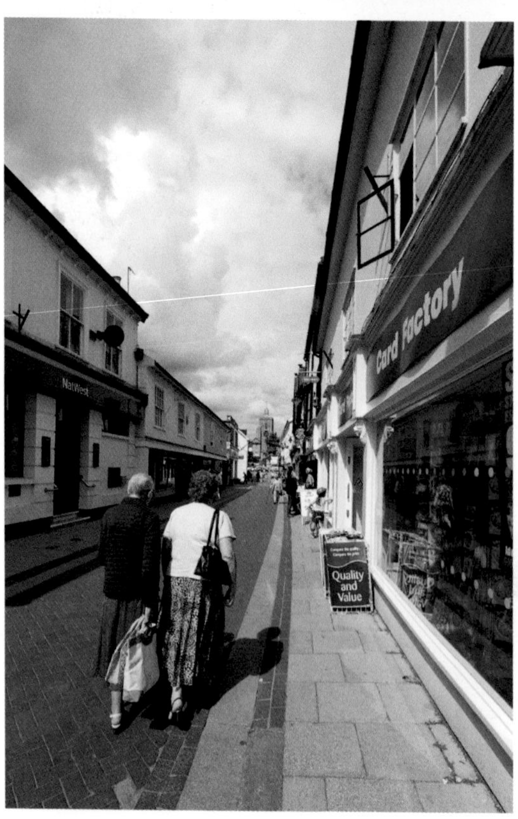

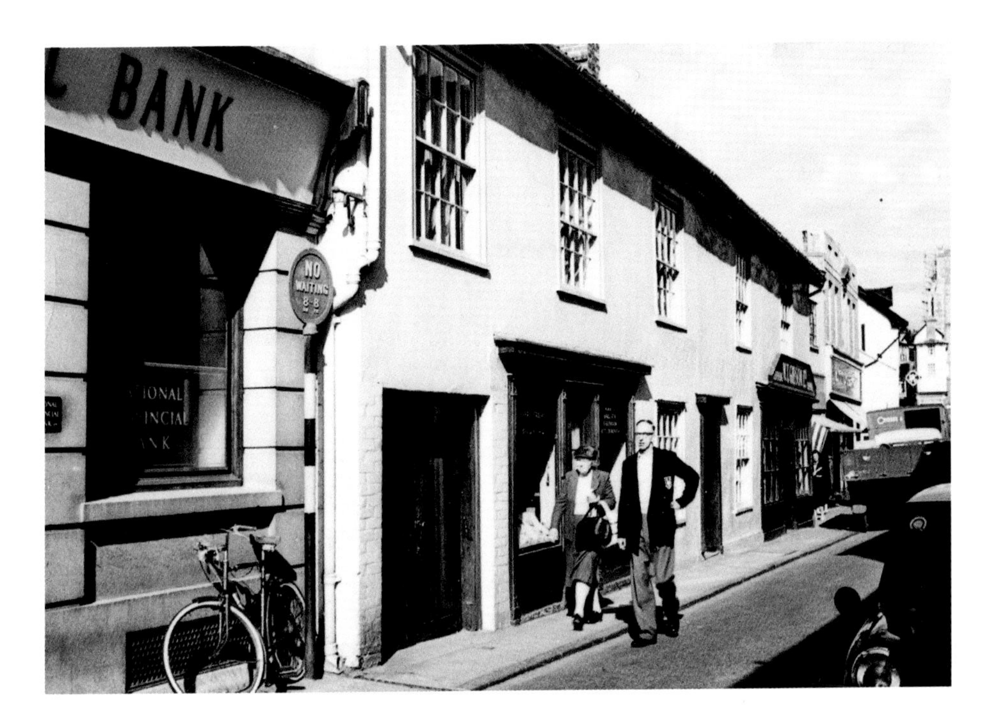

Surveyors' Images

Most of the collection of surveyors' photographs at the Norfolk Heritage Centre were taken in the late 1950s and early 1960s. Wonderfully, they often contain 'before' and 'after' images. These two pictures are both 'old', but they show the change from a traditional shop front to the colonnades that are still on Mere Street today. I particularly love the fashions on show here and I also enjoy the 'Harleston, Fakenham, Attleborough' in Mr Grey's window – move over London, Paris and Milan! (NCC)

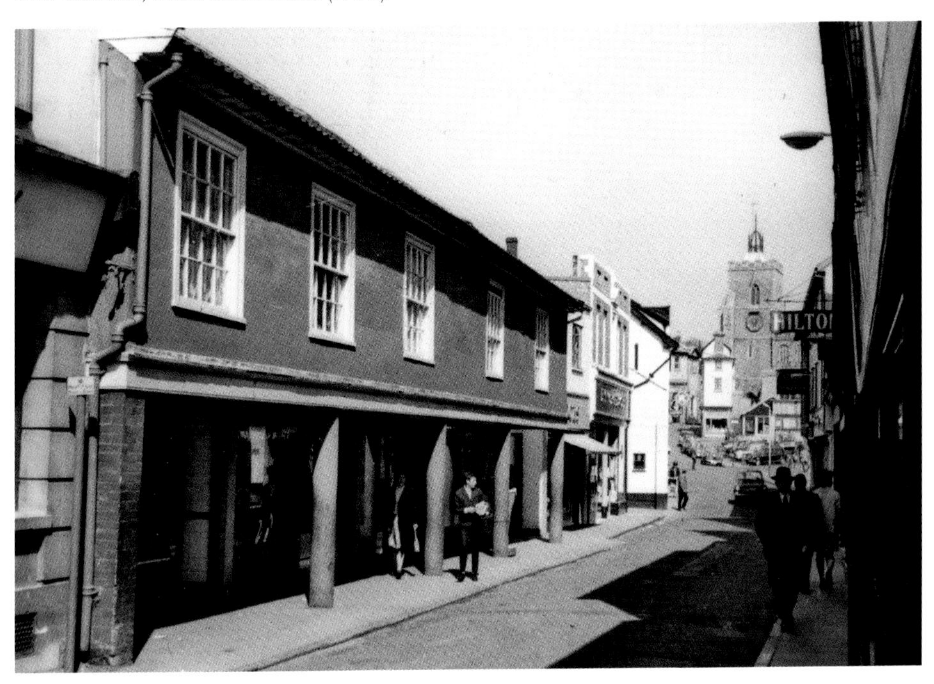

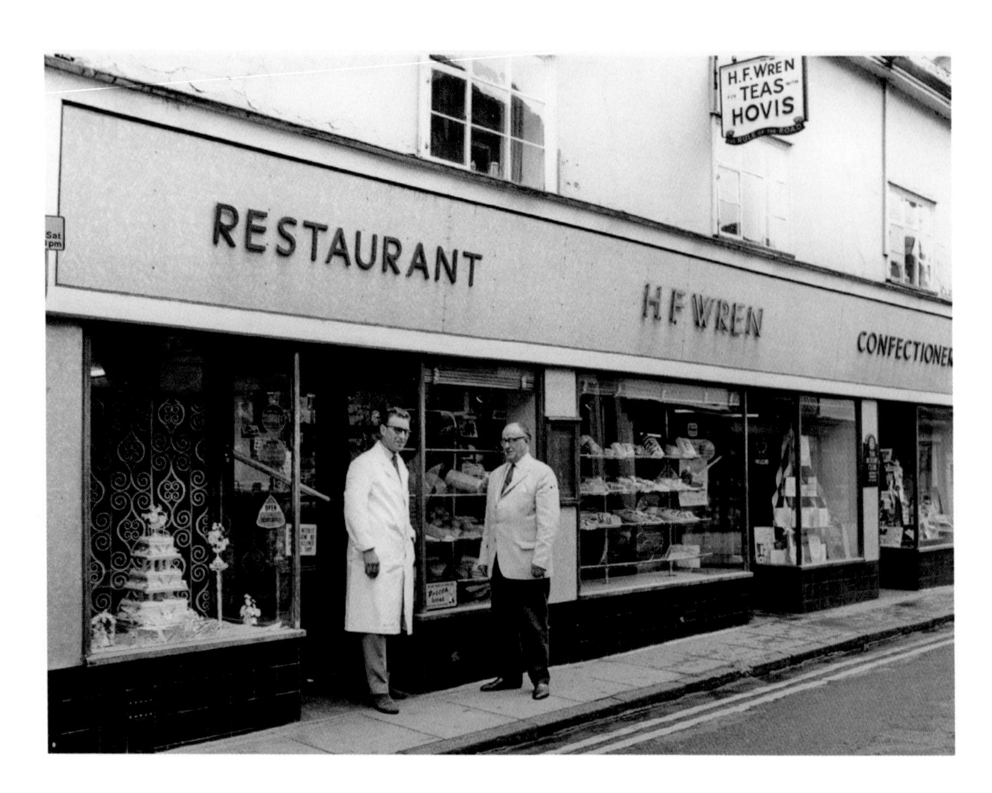

Wren's Restaurant

Continuing along Mere Street, we come to Wren's restaurant. Beyond what you would expect, the premises also played host to many a local gathering. Mr Wren's family provided a site for a new Catholic church in 1952 – the Most Holy Trinity on Stanley Road. This was only recently replaced by the church of St Henry Morse on Shelfanger Road. As the images show, the restaurant has now become an optician's and card shop. (NCC)

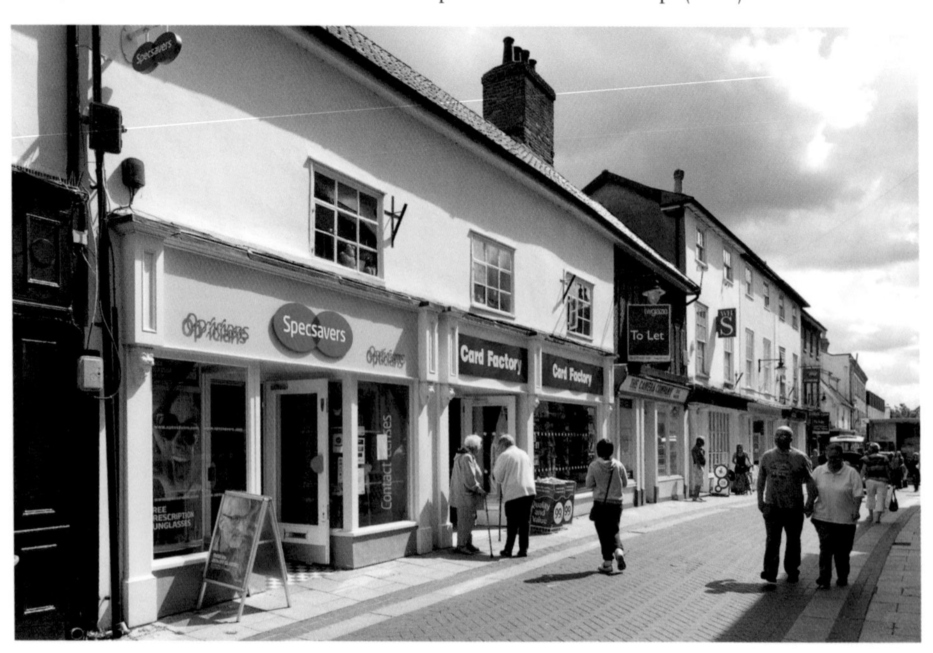

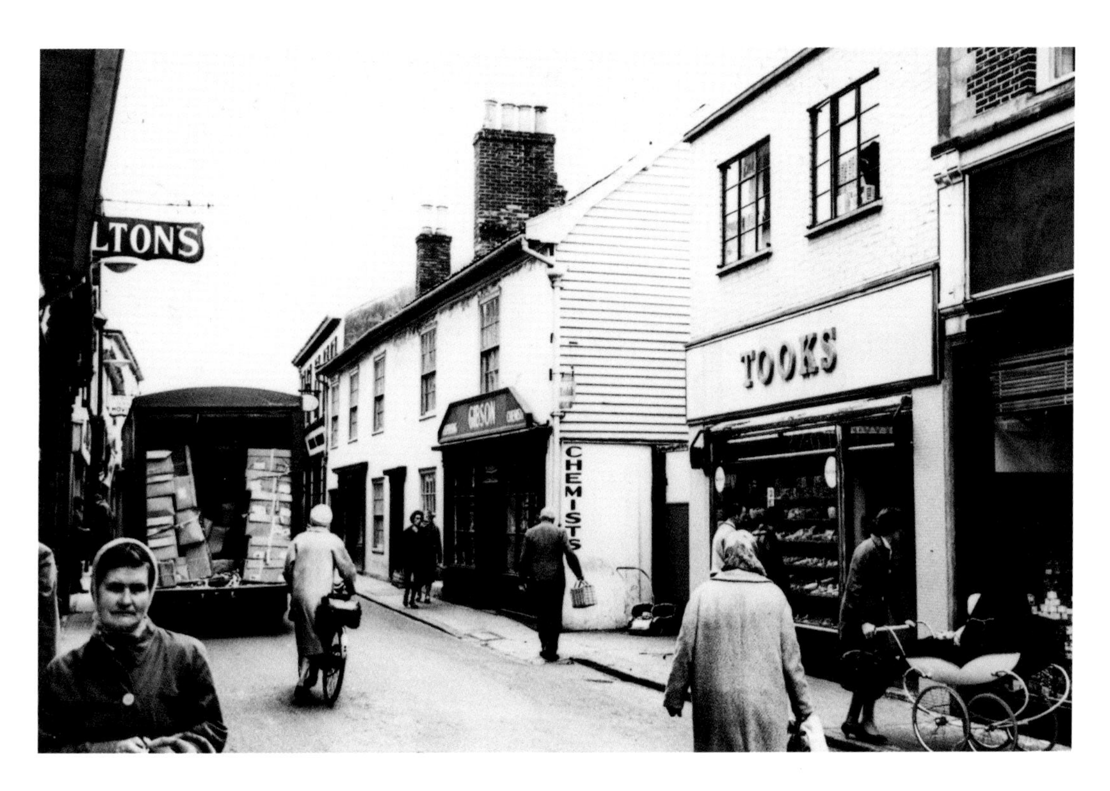

Mere Street

Another surveyor's photograph, here we see the now-colonnaded shops from the other direction. Tooks is now a takeaway and the site of Gibson's Chemist shop became the first of the line of shops which moved back beneath the colonnades, now home to several small retailers. Unfortunately I took this image early on a Sunday, but this is still a bustling shopping area. This part of Mere Street is still very recognisable today, if without such wonderful prams going up and down the thoroughfare! (NCC)

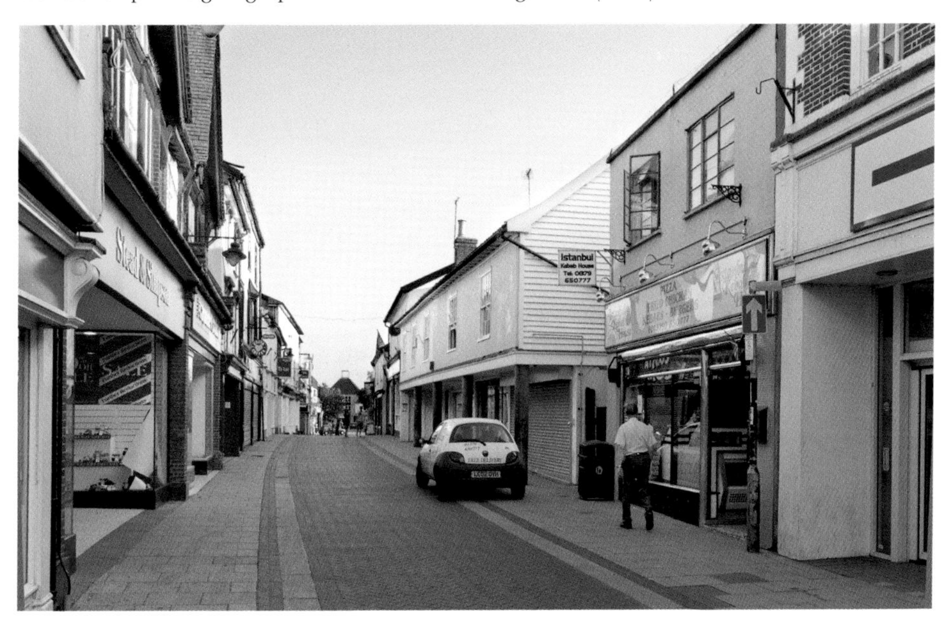

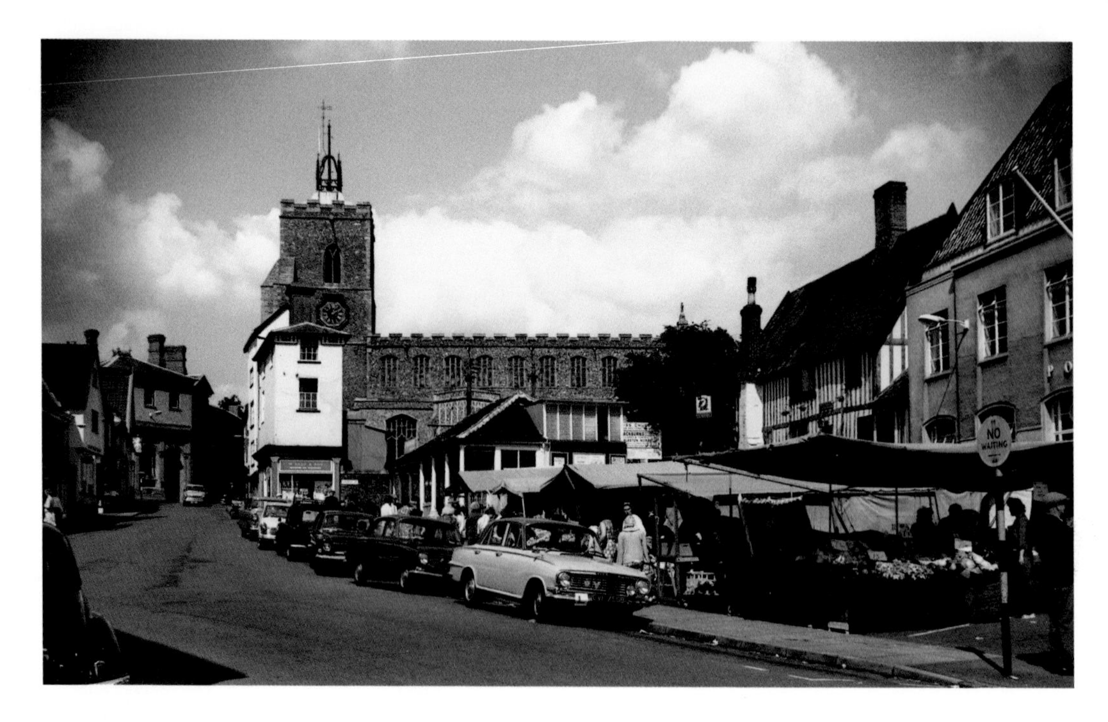

The Market Place

Entering the Market Place, these images show how the area has been remodelled since George Plunkett's visit in 1965. The market has been in the centre of Diss for well over 500 years and still takes place every Friday as it did in 1845 – at that time for the sale of 'corn, swine and provisions'. These days you can still buy provisions (the exact form and variety may have changed!), and market days are still important dates in the calendar for locals and visitors alike. (Plunkett)

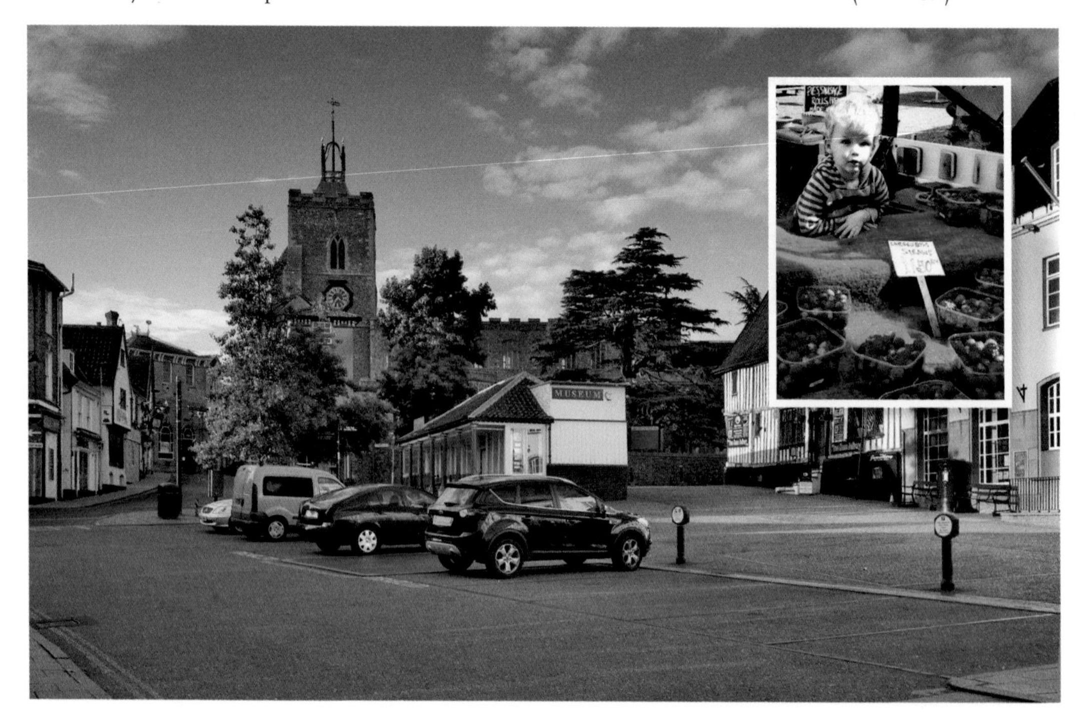

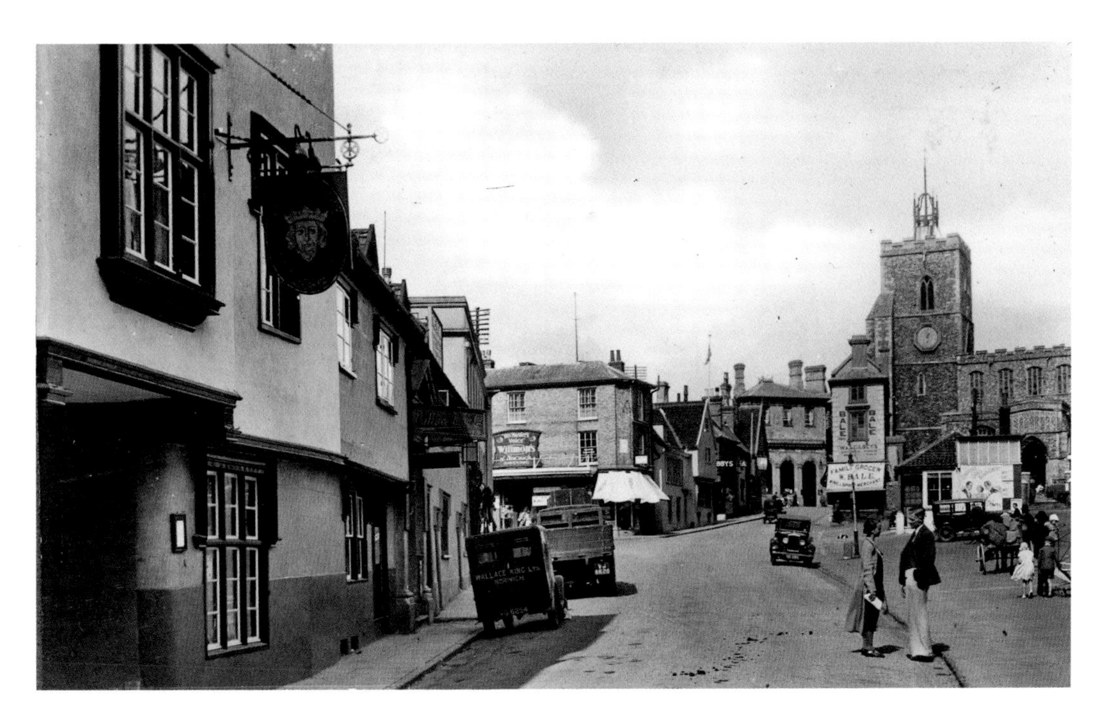

King's Head Hotel

This fabulous old image shows the King's Head Hotel before it ceased trading. Car number-plates suggest a late 1920s/early 1930s date, fitting with the W. Bale's grocer's awning near the church tower. Today, the pharmacy sign hangs from a similar hook and the premises sell not beer, but hangover remedies. Some of the shopfronts have changed a little, but otherwise, Diss Market Place retains its charm. (Untraced; part of image collection donated to NCC)

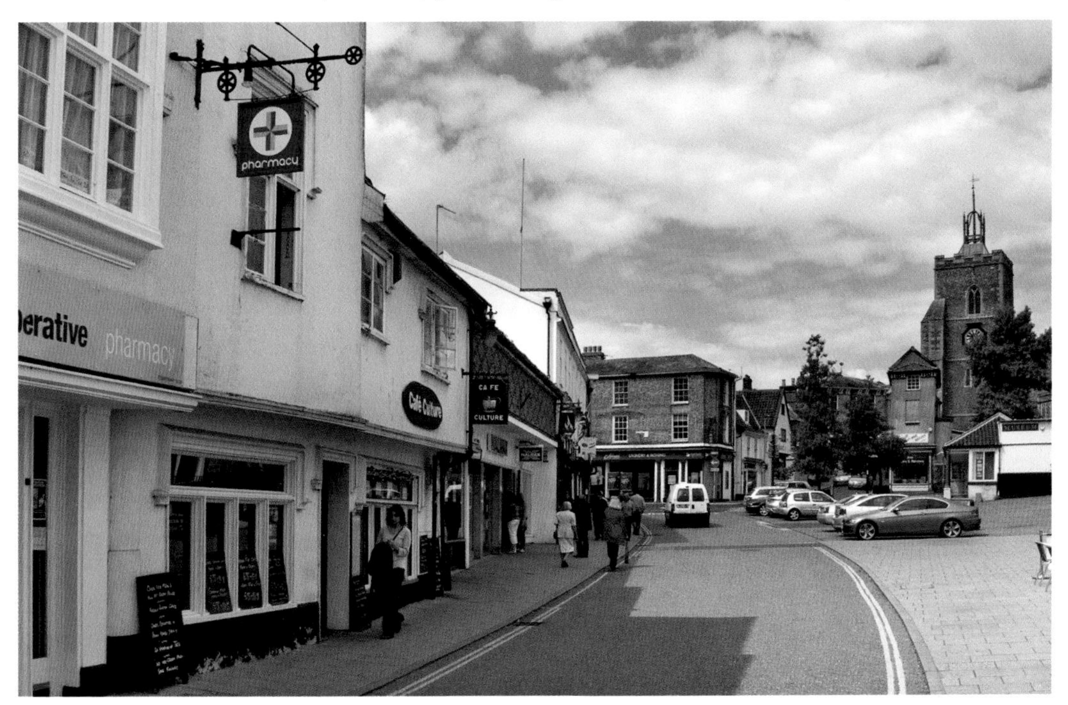

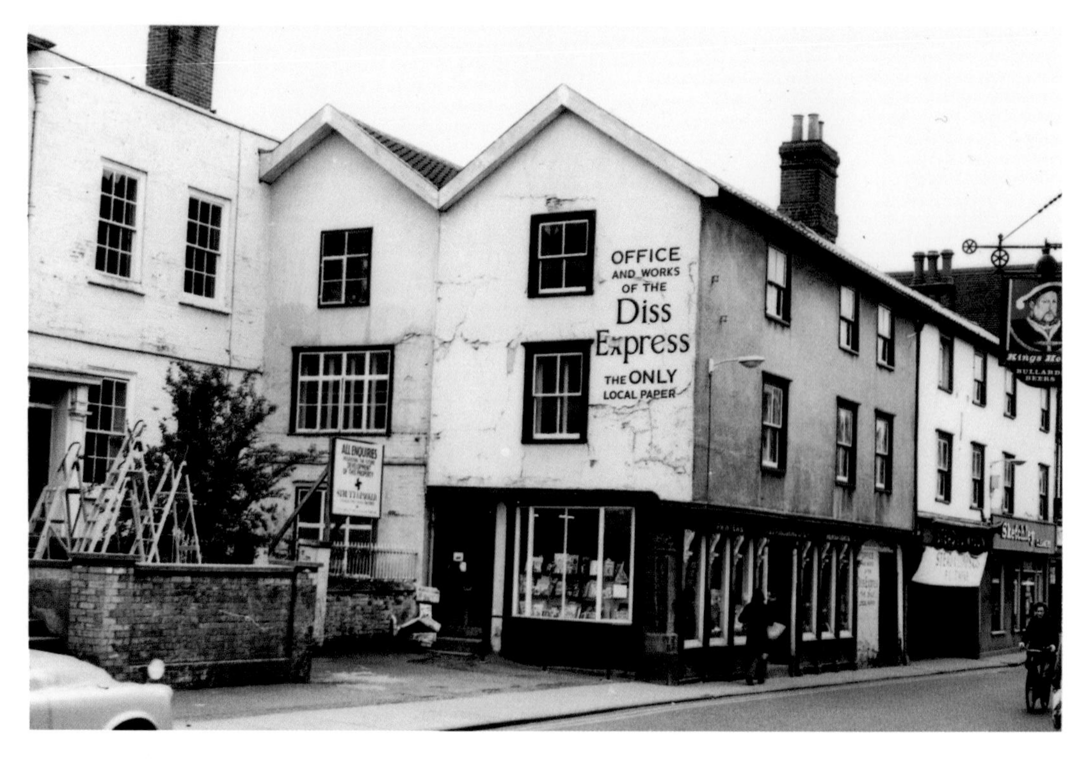

Diss Publishing

Looking back down Mere Street with the King's Head to the right, here we have the old 'Office and Works of the Diss Express' at the Diss Publishing company. The carved post at the corner of the building dates to the late 1400s and provides a clue to the age of the original timber-framed building under the Victorian shopfront. Today these shops are occupied by a health food store, a betting shop and a building society. (NCC)

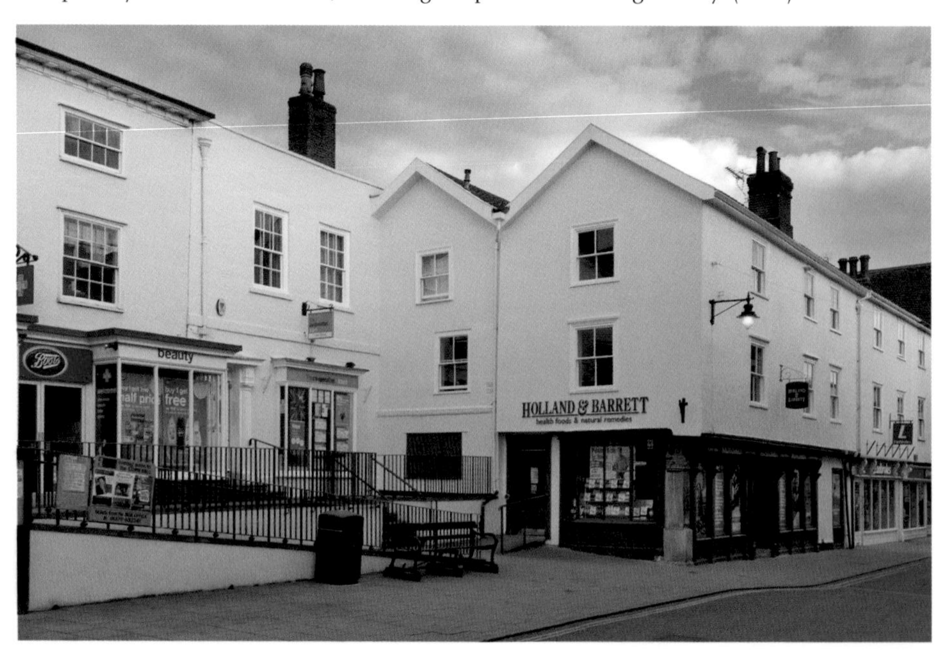

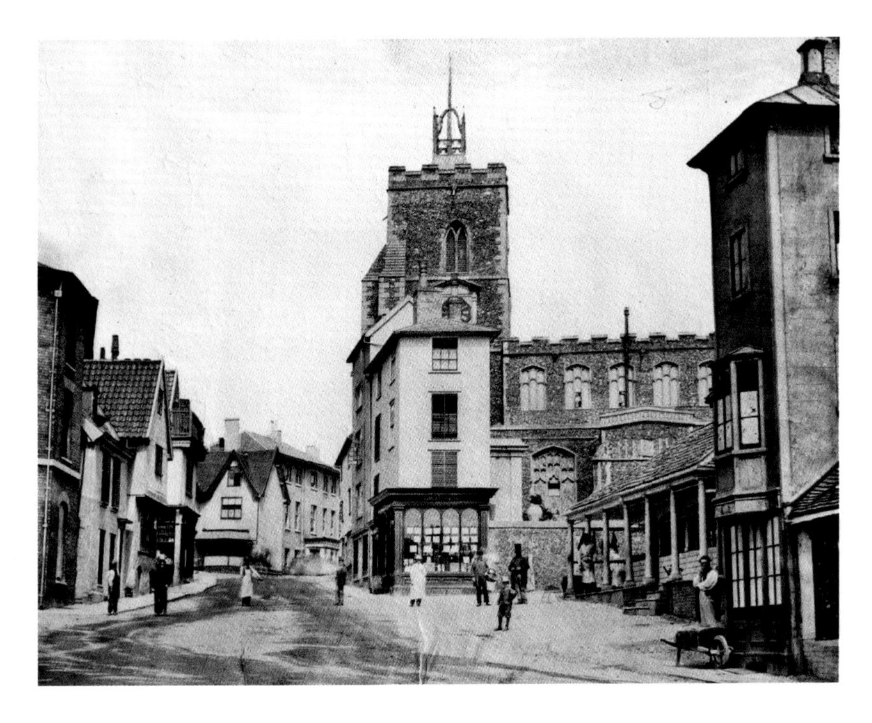

Victorian Diss

Returning to the 'up-hill' view, this pair of images shows the 'Pepper Pot', a building which no longer stands on the modern-day Market Place. Taken well over a century ago by one of the famous Alger family of photographers, this incredibly detailed image gives a feel for the people as well as the place – note the chap with his barrow and the people in their aprons. Photographed in a world before cars, the Market Place still looks remarkably similar to today. (Cleer S Alger Trust; NRO, MS 10825)

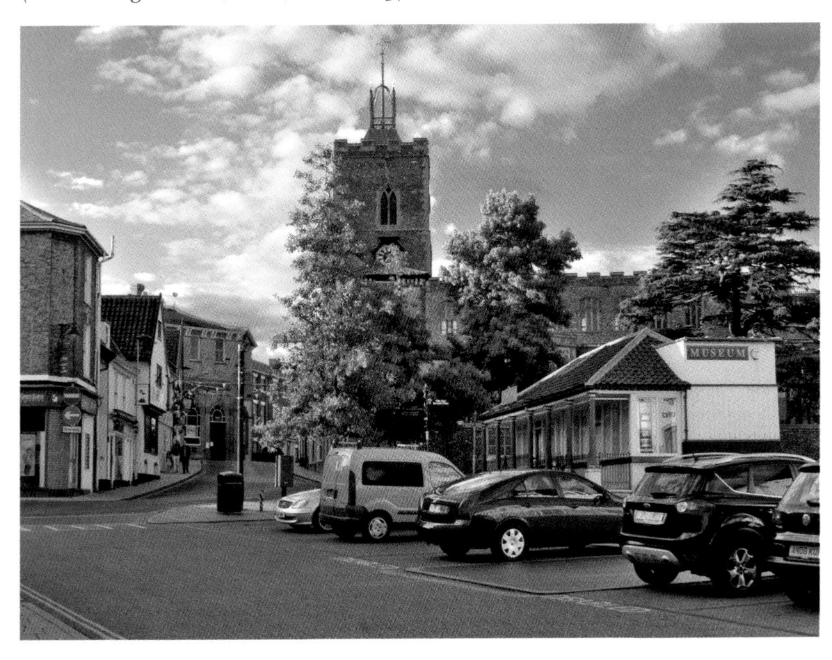

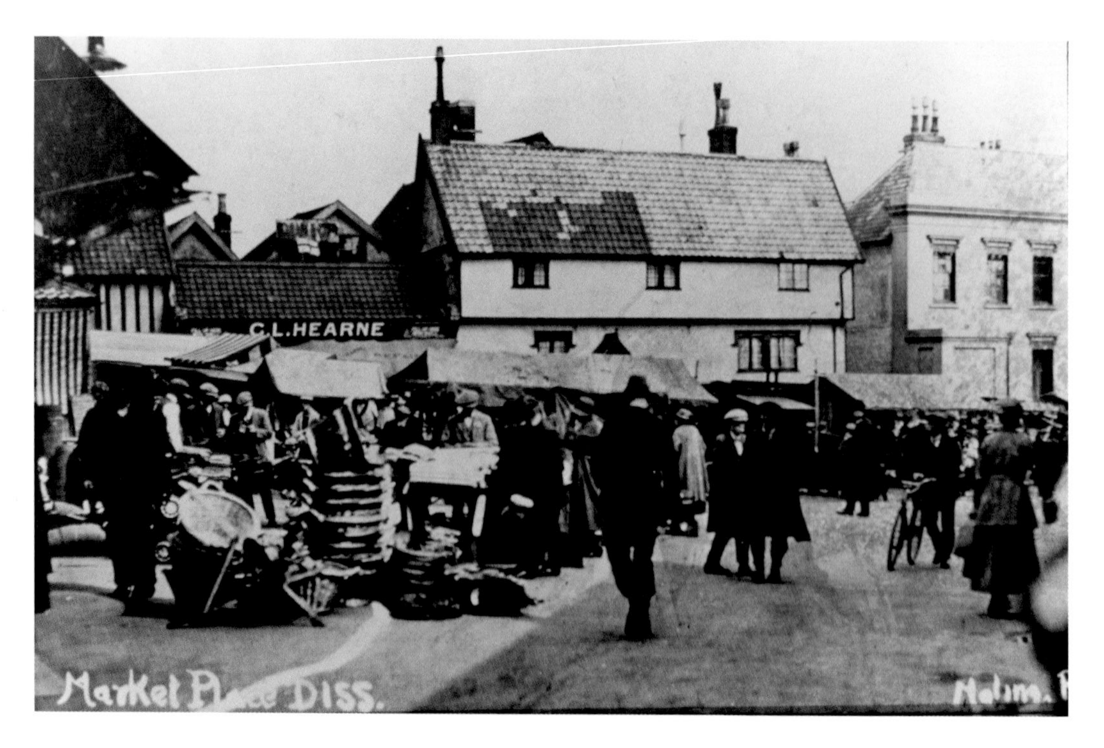

Interwar Diss

Looking across from Market Hill, here we see market day in full swing before the post office was built, probably around 1925–35. In the earlier picture, the Bell public house is next to G. L. Hearne's, a cycle shop. Both buildings were demolished in 1952 to make way for the new post office in the newer picture. The Bell is one of several lost pubs, including The Ship (Mere Street), and the Beehive, now a private house on Denmark Street. (Untraced; part of image collection donated to NCC)

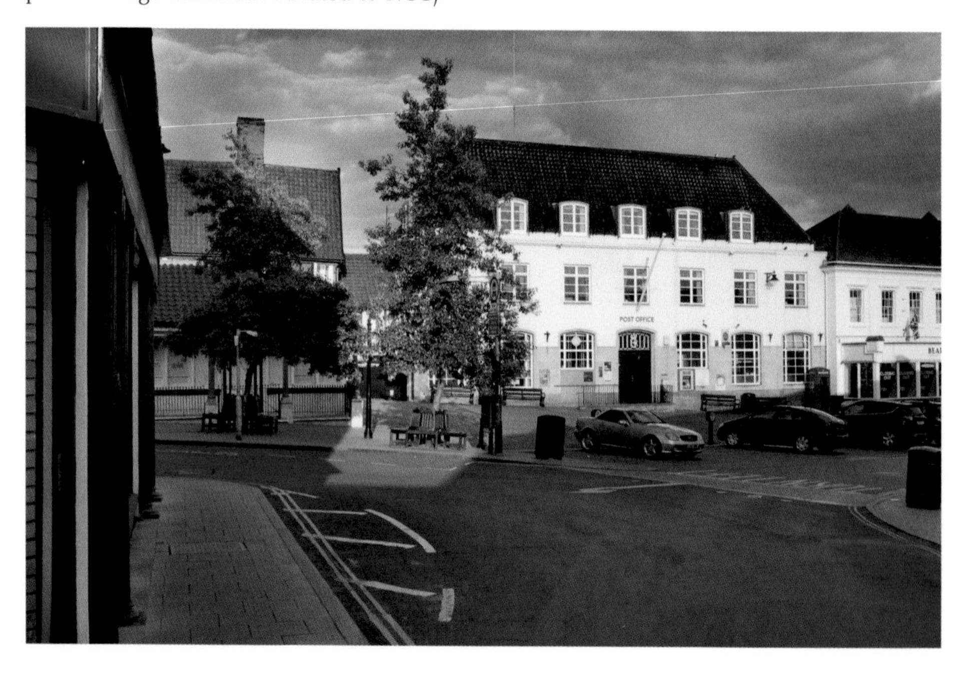

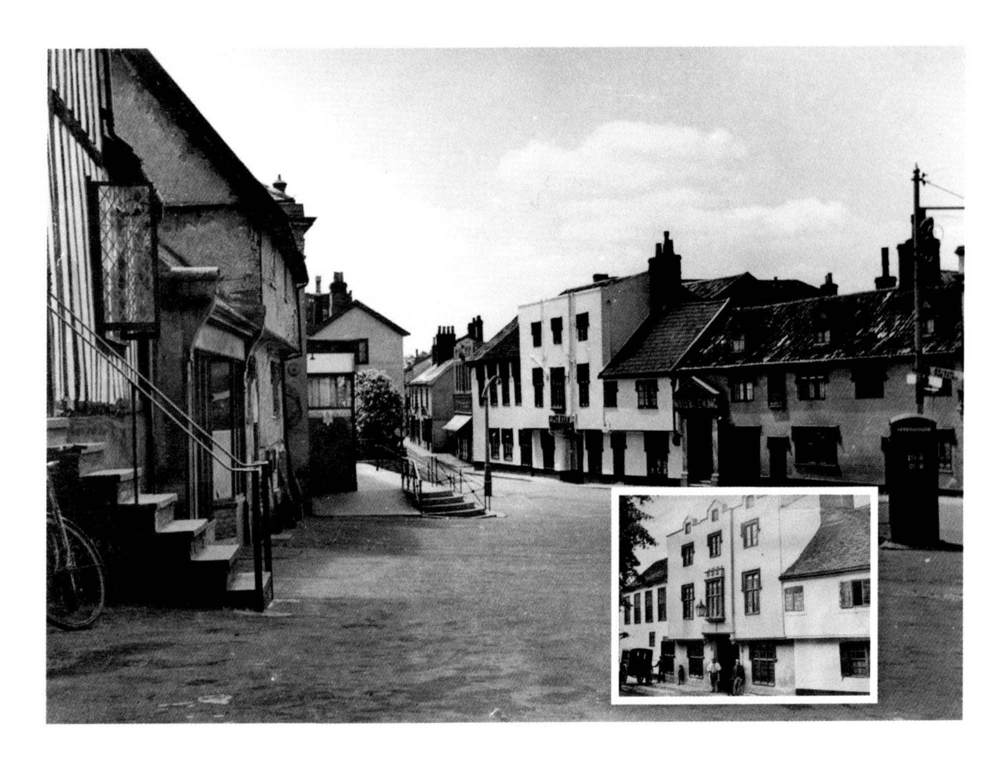

Down the Market Place

This interesting shot was probably taken in the late 1940s or very early 1950s. It shows the Dolphin and the Bell to the left and the King's Head, once home to the town petty sessions, can be seen on the right (behind scaffolding on the new image). A Victorian image of the King's Head is inset. The large door surround is Wallace King's (ironmongers), now a row of smaller shops. There is still a phone box, but it has moved. (Cleer S Alger Trust; NRO, MS 10825/NCC)

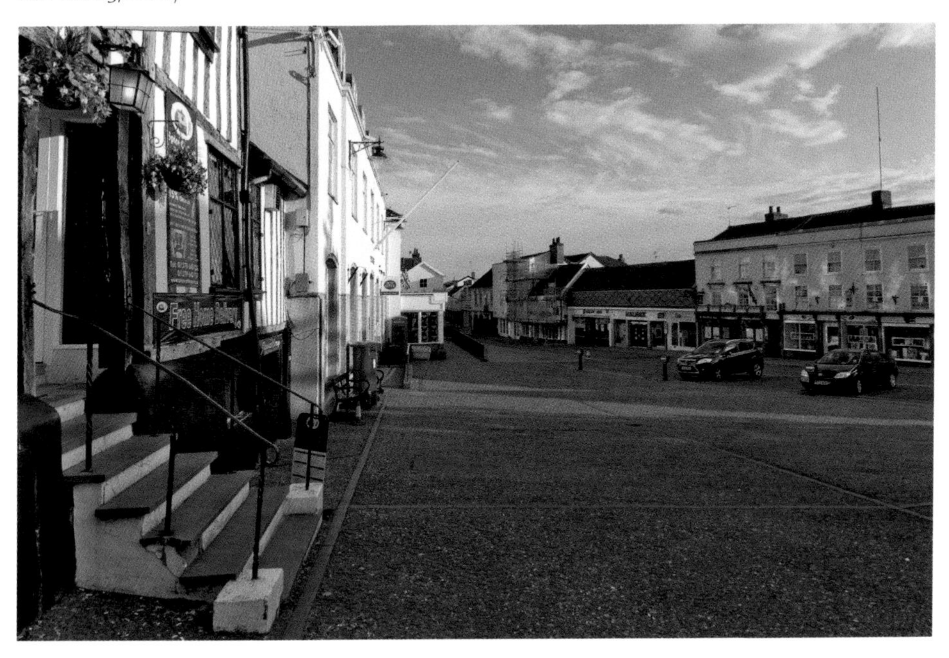

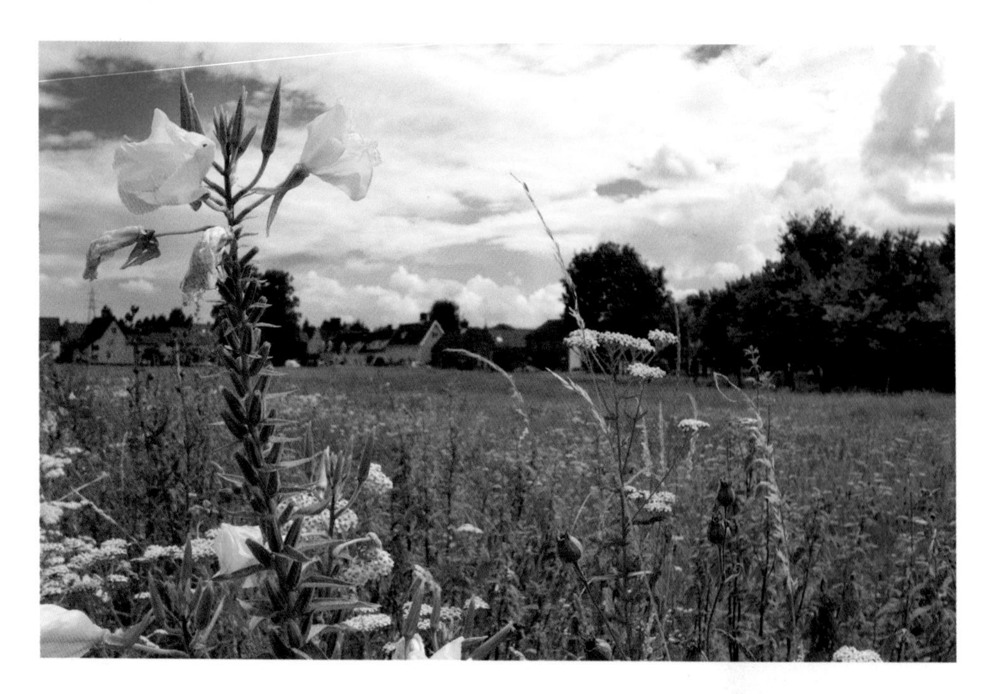

High and Low

Two of my favourite Diss images, these are my idea of the top and toe of the town. The older (and cover image) originally appeared in the *Eastern Daily Press* on 18 June 1954 and shows Mr Starling and Mr Dawson stripping lead from the roof of St Mary's church before recasting and replacing it. Behind them, the Market Place stretches into the distance, with bunting across Mere Street. From a different altitude, the new picture shows the picturesque Denmark Green looking across towards the end of the street as it nears the bridge. (Archant)

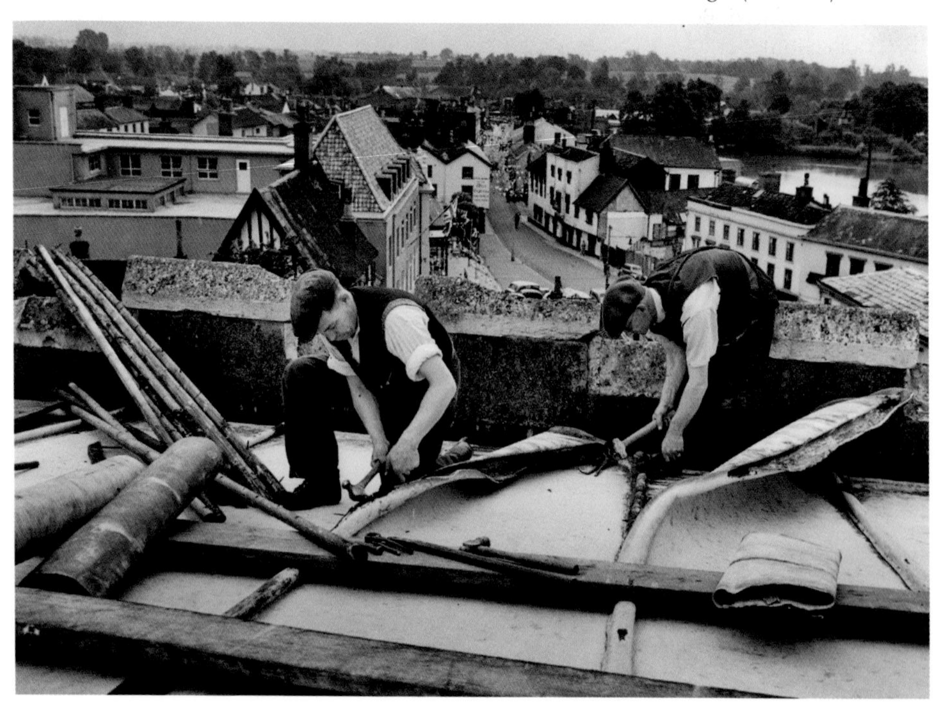

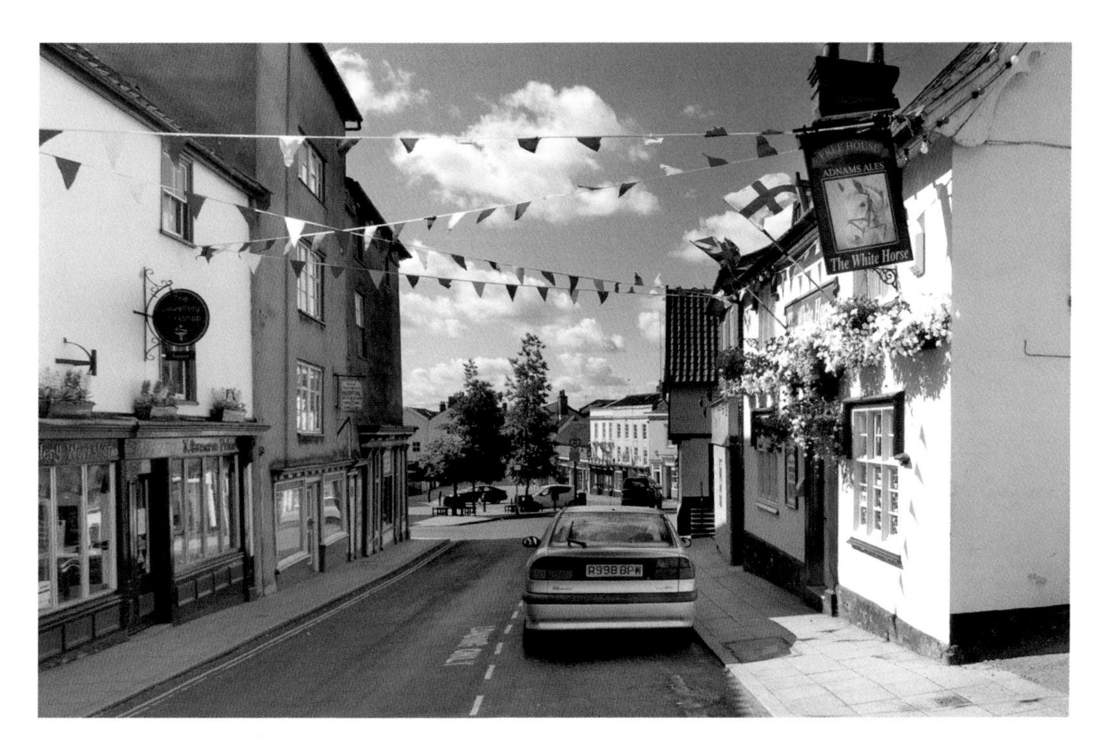

Top of the Market Place
Past the church and heading up towards Mount Street, we meet The White Horse pub. The older image shows Cory's, selling footwear (previously a saddler's), opposite the inn – these days it's a jewellery shop. Looking downhill, there are antique shops where once were grocers and, later, travel agents. Harvey's hardware store once stood next to the White Horse but the building has since been replaced. Between 1912 and 1916, Harvey's moved to St Nicholas Street. (The Francis Frith Collection)

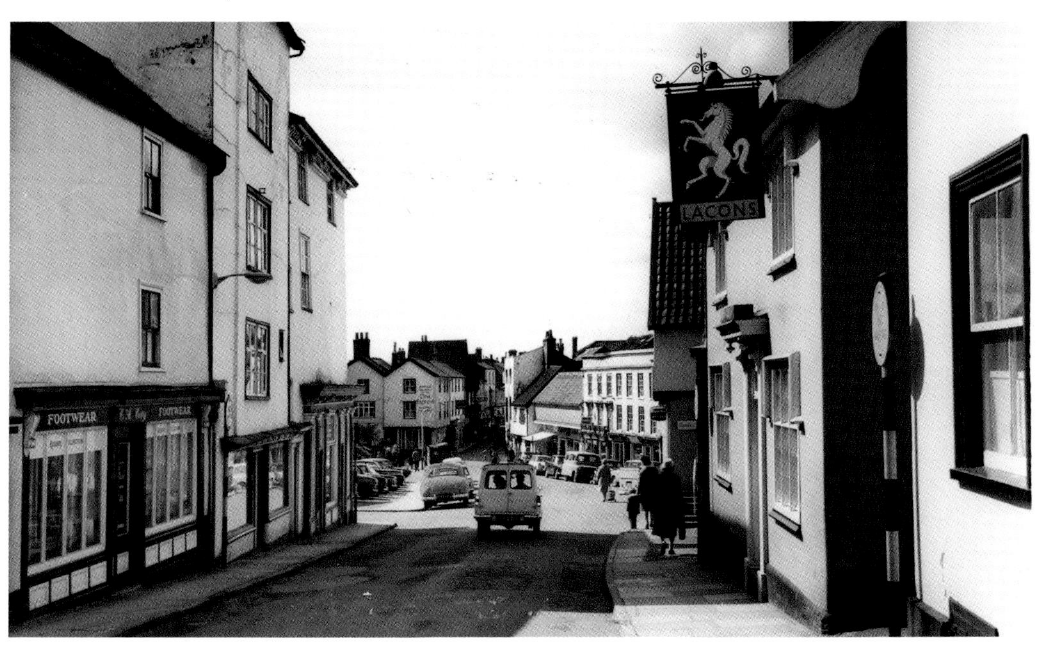

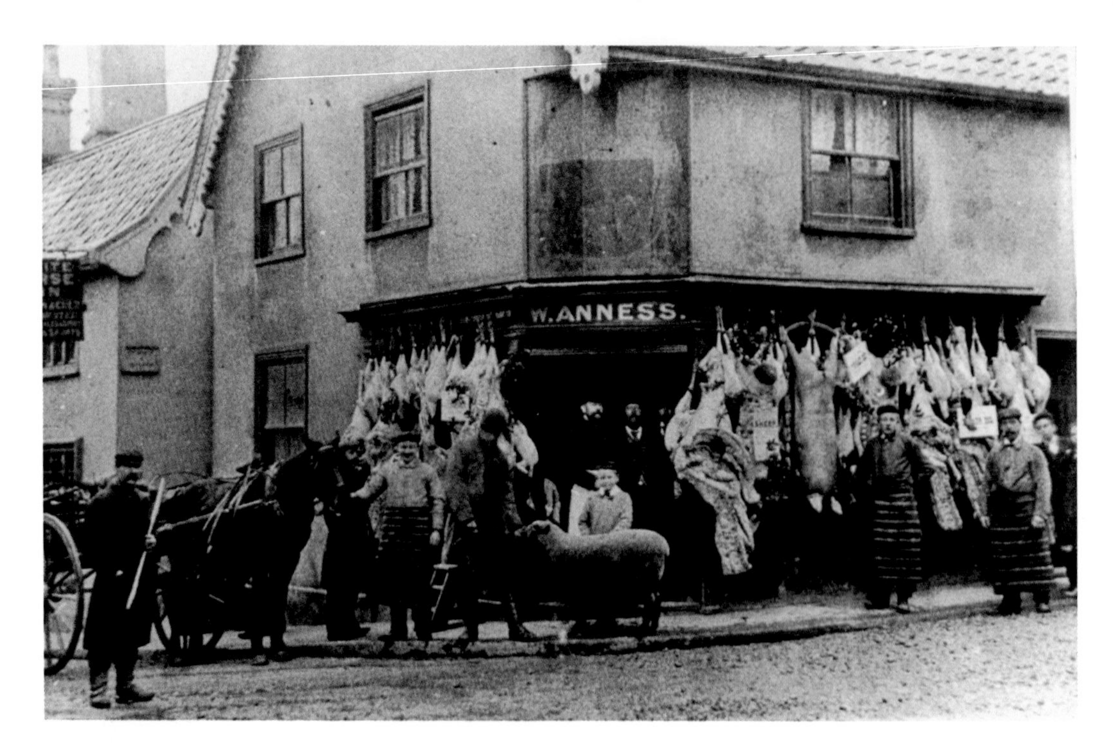

Butchers'

This untraced image comes from a collection of slides in the Picture Norfolk archive. The shop is still a butcher's today, although W. Anness is now D. A. Browne & Son. Walter Anness' butchers could be found in Diss from the late 1870s until at least the 1930s. These days, you won't find such an array of livestock at the entrance (living or dead!), but the painting over the doorway is still there. D. A. Browne & Son was founded in 1934. (Untraced; part of image collection donated to NCC)

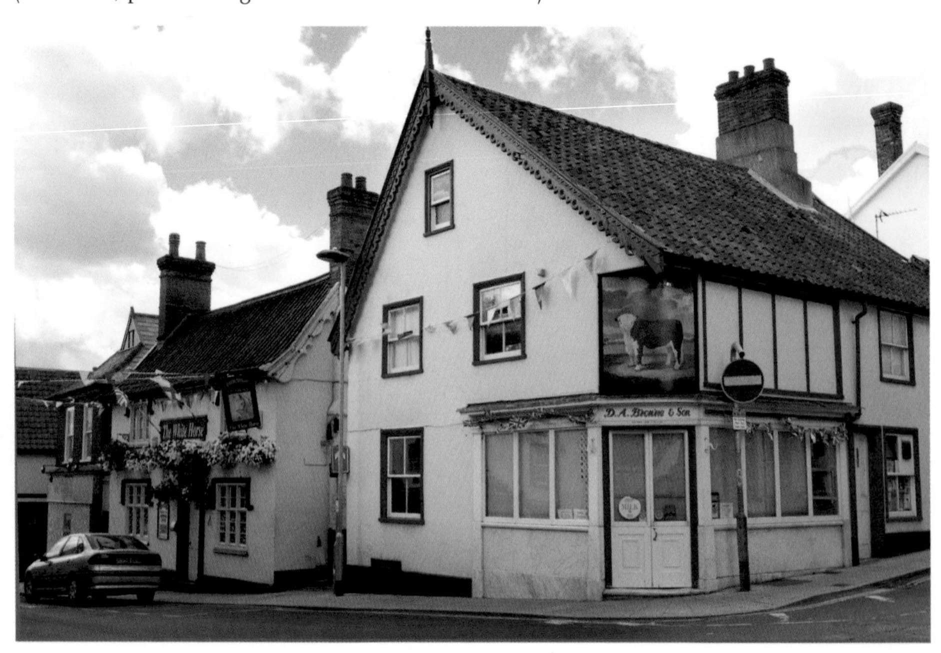

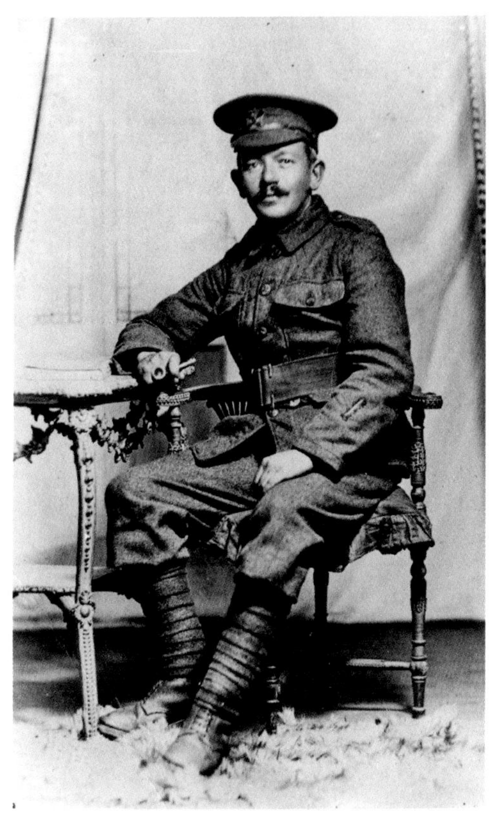

Lest We Forget
As a reminder of the sacrifices made by men and families all over the Diss area during wartime, I include images of Diss soldiers here in order to put faces to some of the names on the town's war memorial. These two gentlemen are William Harold (upper-body image, below) and Thomas Edgar Harold (full-length image, right). As well as being on the memorial erected in 1921, they are also remembered in the Great War soldier portraits collection at the Norfolk Heritage Centre. Further names were added after the Second World War. (NCC)

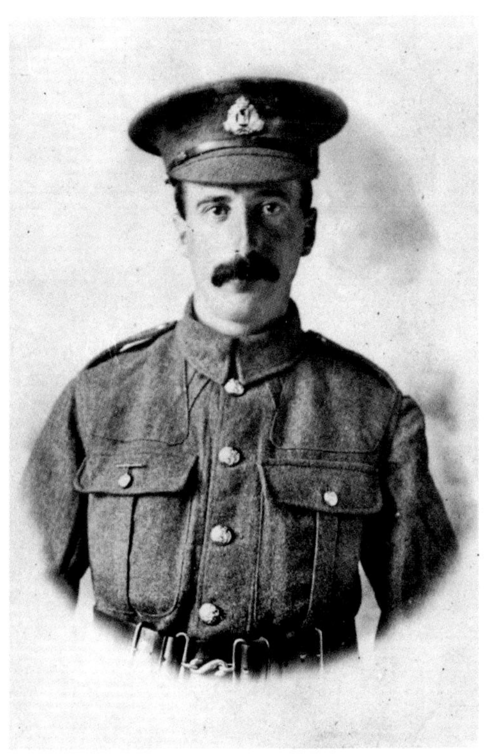

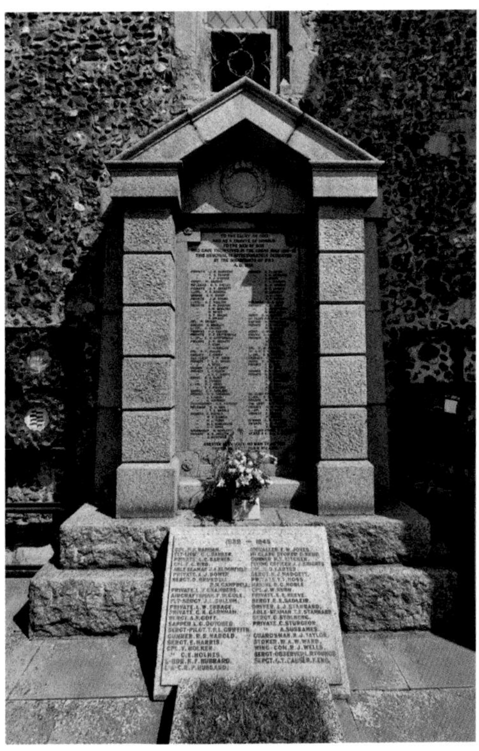

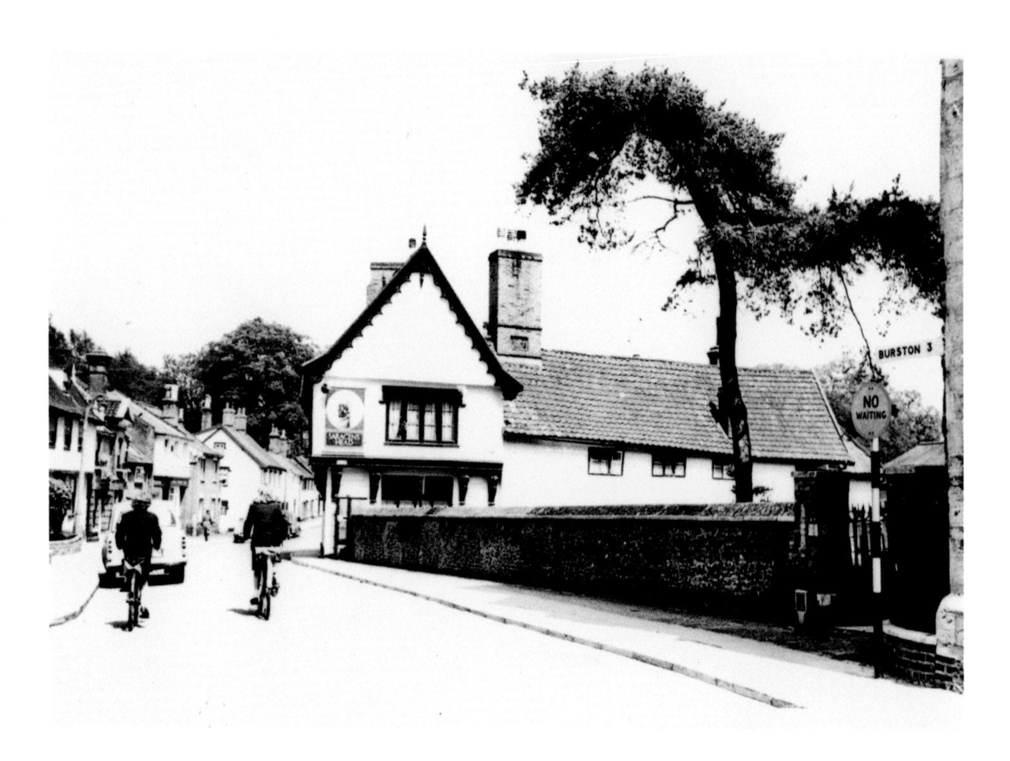

Saracen's Head

The Saracen's Head on Mount Street is another old pub, now in at least its fourth century. It was a hall for the Weaver Guilds even before that, and once plainer to look at – older images show the building without Victorian additions. At one time there was a bowling green here, and the pub was the location of Friday stock sales by Messrs Slater, Simpson and Sons (which alternated with Gaze's sales at the Crown Hotel up the road – *White's*, 1890). (NCC)

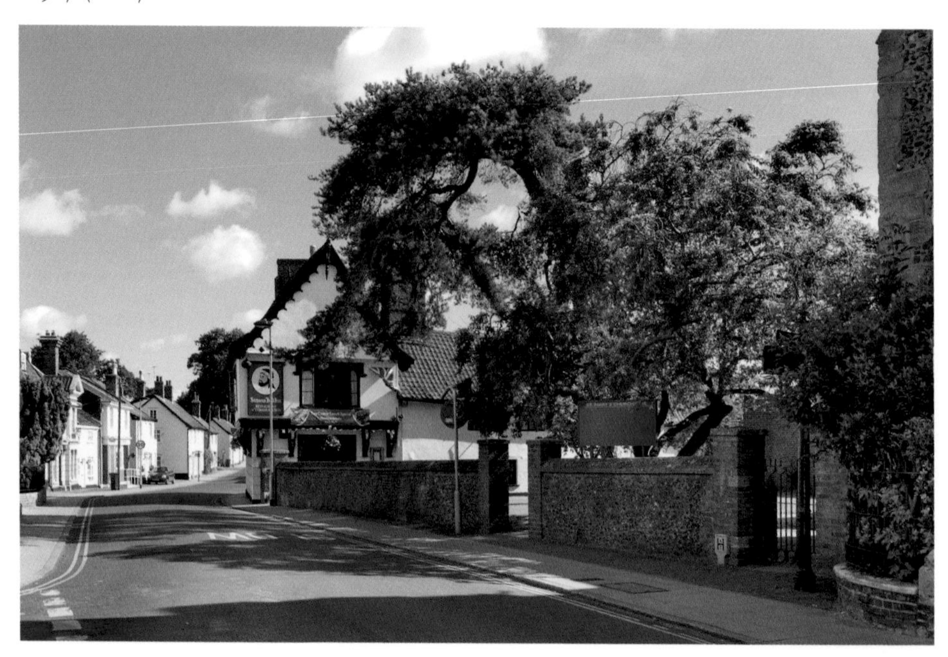

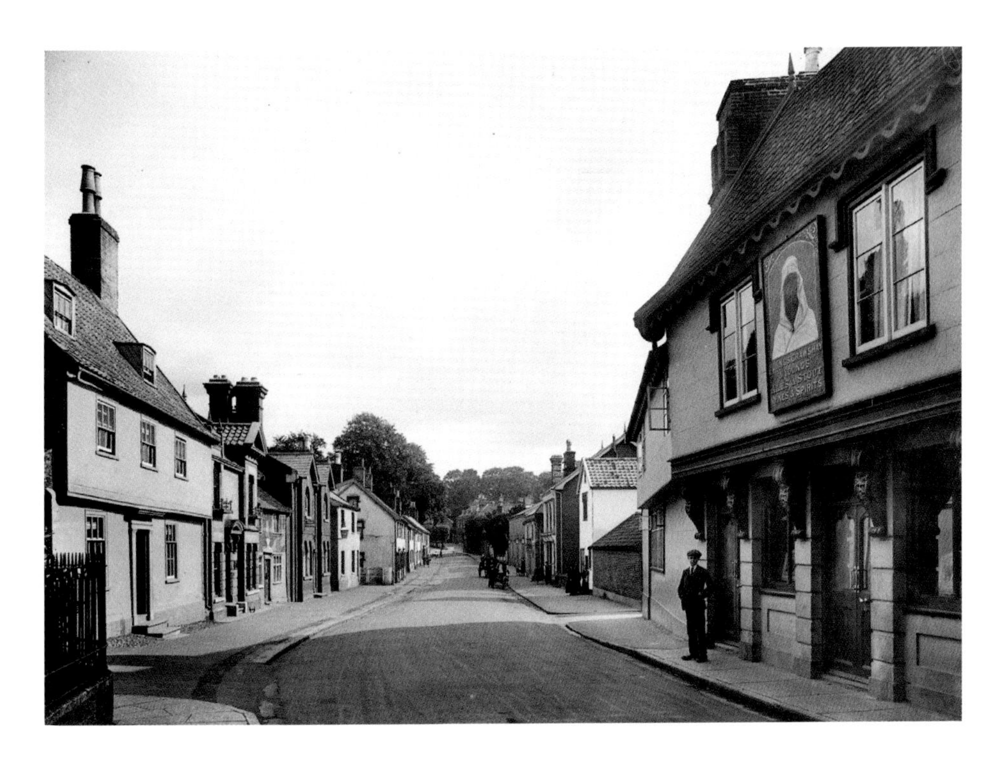

Mount Street

Moving closer to the Saracen's Head, this fantastically detailed image of a bygone Diss shows a lad standing outside the pub, and many more people down the street. On the pavement, a group of ladies have a chat while behind them are two men moving furniture and someone walking their dog – perhaps a Labrador. In the street, a boy pulls a handcart and behind him another walks beside a horse. The buildings, however, remain much the same. (The Francis Frith Collection)

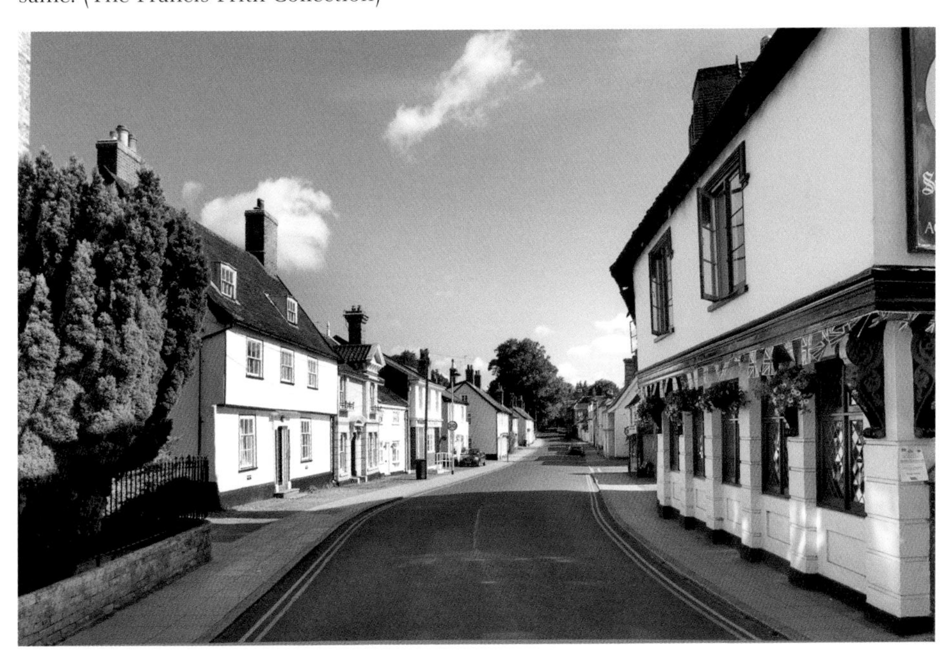

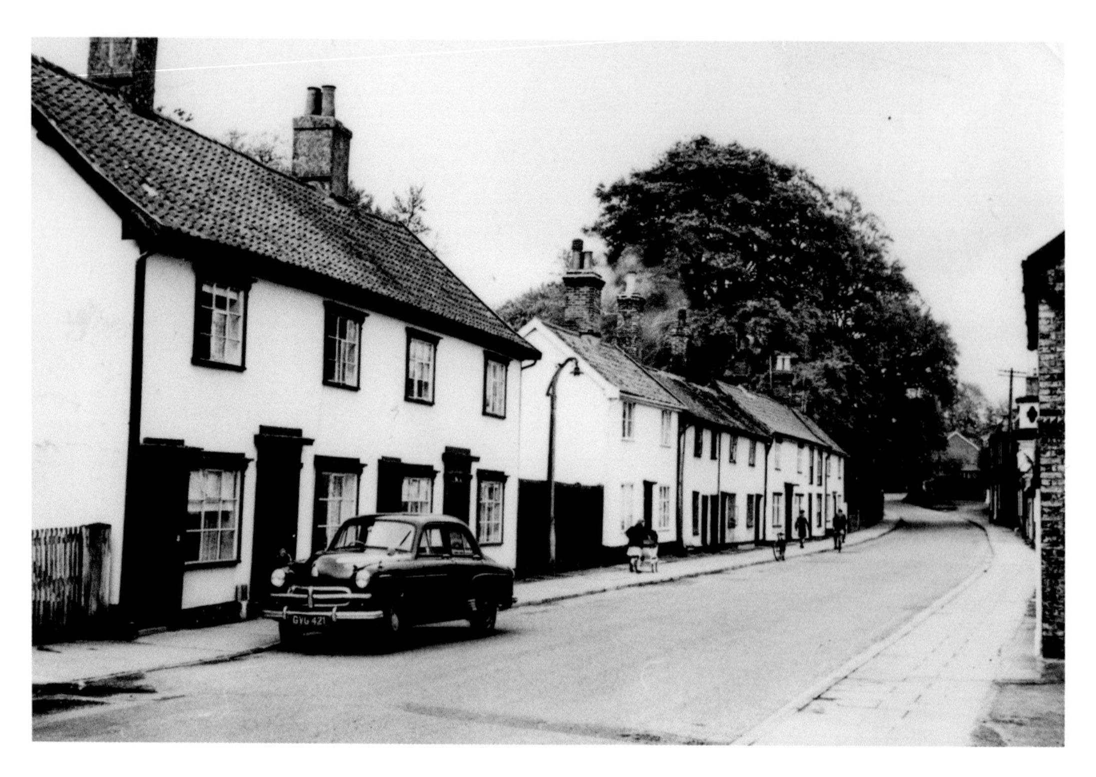

Pot of gold

Moving further north, I ask for a little artistic license for this pair of images, showing both sides of Mount Street. The 1950s/60s view above does not look so very different from today, and I was lucky enough on one of my visits this summer to catch a beautiful double-rainbow over houses on the other side of the road. Mount Street has long been one of the most respectable and pretty streets in Diss, and it's still lovely today. (NCC)

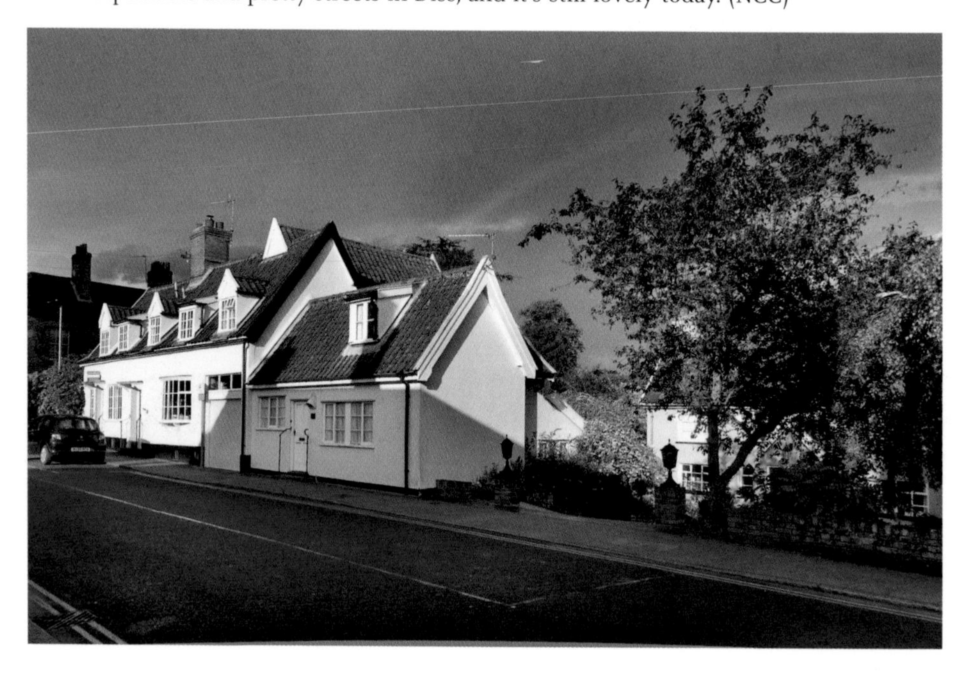

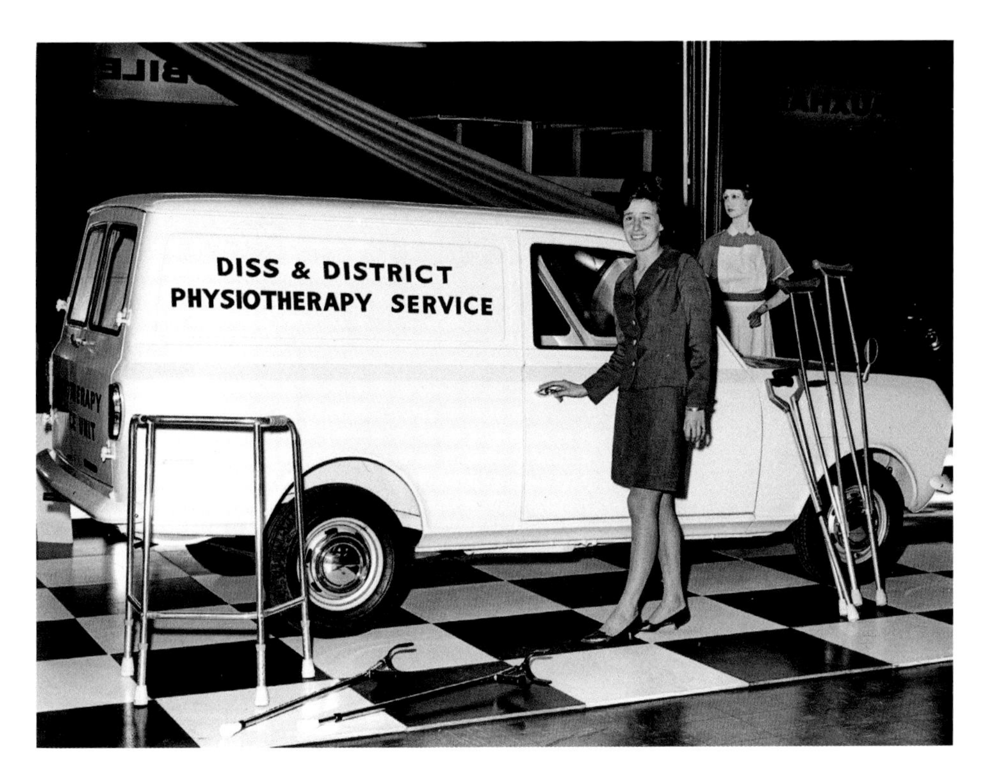

Healthcare
Grassmere was once home to a hospital, after the building's conversion from a school, and later, a house. Uplands (now the Sixth Form Centre) too was a Voluntary Aid Detachment (VAD) hospital during the Great War. This image shows the 'Diss and District Mobile Physiotherapy Service' which operated from 1968 until the 1990s. Today, the town has a purpose-built health centre on Mount Street, where, in 1841, William Mines and Charles Thompson were enumerated as surgeons. (Archant)

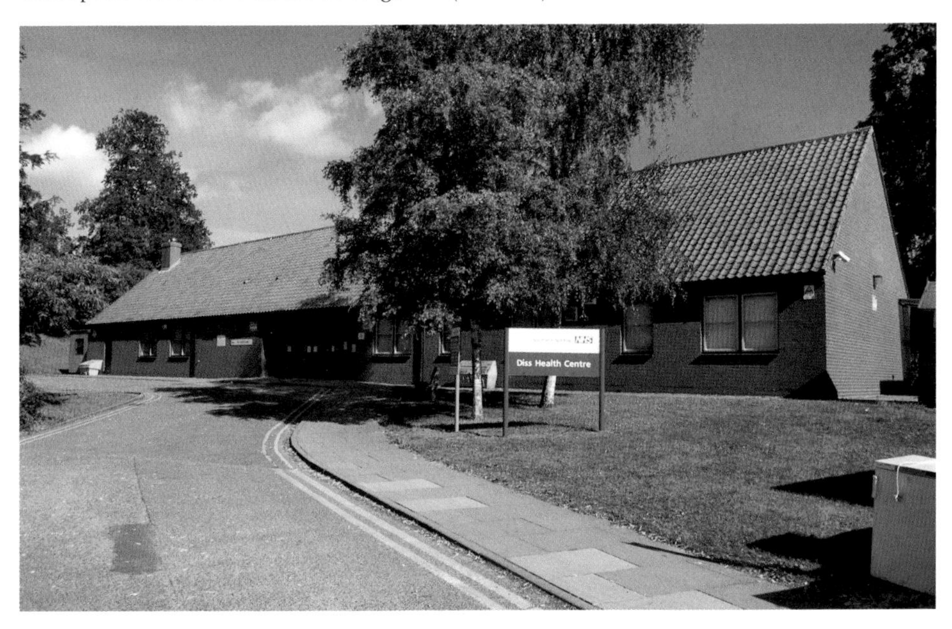

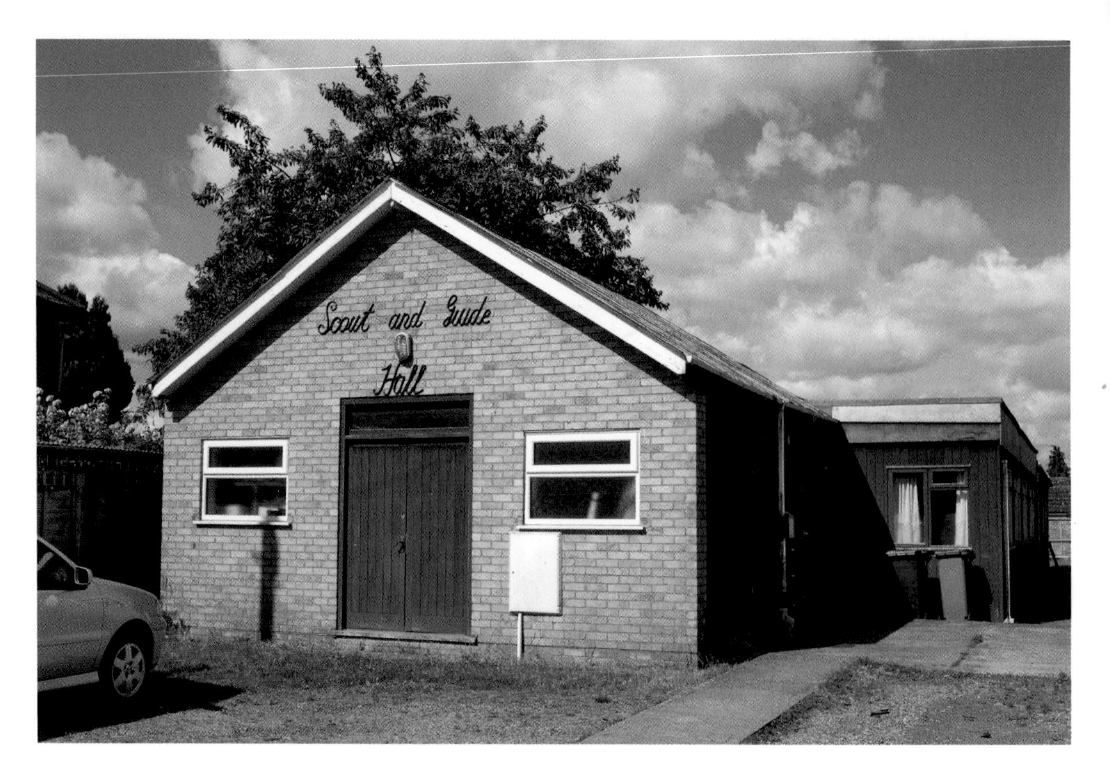

Keeping the Guide Law
This great picture of the 1st Diss Guides was perhaps taken in the 1960s. Girlguiding is still going strong in the area, with groups meeting at Diss, Garboldisham and Roydon. These days, there is a Scout and Guide Hall on Heywood Road, used by local groups for all sorts of events, including road races and table tennis, as well as by youth groups. The site was once home to a corset (or stay) factory, at one time a significant industry in Diss. (NCC)

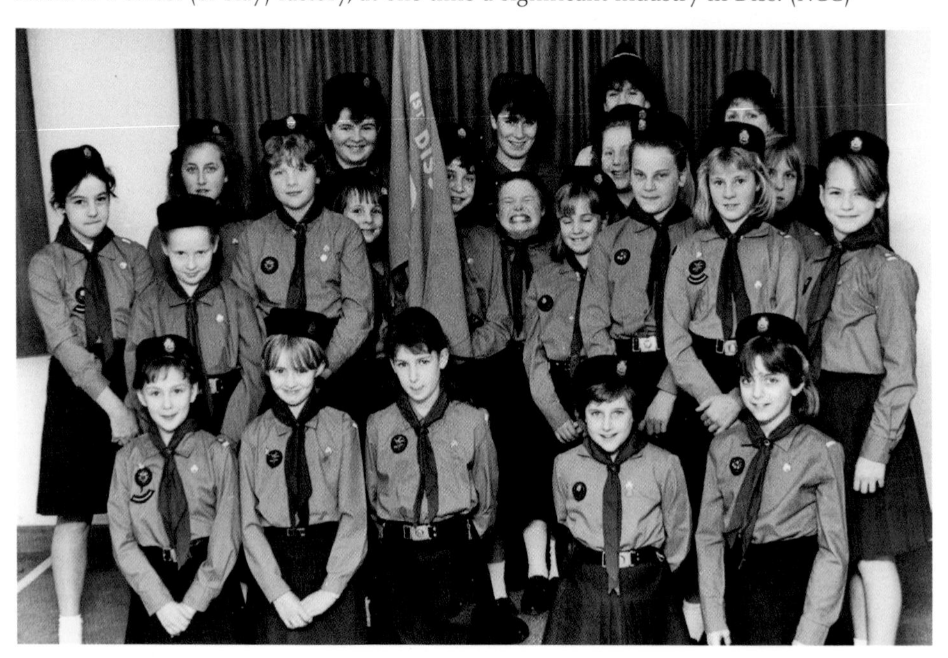

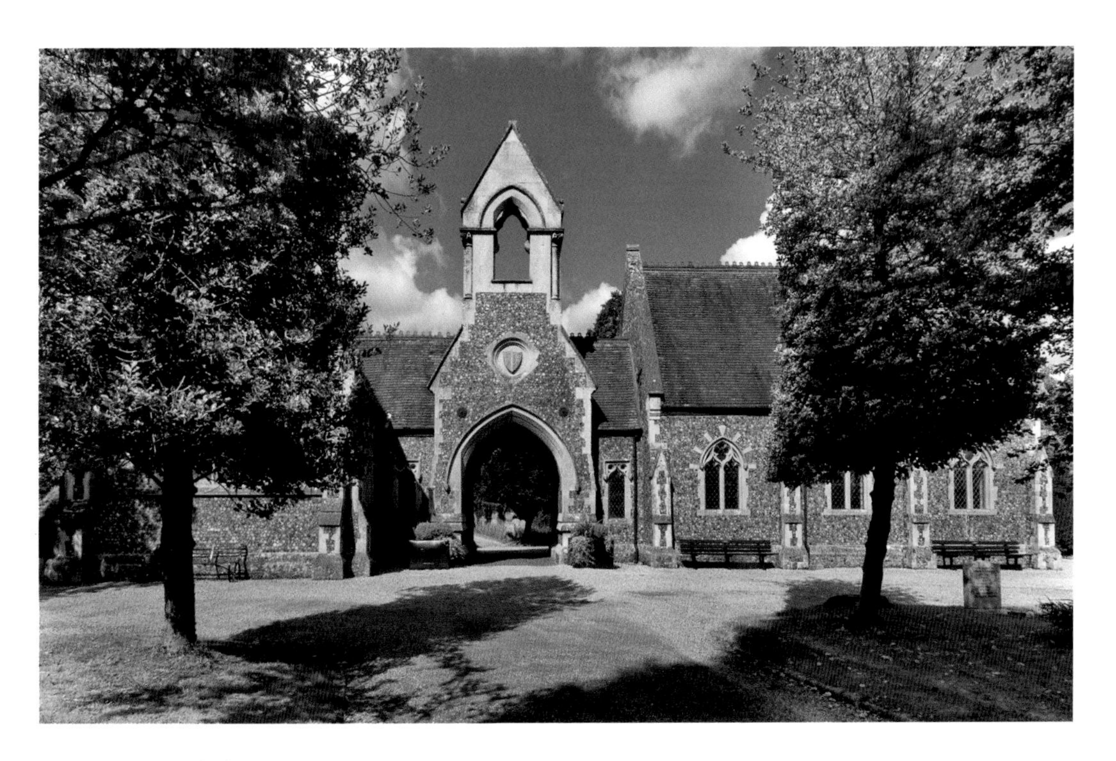

Garden of Sleep

Moving further up Heywood Road, this painting shows the non-denominational Chapel of Remembrance in Diss Cemetery shortly after it was created in 1869. Before the cemetery was opened, this area was open grassland on the far edge of the town. Today, the cemetery has become the peaceful final resting place of nearly 150 years' worth of townsfolk. More recently, the cemetery has created two pretty Gardens of Remembrance. (NRO, MS 10825)

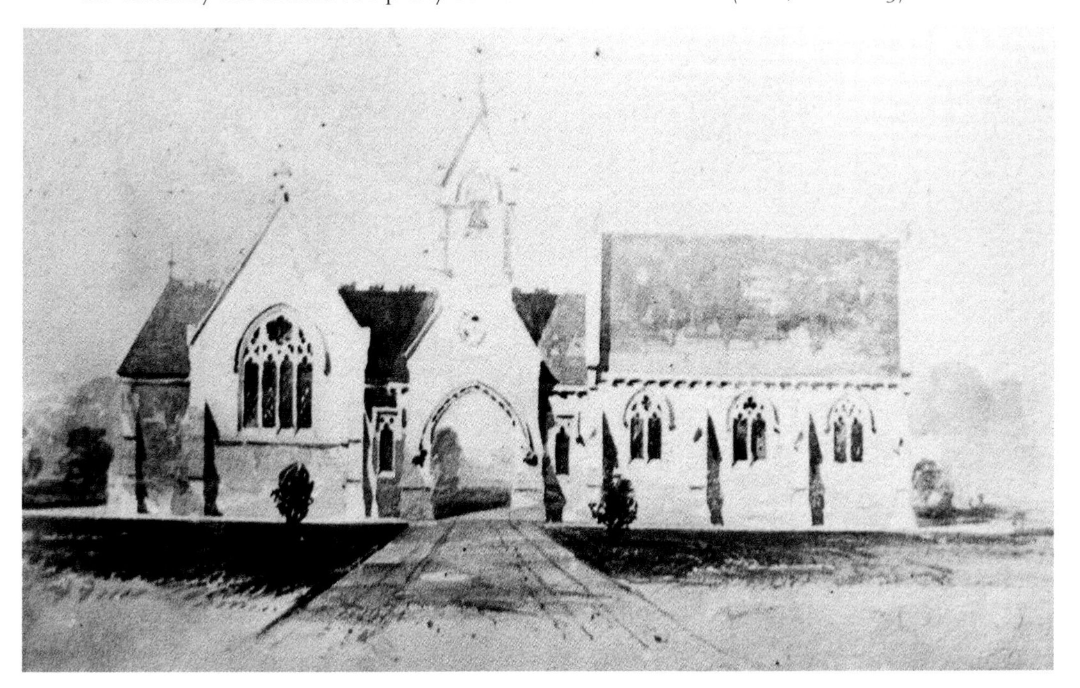

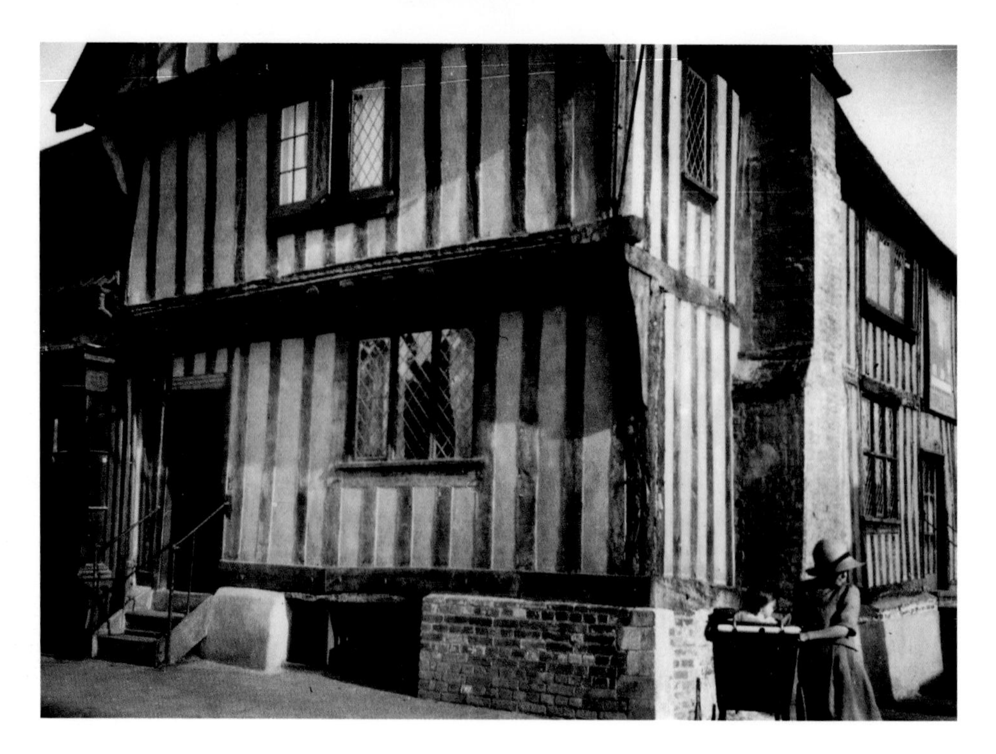

The Dolphin

Returning to the Market Place and heading east we meet The Dolphin – instantly recognisable to anyone familiar with Diss. The older image shows the pub as it was, probably in the 1920s. Today, Dolphin House (as it's now known) is home to more than one local business, including an Indian and Nepalese restaurant. The building dates back to at least the 1500s and the aisled hall on the first floor suggests it may once have been a merchant's home. (Untraced; part of image collection donated to NCC)

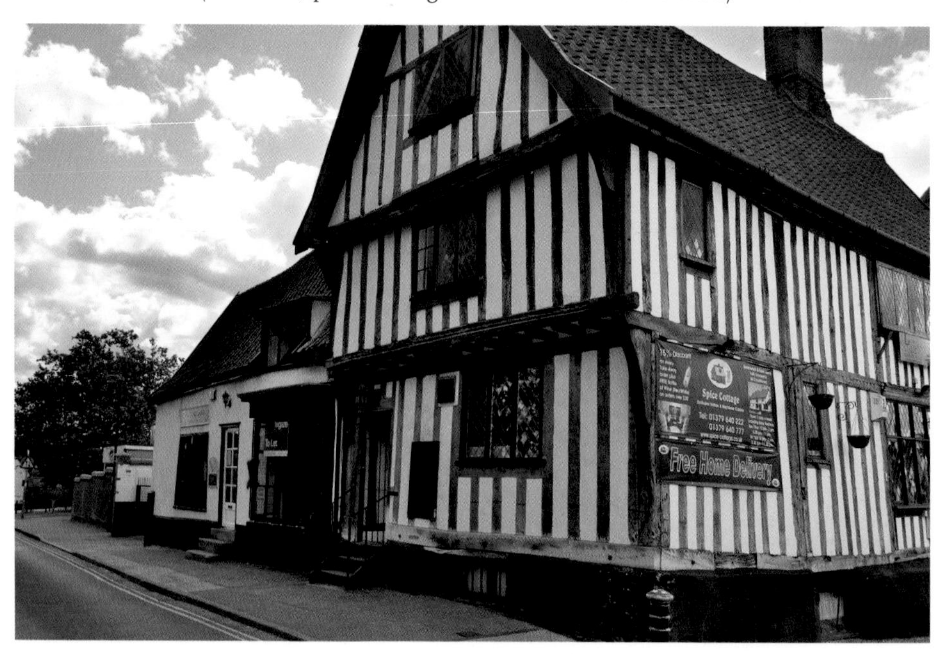

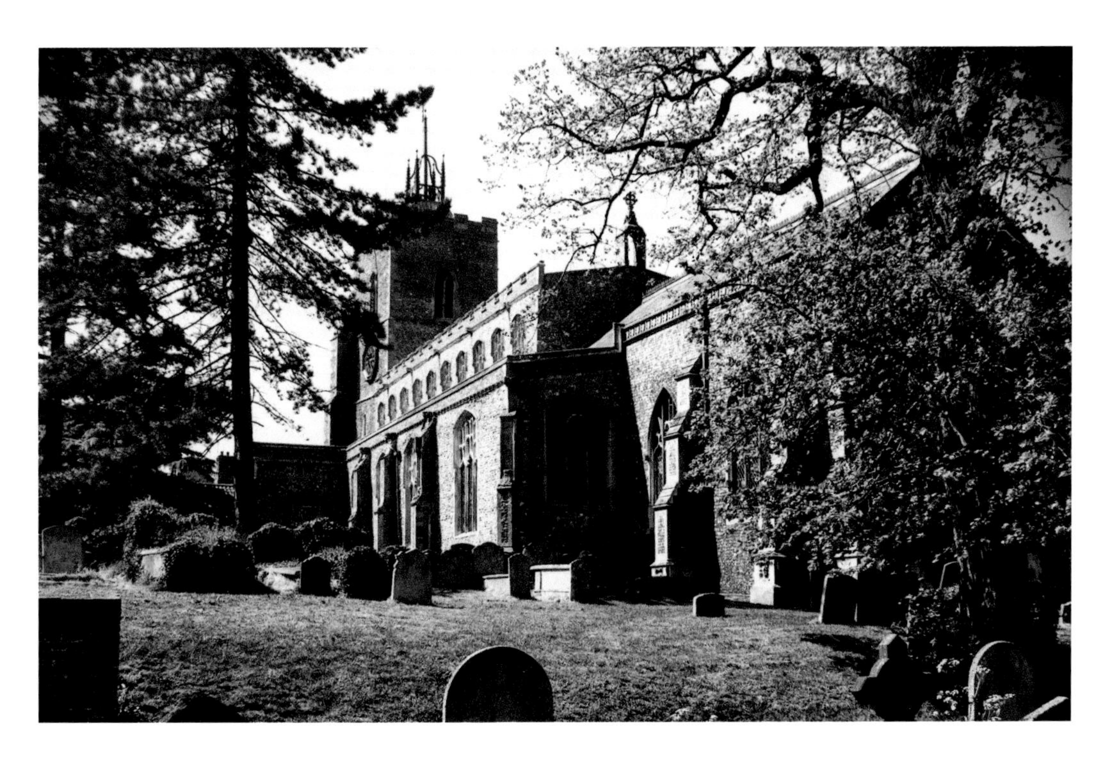

Parish Church
The church of St Mary the Virgin sits at the top of the Market Place, presiding over the narrow streets and old buildings. Founded in 1290, it was described in 1845 as 'a large and handsome Gothic structure ... founded by the Fitzwalters'. A new peal of eight bells was installed on 6 January 1832 which were 'allowed to be as musical and perfect as any in the kingdom'. Plunkett's image, taken nearly thirty-five years ago, could almost have been taken yesterday. (Plunkett)

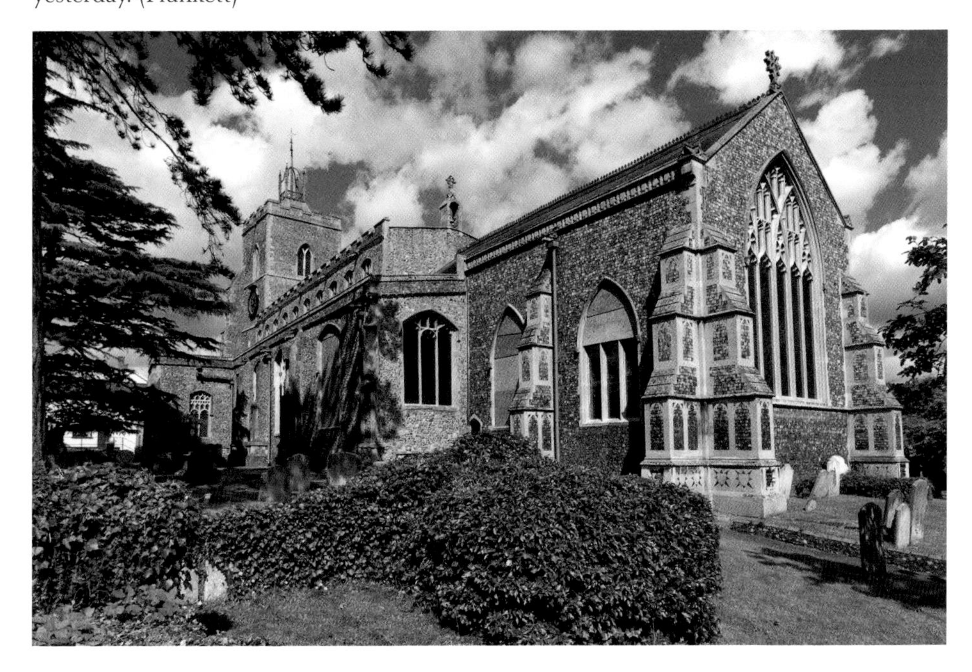

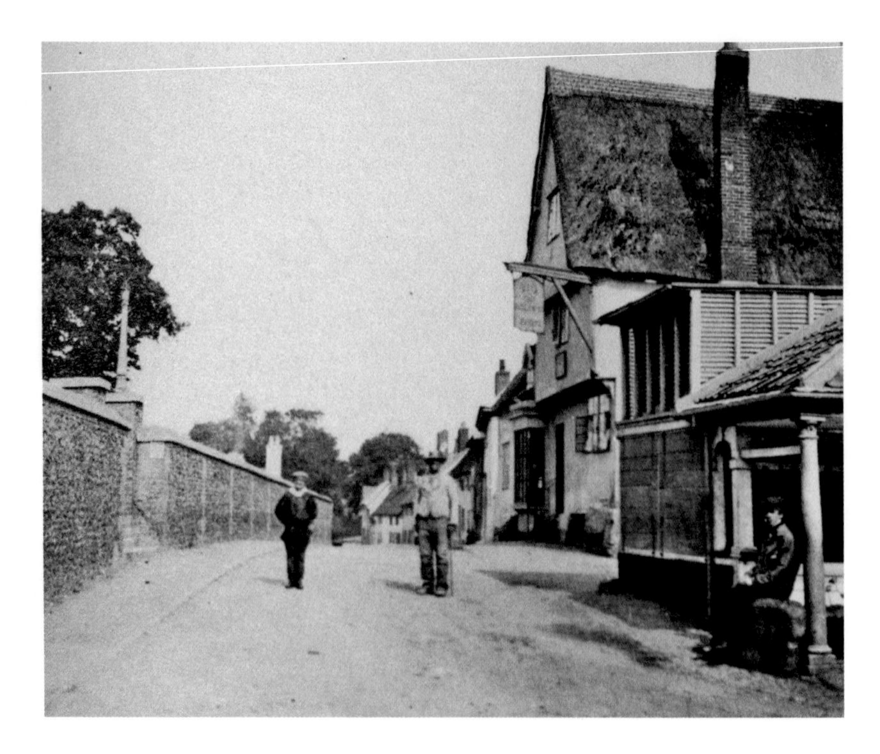

Church Street

Another fabulous Alger image, this one depicts a man and boy outside the still-thatched Dolphin, standing in the middle of Church Street. About 150 years later, my husband does the same, creating a modern-day comparison. Another man sits under the canopy of The Shambles, now the town's museum but once two butchers' shops. The museum hosts changing displays, most recently events tying in with the American Connections project, celebrating the area's close links to the so-called 'Friendly Invasion' during the Second World War. (Cleer S Alger Trust; NRO, MS 10824)

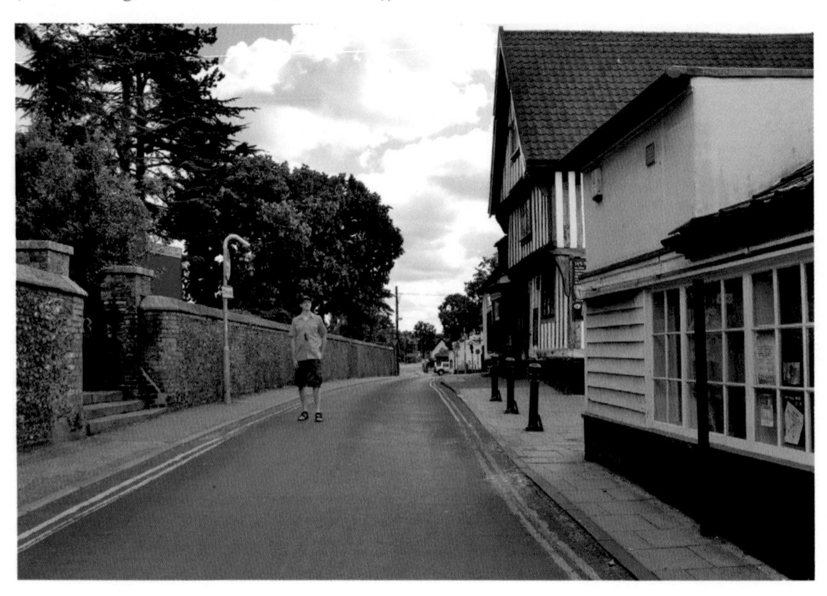

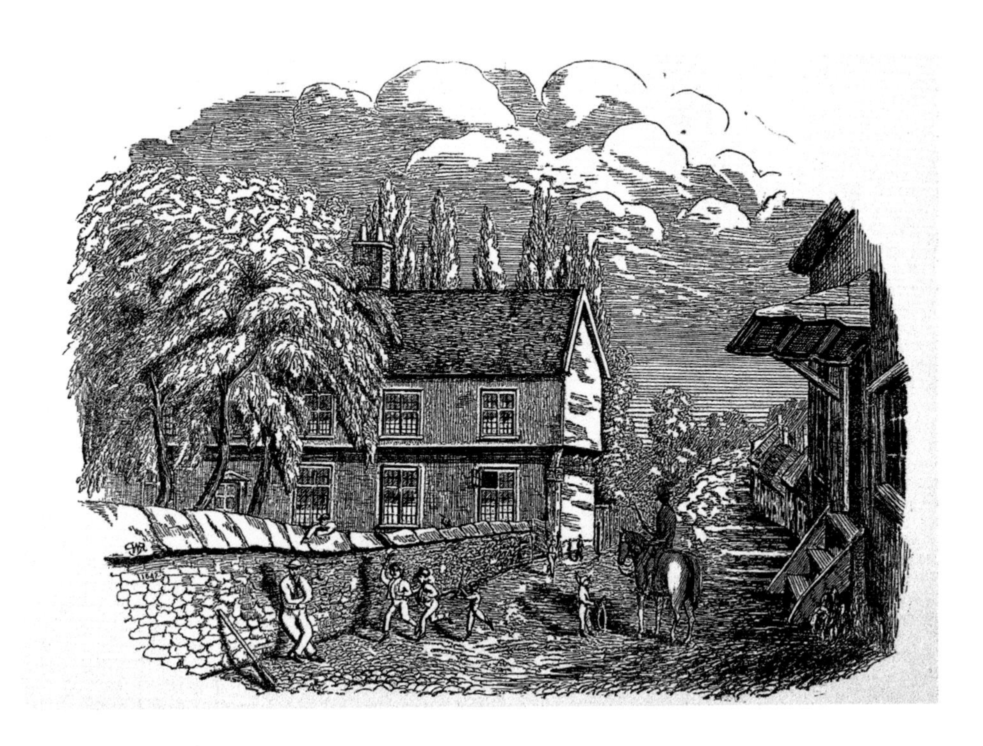

Grammar Schools

The Guildhall Grammar School, where the Norfolk historian Francis Blomefield began his education, once stood in ground which is now part of the churchyard – the building was taken down in 1846 according to the 1864 *White's Directory*. It is not the only school in Diss to have come and gone; the newer image shows Scholar's Walk housing estate, previously home to Diss Grammar School (originally Diss Secondary School), built in 1908 and demolished in 1991. (NRO, MS 10825)

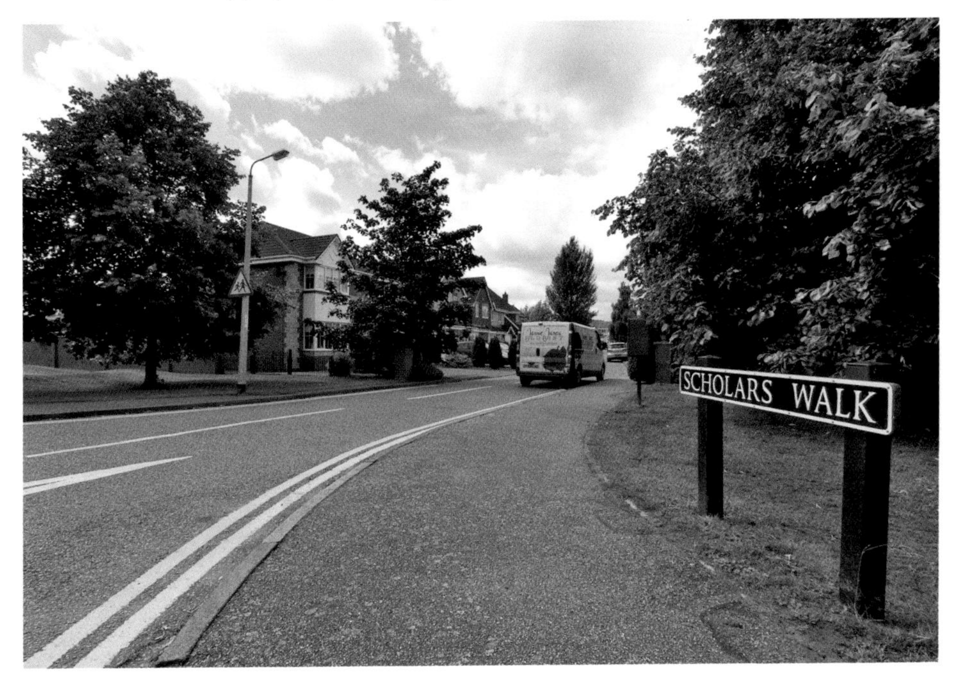

DISS PUBLIC LIBRARY

AND SCIENTIFIC INSTITUTION.

THE COURSE OF LECTURES for the present season will comprise the following subjects:

ASTRONOMY ......BY MR. JAMES DUNBAR.

OPTICS .... BY MR. S. W. RIX.

PNEUMATICS......BY REV. C. VALENTINE.

HISTORY .... BY MR. B. MUSKETT.

BOTANY ....BY MR. DUNBAR.

These subjects will occupy six or seven Lectures.

Tickets of admission may be had of Mr. Abbott, the Librarian, and of Mr. Marsh, *to the Course* price Four Shillings and Sixpence, and to single Lectures price One Shilling.—Schools will be admitted at half price. —Shareholders have the privilege of attending the Lectures gratis.

Library

Diss has been home to a library for a long time – a book club started as early as 1777. This poster promotes upcoming lectures at the Public Library and Scientific Institution around 1870. By 1864, the Public Reading Room and Library at the Corn Hall had 3,000 volumes, and another 6,000 were available at a separate book club on Mere Street. The new library on Church Street pictured here was officially opened on 17 March 1964 by Rear Admiral A. H. Taylor. (NRO, MS 10824)

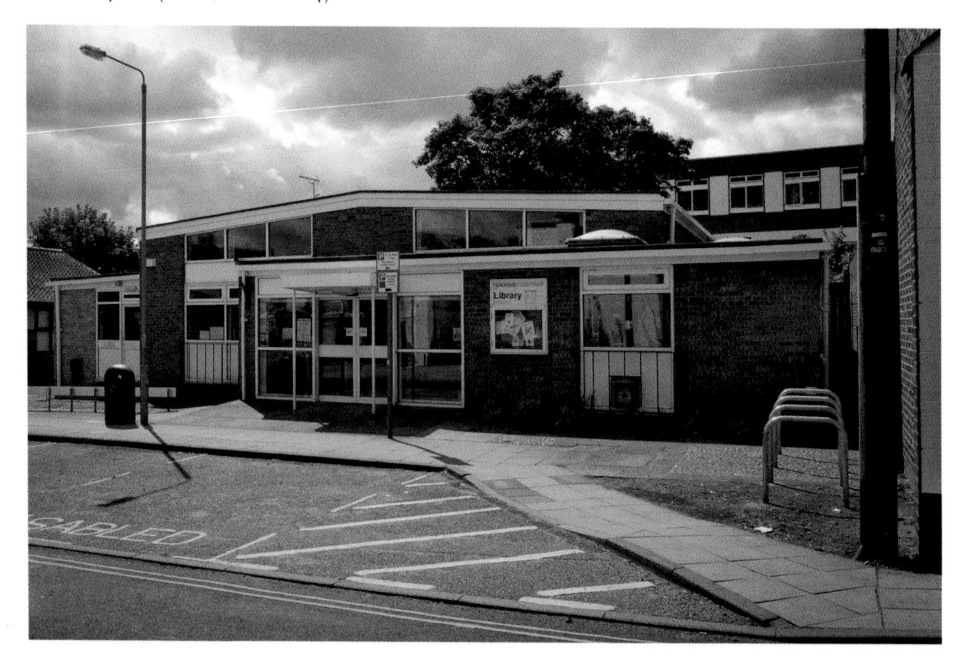

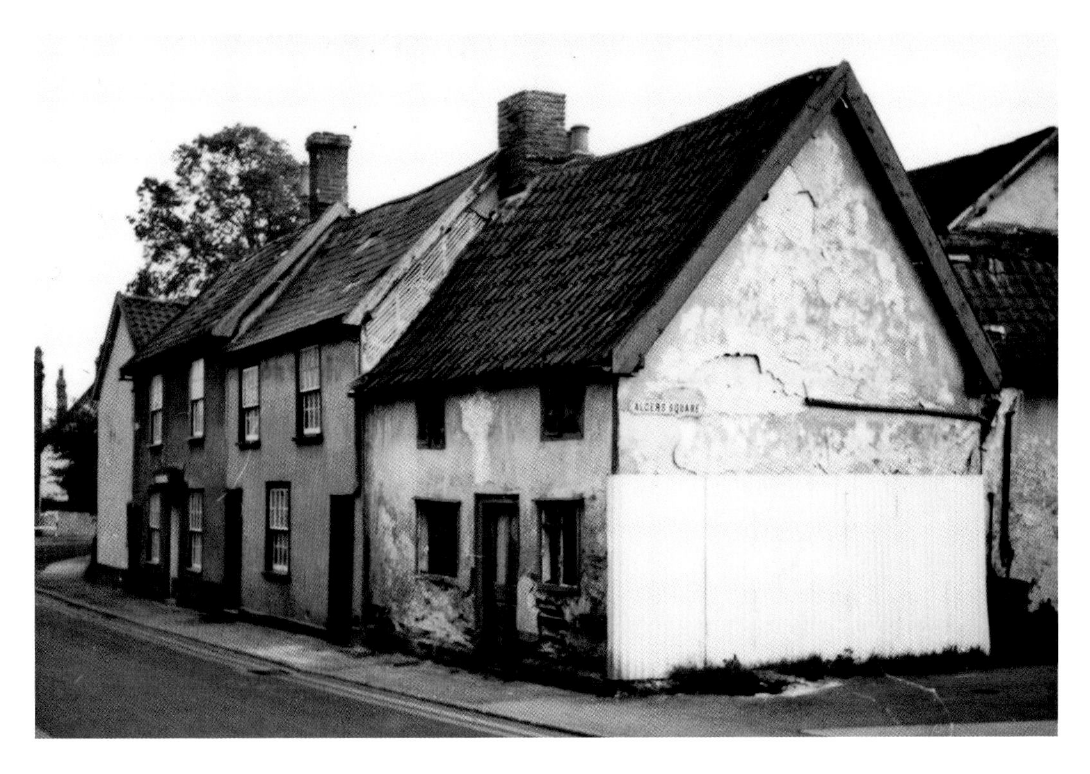

Change on Church Street

These views from Church Street show a great change. Alger Square, pictured above, was demolished not long after this was taken. The small square was the namesake of a famous local family, the Algers, best known for their early photography of the area (they were also surveyors and lithographers). The site is now home to a modern Job Centre Plus. Look closely, and the tree and the house behind the building can be matched up. (NCC)

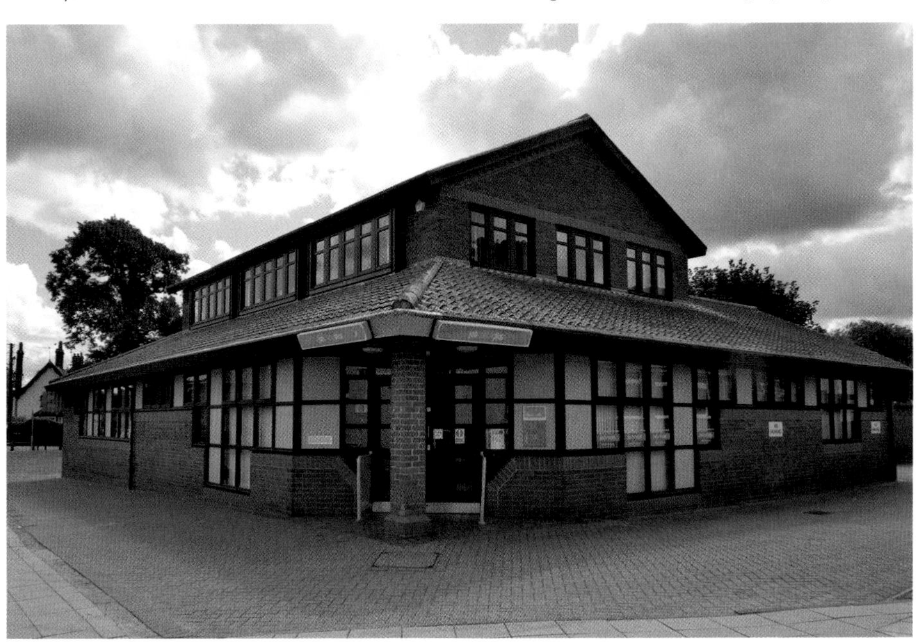

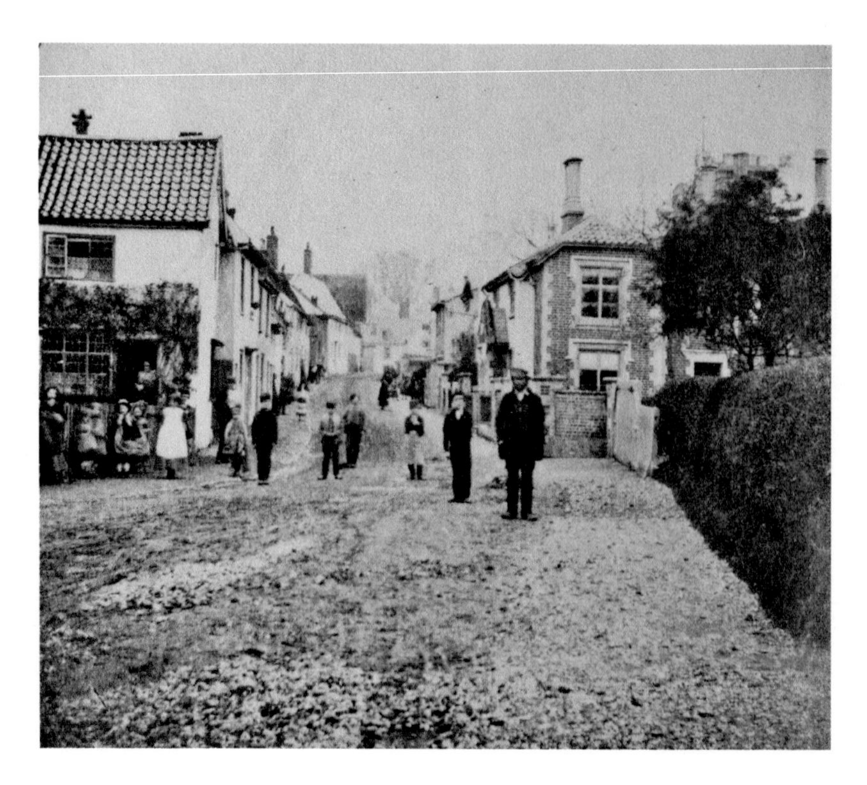

For Better or Worse

In 1885, except for Mount Street, this was effectively the northern boundary of the town centre. By 1946 the beginnings of streets running northwards were evident, but much of the development between here and Walcot Road is relatively modern. On Church Road itself, almost all the houses to the left of the older shot have gone, making way for newer buildings. Much of the right-hand side is recognisable however. Which image is the more attractive? I will leave that up to you to decide! (Cleer S Alger Trust; NRO, MS 10824)

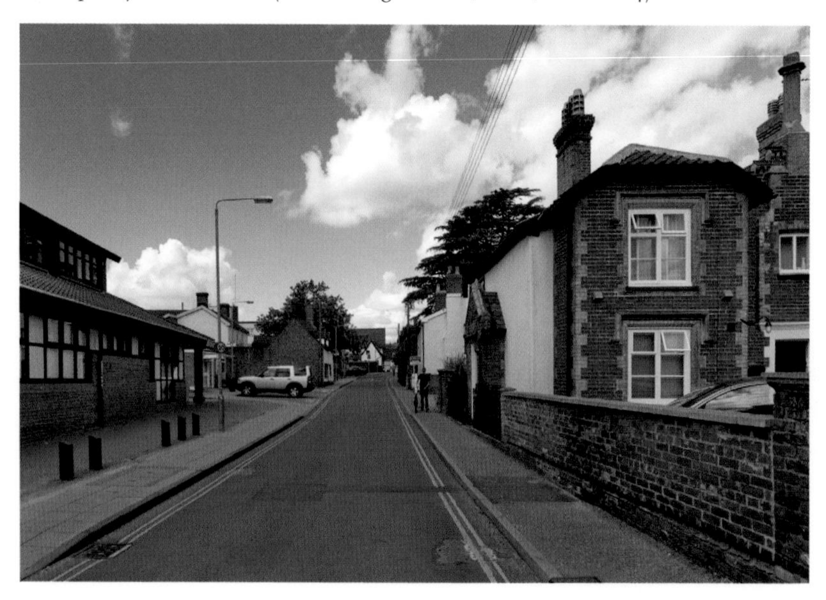

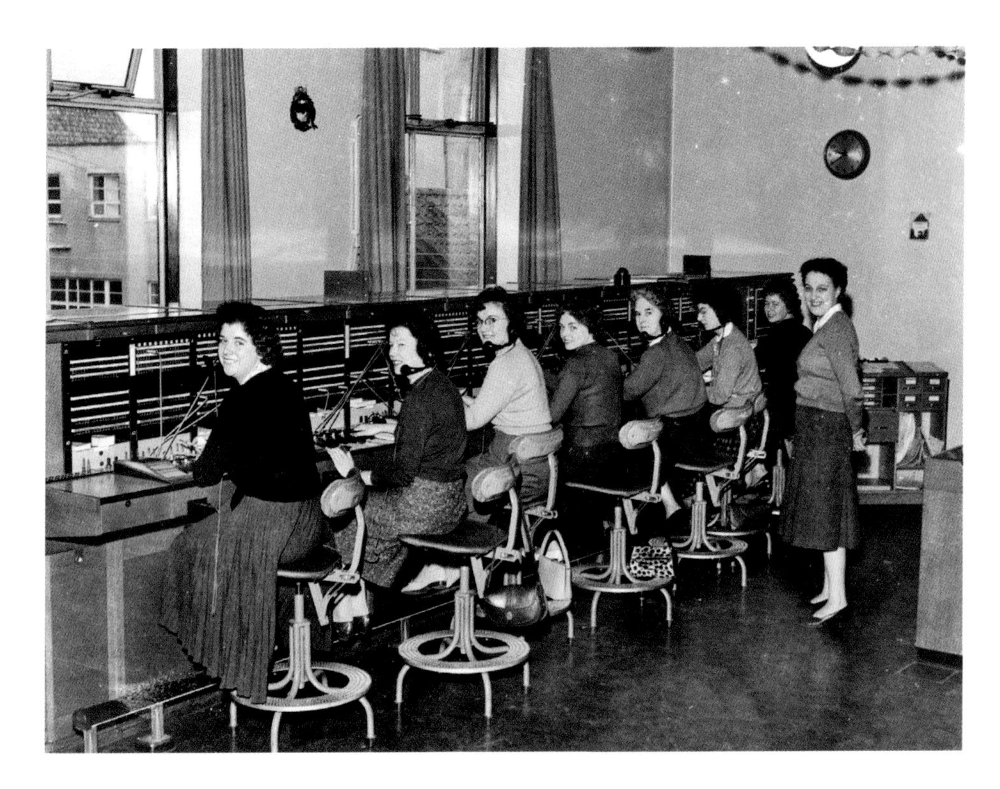

Operator Speaking
This is one of my favourite 'old' images in this book. In a bygone era before 3G and Wi-Fi, here we see women working at Diss telephone exchange at 9.40 a.m. one morning in the middle of the last century. The skies were somewhat ominous when I returned to take the newer image of the outside of the BT building on Chapel Street this summer, but you can just about see the back of the post office buildings in both images. (NCC)

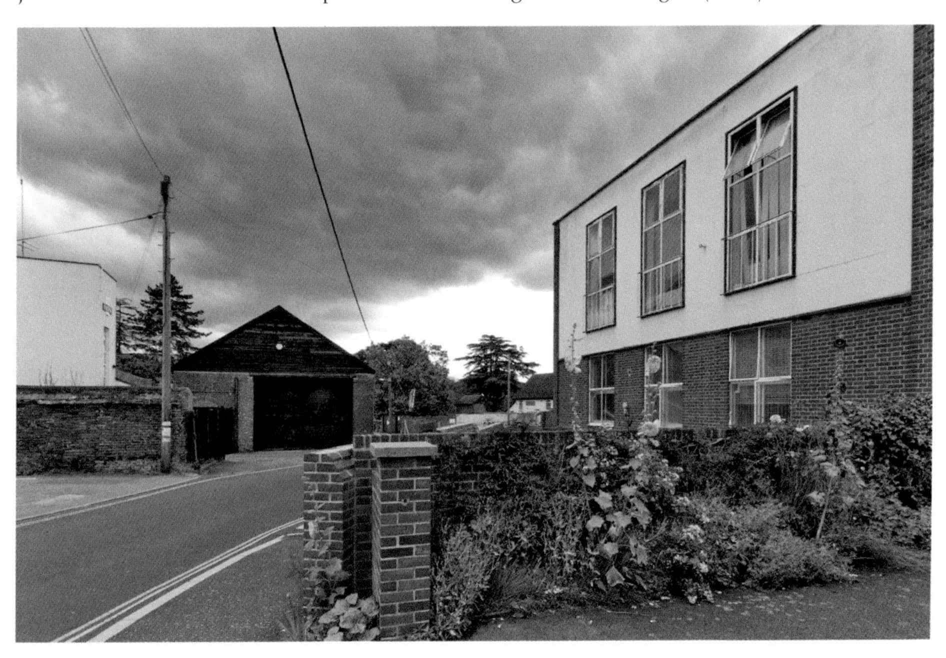

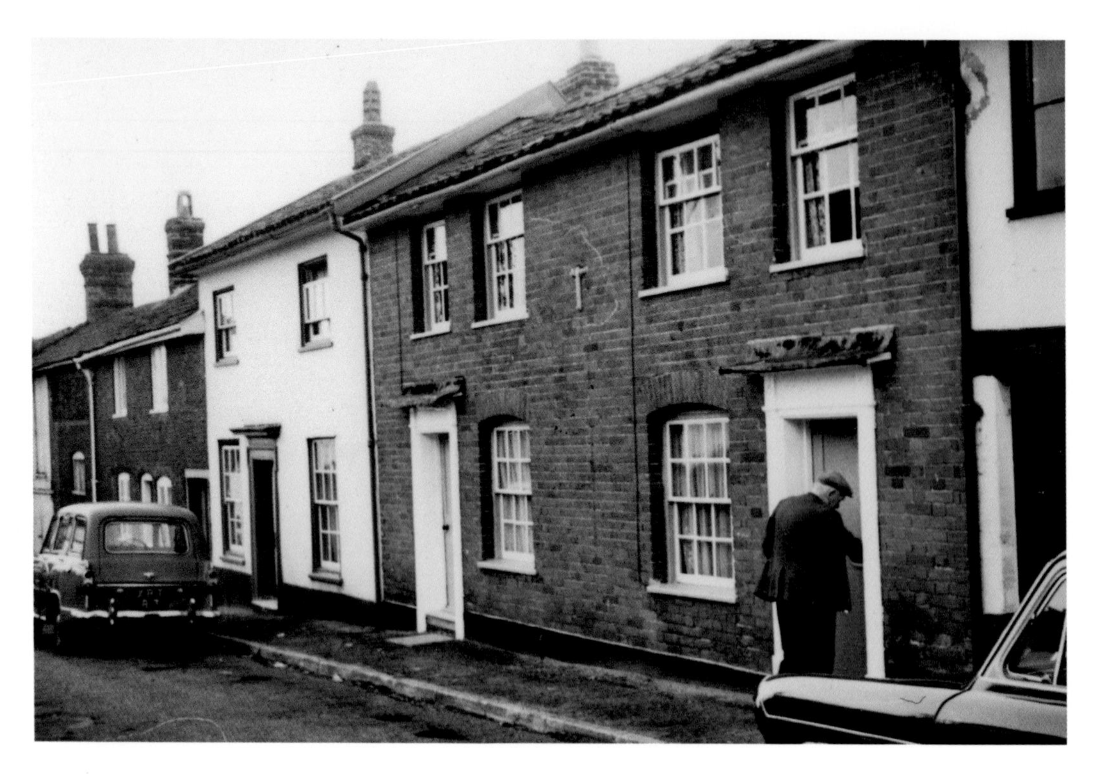

Chapel Street

Many will recognise the 'RT' in the number-plate, issued to vehicles in East Suffolk; my own first car was an 'SRT'! While this terrace has changed little since the 1960s, the rest of Chapel Street, particularly to the north where it meets Church Street, has changed somewhat from that which our ancestors would remember. I wonder what the Victorian inhabitants of the town would make of the modern-day guitar shop in Wills Yard, the former home of the fire station? (NCC)

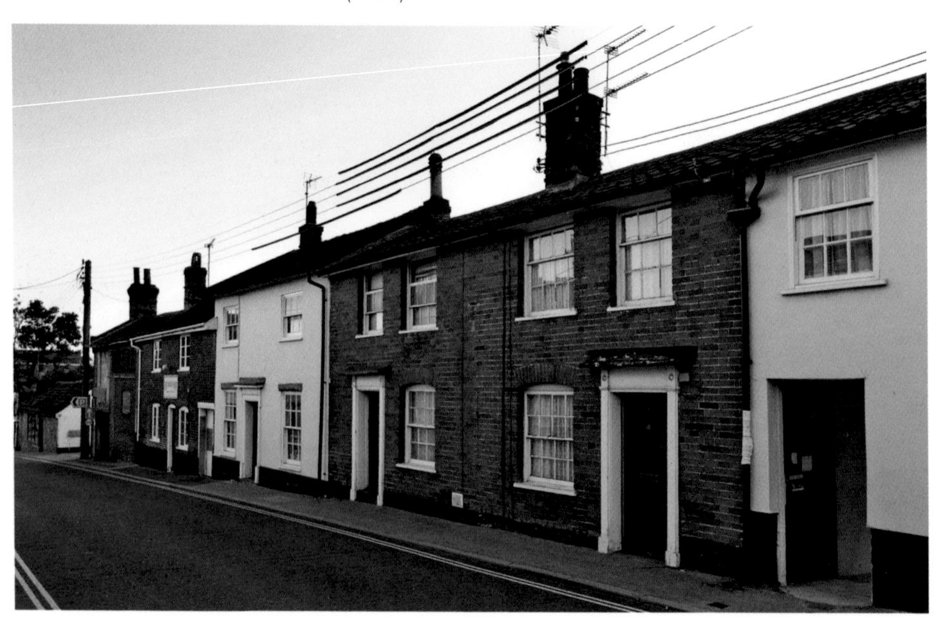

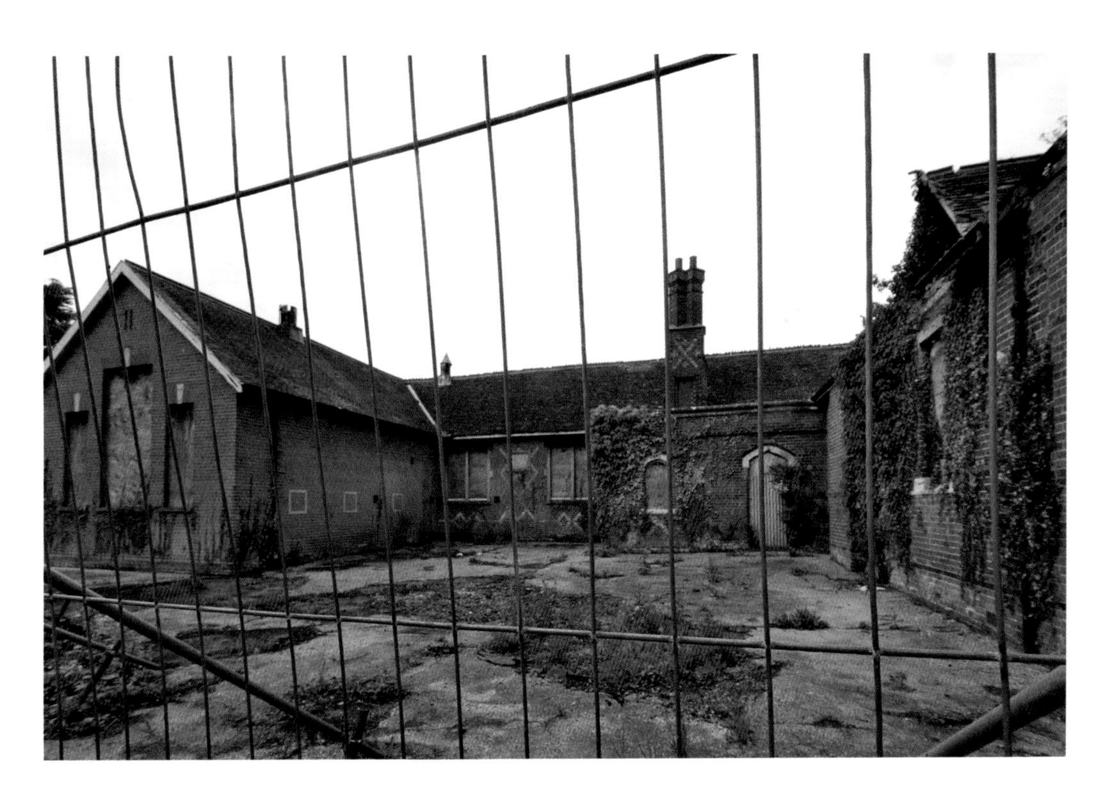

Victorian Schools

By 1845 there were already national and British schools in Diss for boys and girls, as well as private and church schools. The new British school was built in 1860 and two years later a new building for the national school was erected for 120 children; both were later enlarged. The national school is pictured above, now the Junior School. The British school, later an Infant school, is now derelict and awaiting redevelopment – the Infant school has moved to a new site.

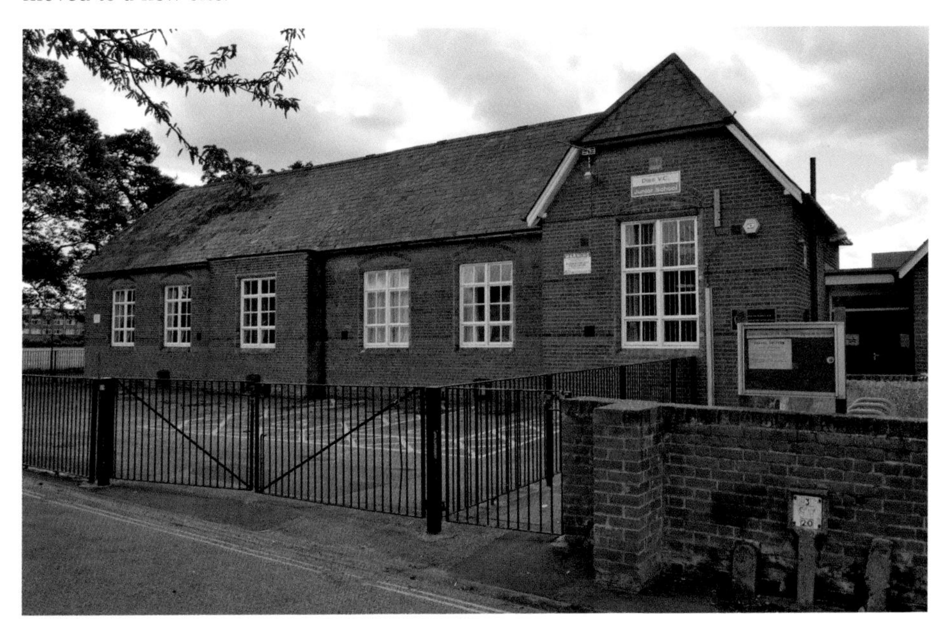

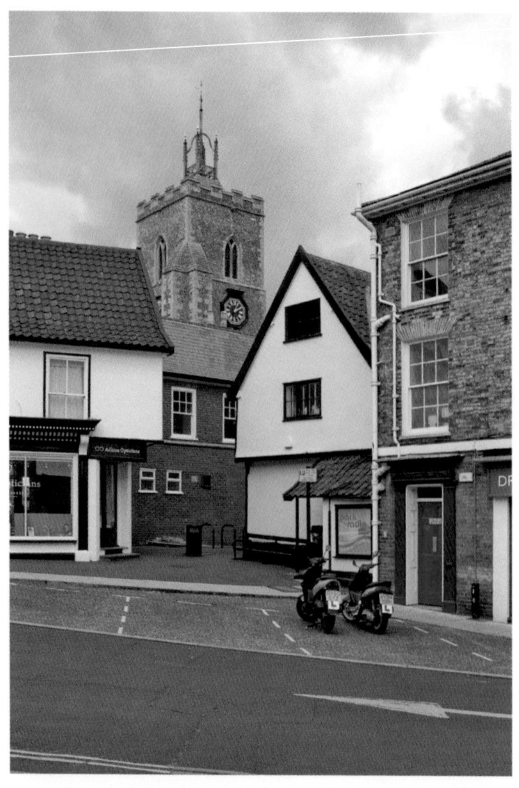

Market Hill

Returning to the Market Place and this time heading west up Market Hill, we find this little corner of the town that has only changed a little in the past fifty years (and most likely more than that!). The door on the building in the middle has moved, parking spaces have been laid out and the ghost signing has been painted over, but while the choice of vehicle may have changed a little, this is still a very recognisable scene. (NCC)

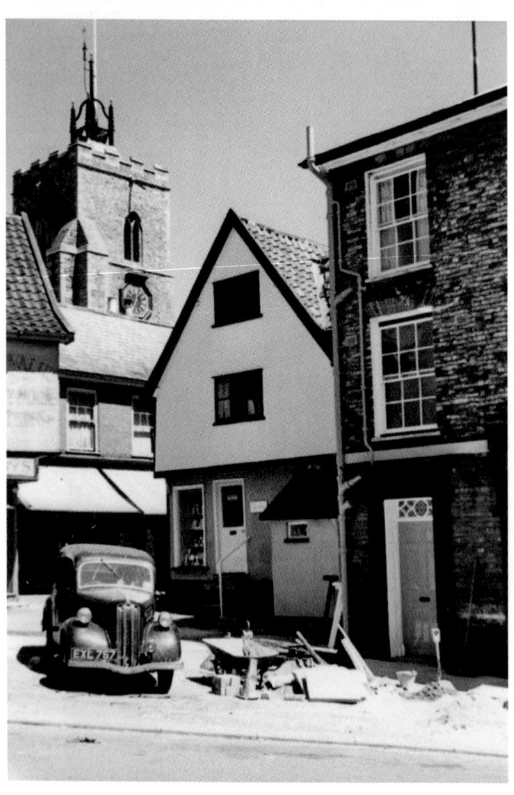

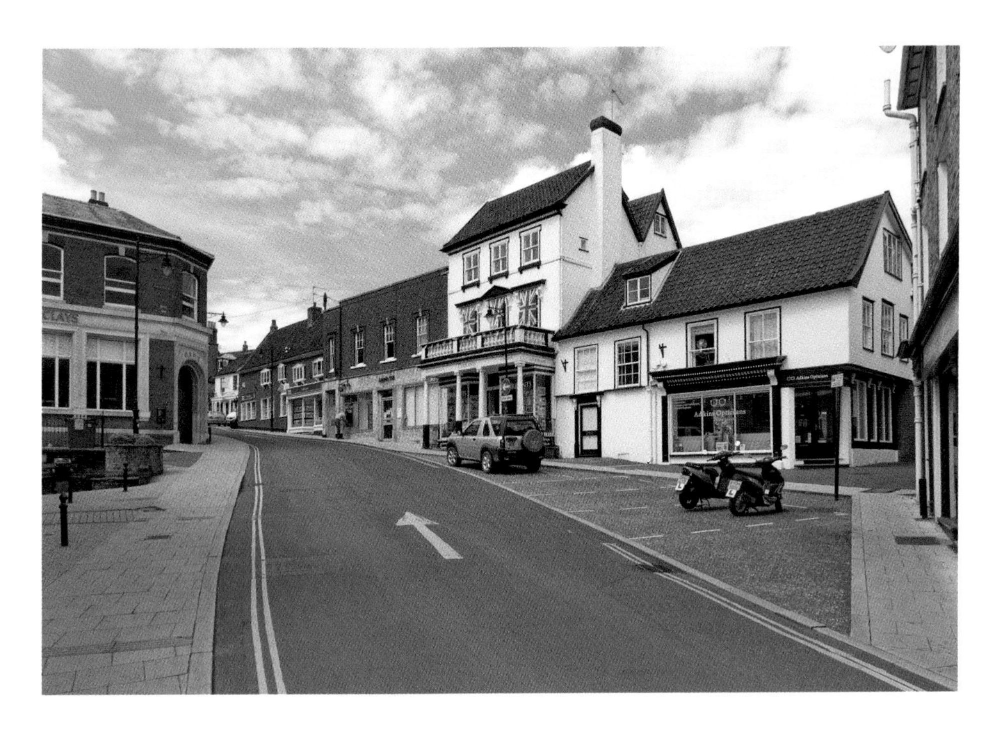

Local Banking

This image shows Barclays as it was fifty years ago – the memorable arch over the door remains a feature today. My Dad informs me that the older image shows a Bianchi Orsetto Scooter, a Ford Anglia 105E and probably a Ford Consul MkII (perhaps a Lowline version). Today, you might guess that I visited during the Queen's Diamond Jubilee celebrations and the London 2012 Olympics, as several of the images include union flags. The Wireless Shop is on the right of the older image with a canopy above the window. (NCC)

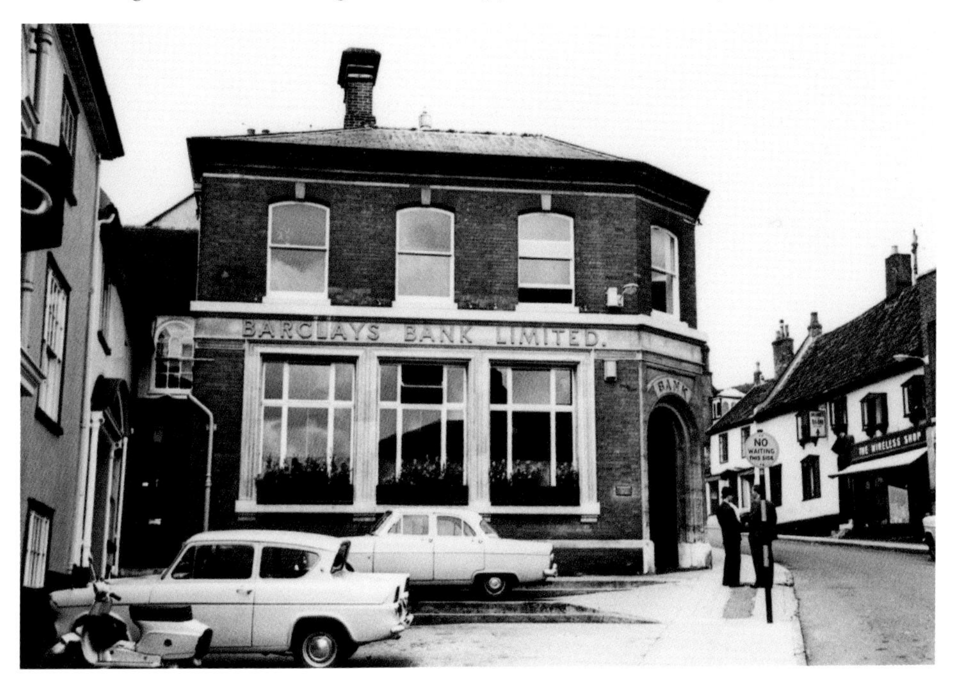

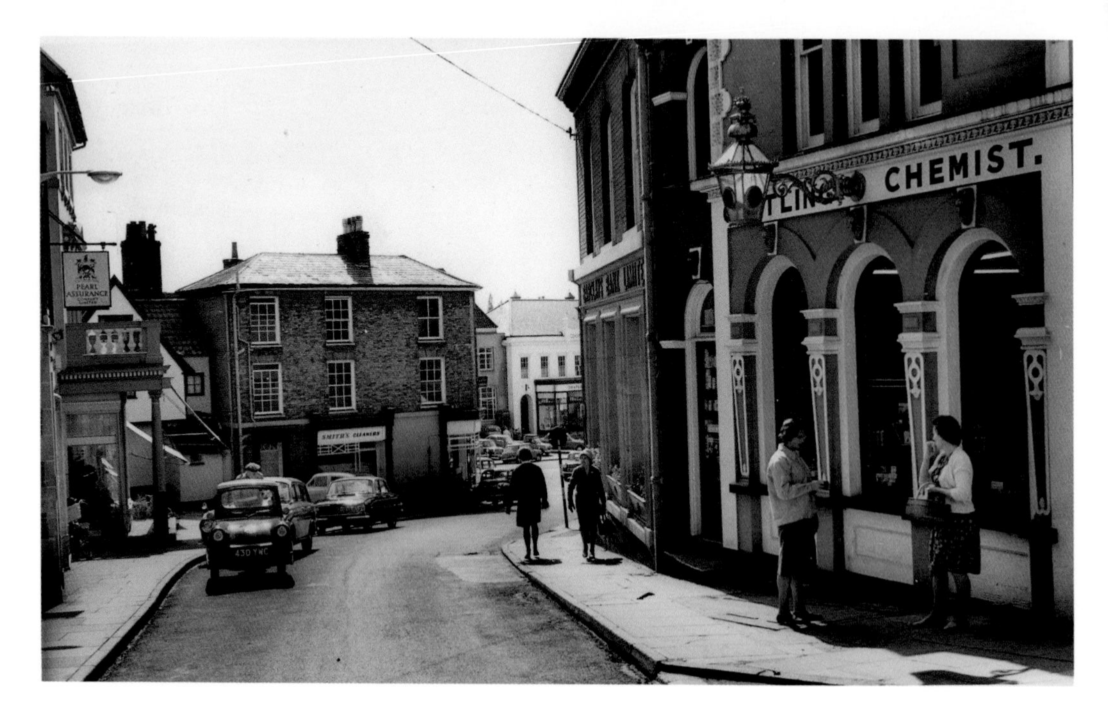

Looking Downhill

Moving further up the Market Hill, this great image shows ladies having a chat outside Gostling's Chemist (once one of several stores owned by the family). The sign for the Pearl Assurance Company, now a high-street bank, swings opposite and Gurney's bank is down the hill. The cars mark this out as an image from around 1965, and include what I am told is a Thundersley Invacar, probably a Mk12, heading up the hill towards the camera. (The Francis Frith Collection)

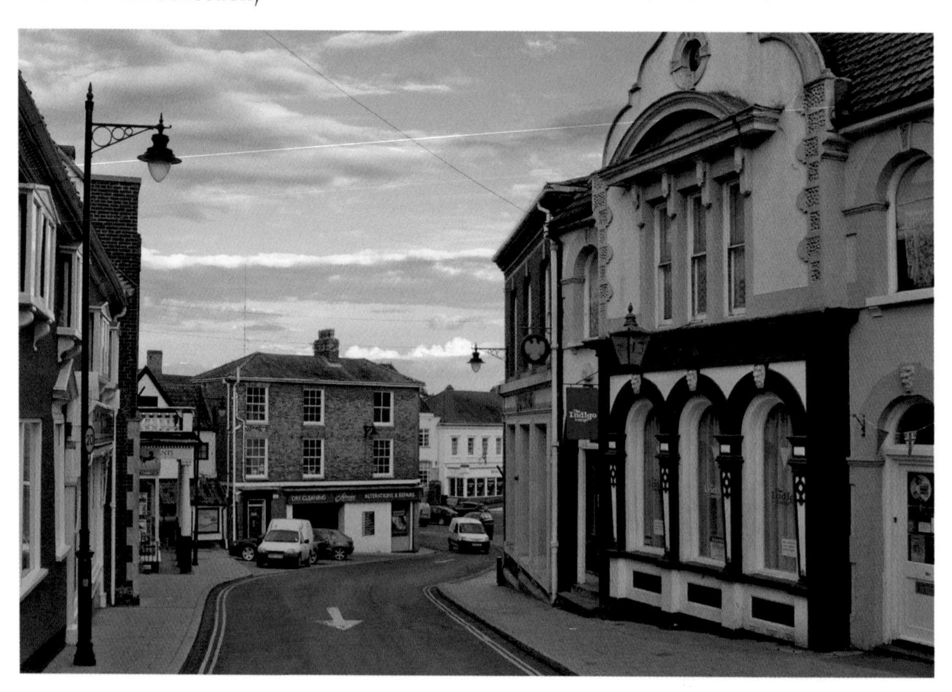

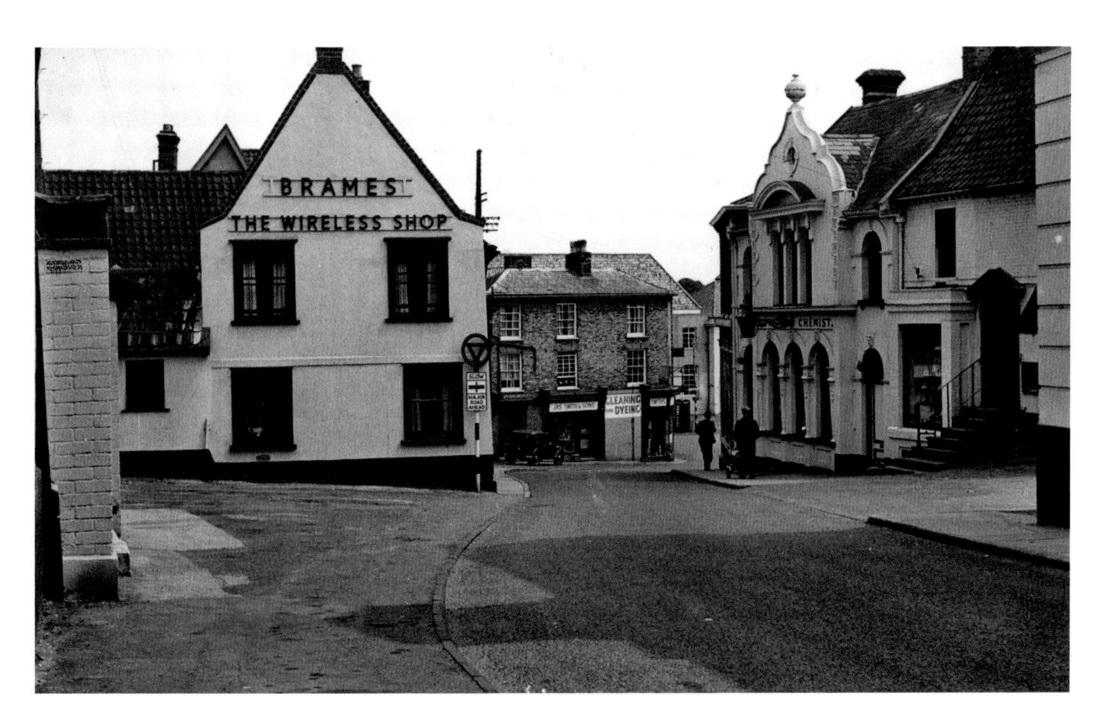

From the Top

Still very much in the heart of Diss, Market Hill (or Pump Hill) appears to have changed little since this image was taken (although the former Gostling's Chemist shop has lost a decorative ball from the roof). Brames' Wireless Shop operated from the 1920s (although not always on Market Hill – the 1925 *Kelly's* gives the address as Frenze Road) and finally closed in 2001. The premises of James Smith and Sons Cleaners Ltd (dyers and cleaners) remain a dry-cleaners' today. (The Francis Frith Collection)

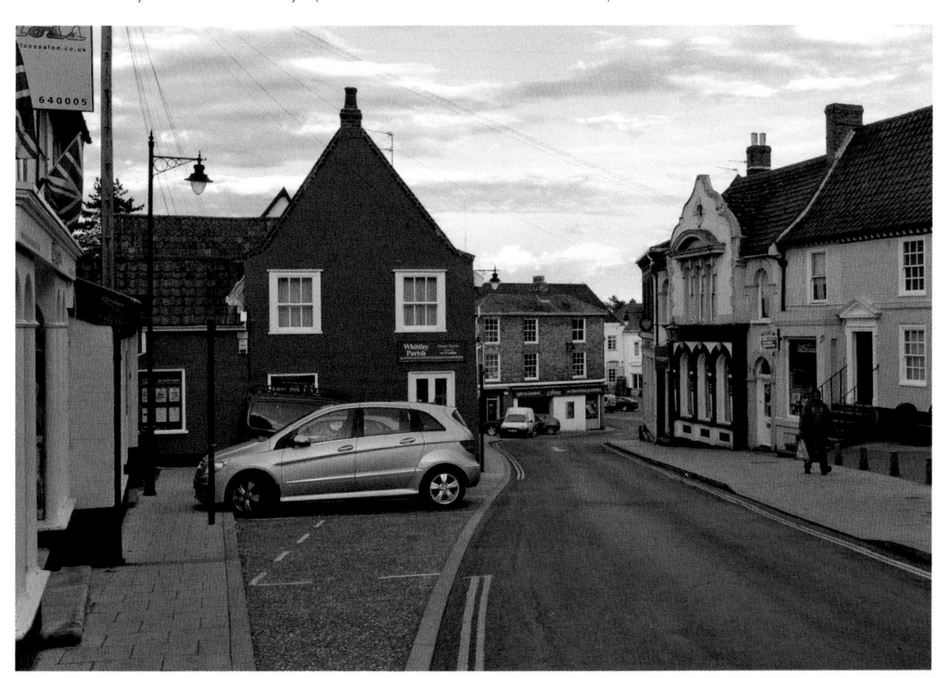

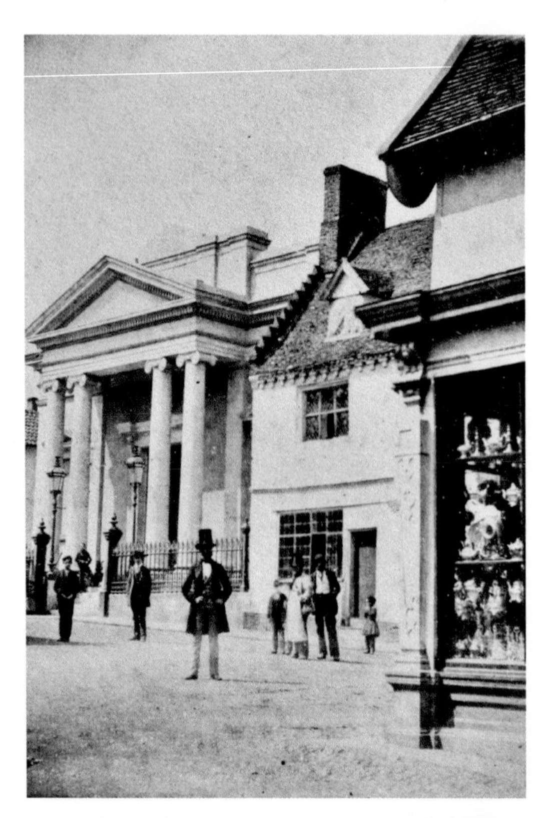

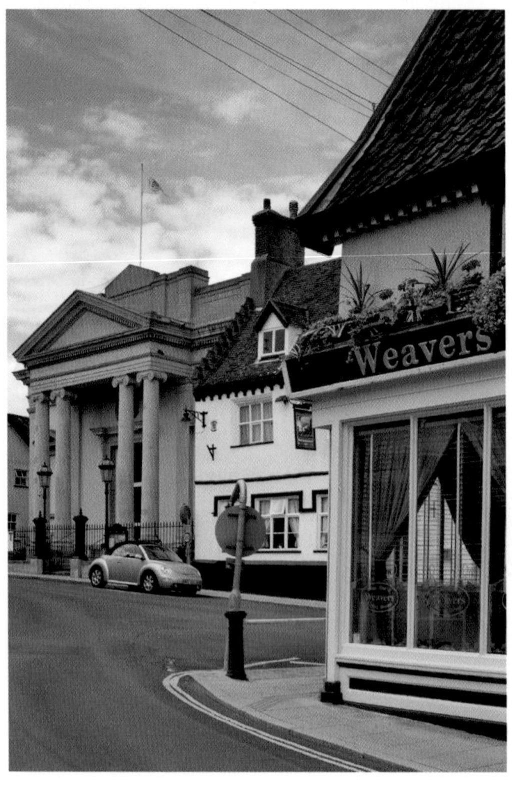

Corn Hall

The 1922 *Kelly's Directory* described the Corn Exchange (now the Corn Hall) as 'a structure of brick with a lofty stone portico in the Ionic style, designed and erected by Mr George Atkins, of this town: the hall is 77 by 42 feet, lighted from above by an iron and glass roof, and contains an organ, presented by the late Miss Taylor'. The building was paid for by Thomas Lombe Taylor. The Victorian scene shows the Corn Exchange in its early days. (Cleer S Alger Trust; NRO, MS 10824)

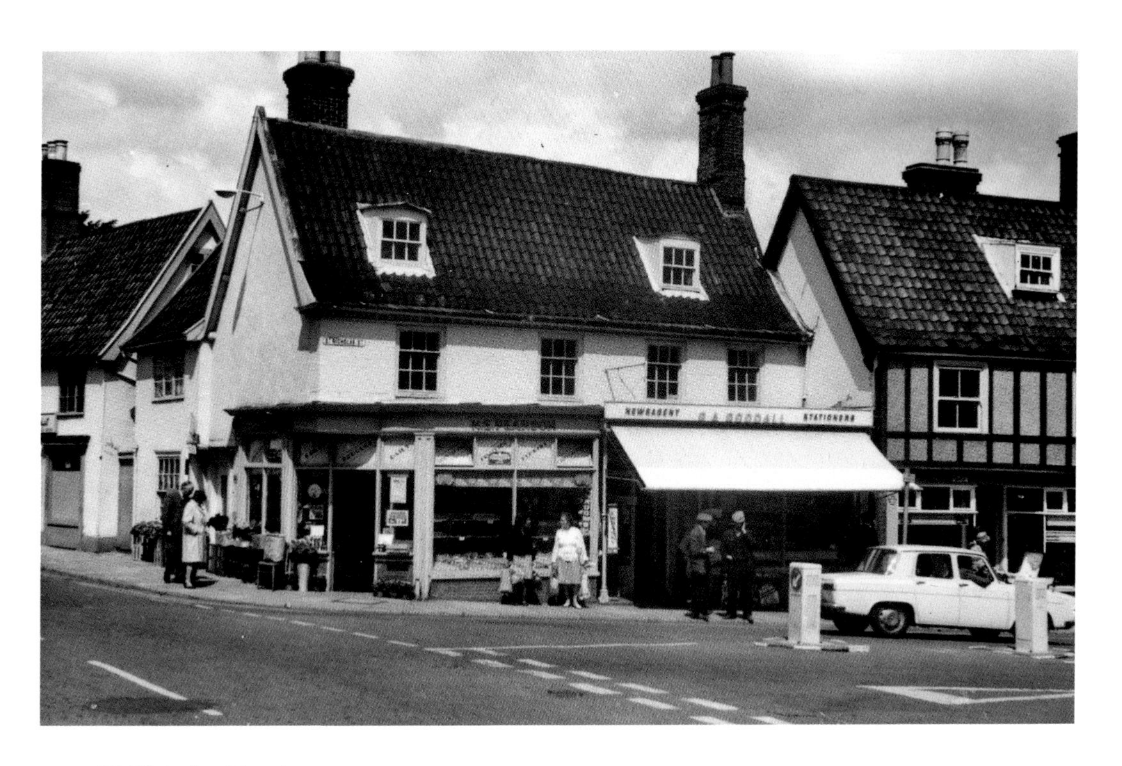

St Nicholas Street

Moving to the top of St Nicholas Street (once Crown Street) from Market Hill, we can look down the street towards the church. Another surveyor's photograph, the building pictured here once housed Pearson's corner shop and Goodall's newsagents and stationers. Today, it provides a home for a copy shop and a home-brewing company. Changes to the building include the removal of windows in the roof, and the addition of a new one in the side of the building. (NCC)

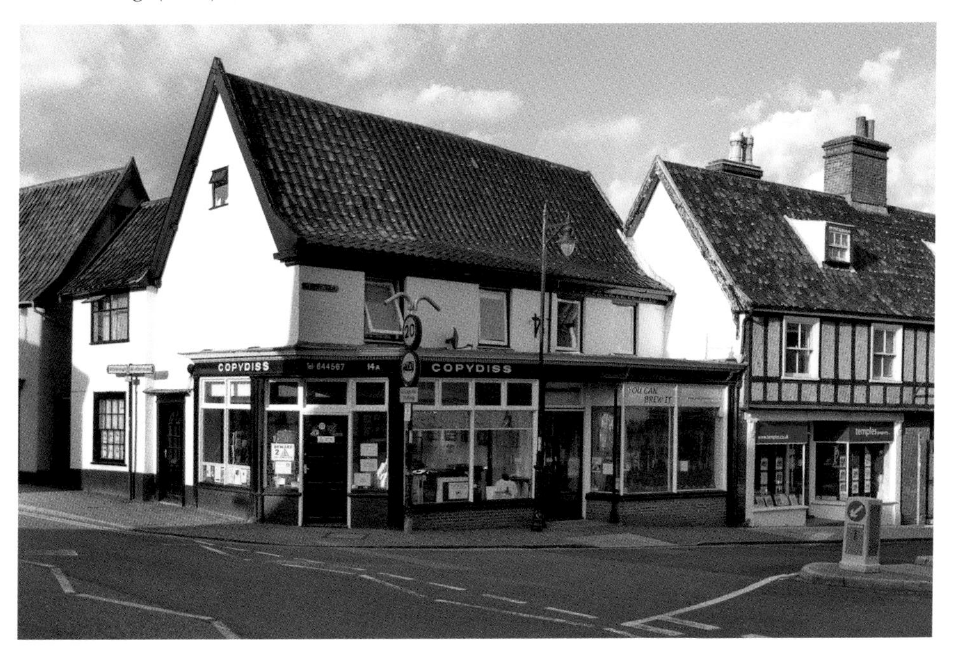

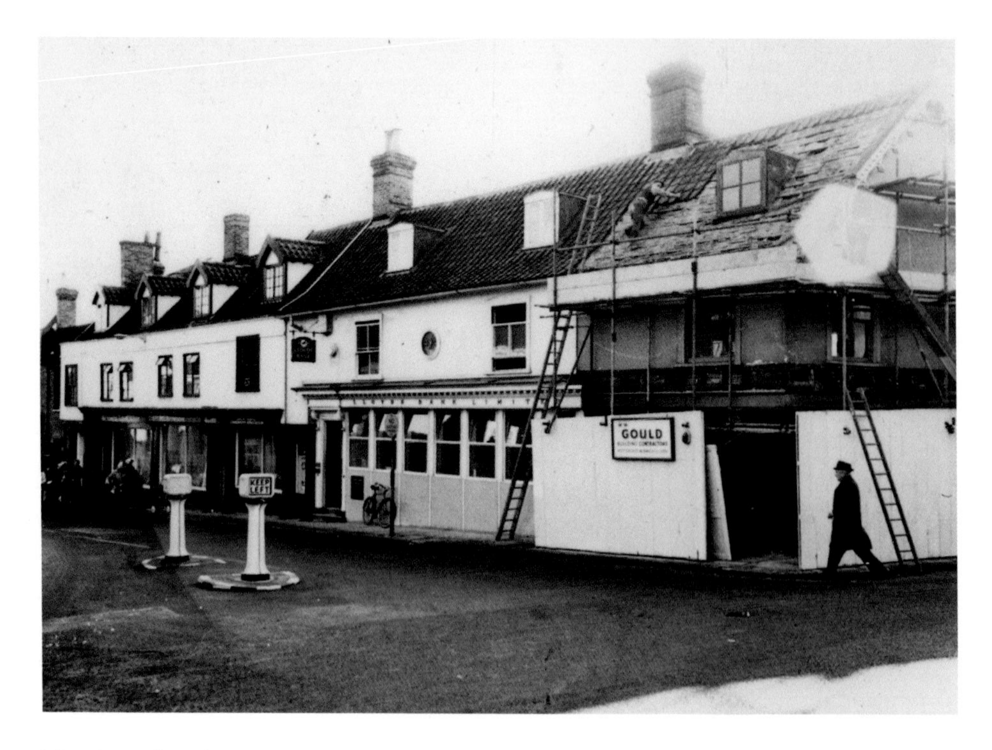

The Opposite View

On the other side of the road, another surveyor's photograph shows work being done by Norwich firm W. W. Gould on the corner with Denmark Street. The round clock on the wall of the old Lloyd's bank is still there, but the change in the shape of the building altered the layout of windows and doors (*inset*). The old 'keep left' bollards have since been replaced, and there is now also a zebra crossing on Denmark Street between this building and the Crown. (NCC)

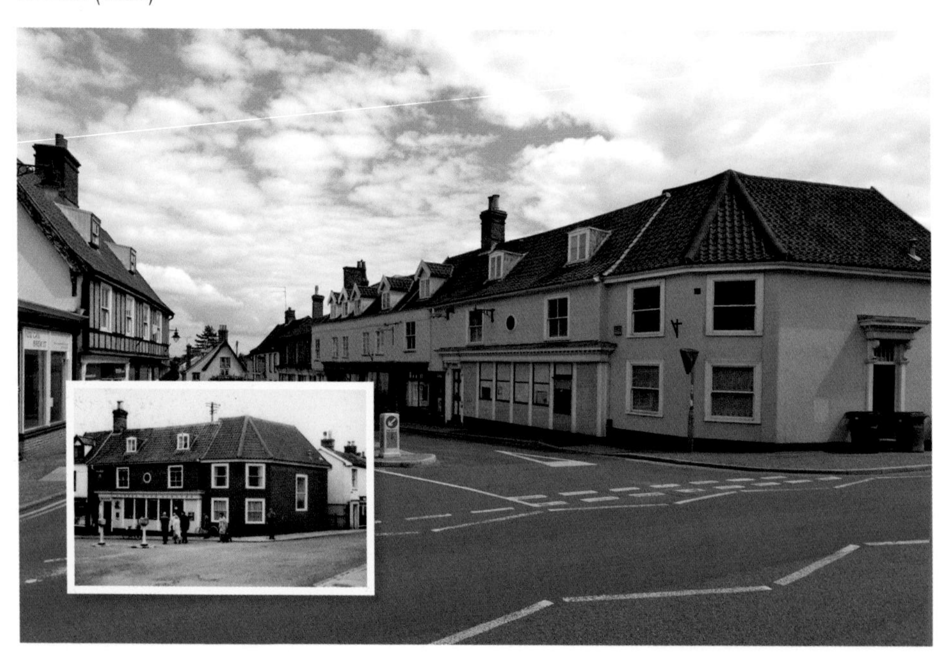

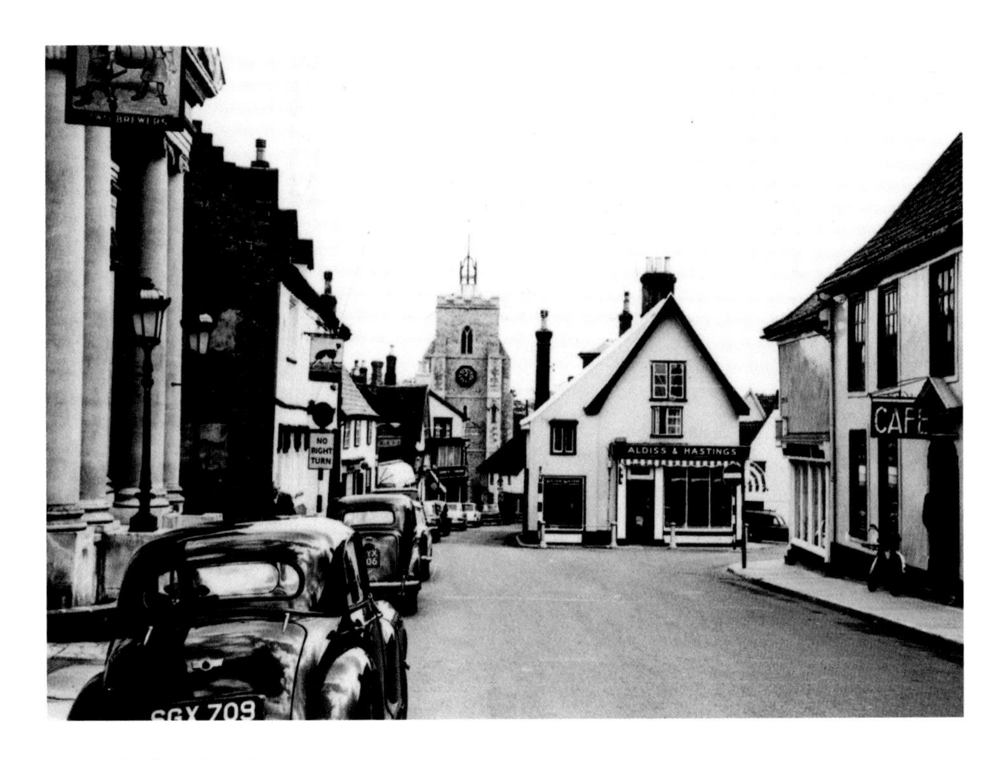

Towards the Church

This great surveyor's image shows the church from a vantage point on St Nicholas Street. The Two Brewers has become the Nutbush, while the Greyhound remains recognisable and in business. Aldiss and Hastings' men's outfitters has become the Weavers restaurant (this is the site of the Chapel of St Nicholas, belonging to the Guild of St Nicholas, which was suppressed in the 1500s) and the café, while still selling food, now serves Chinese cuisine. (NCC)

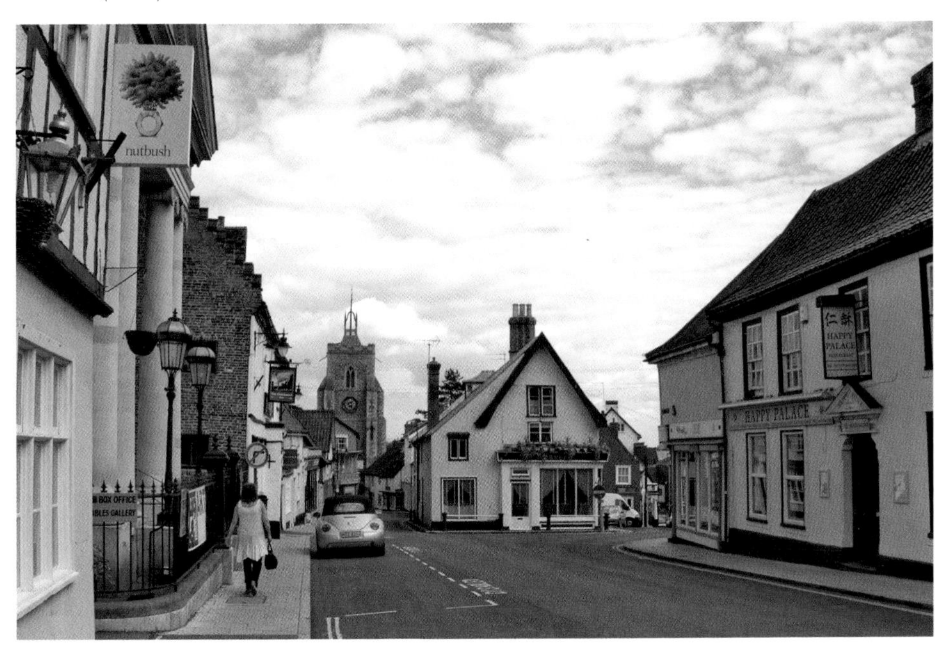

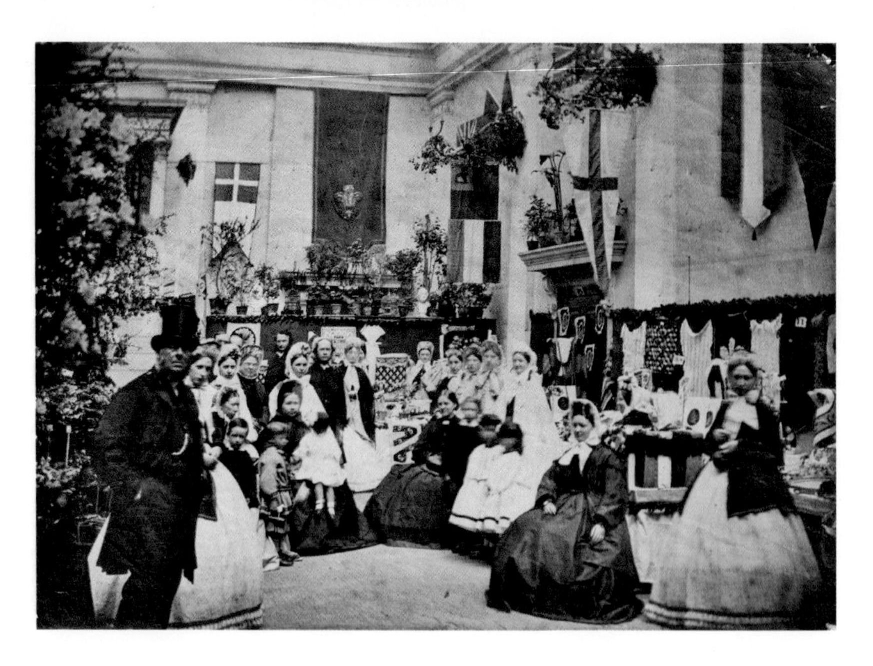

Musical Entertainments

Erected in 1854, the Corn Hall has always provided space for concerts and public meetings as well as the activities of local corn merchants. Rooms inside were also used for magistrates' meetings and a public library and reading room. Over time, a huge number of events have taken place here, including the concert (*below*) by the Alex Pettit band on the occasion of the Queen's Coronation in 1953, and a school fundraiser in 1864 (*above*). The Musical Society and Sacred Harmonic Society were also meeting here in 1864, and the hall is still used for cultural events today. (Cleer S Alger Trust; NRO, MS 10824/NCC)

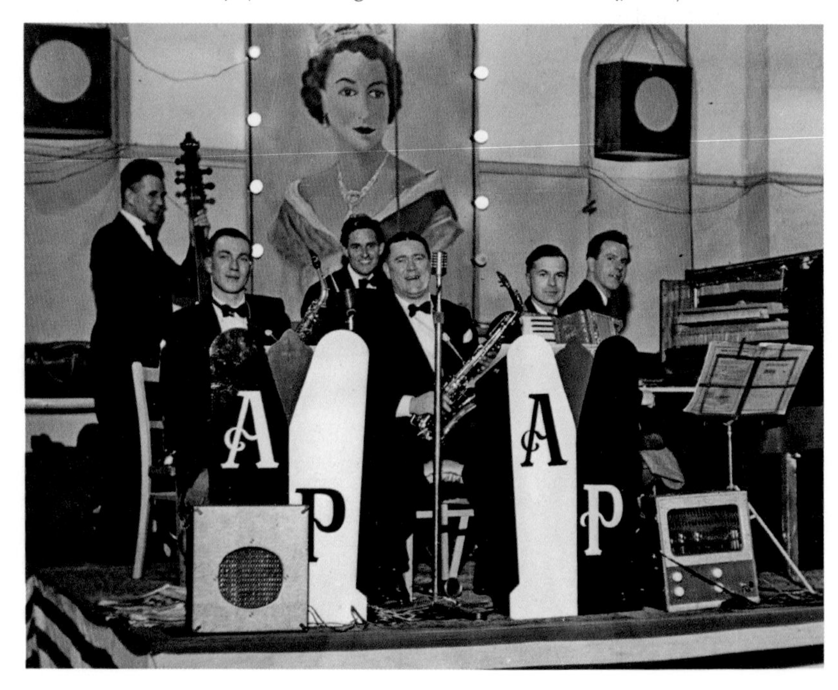

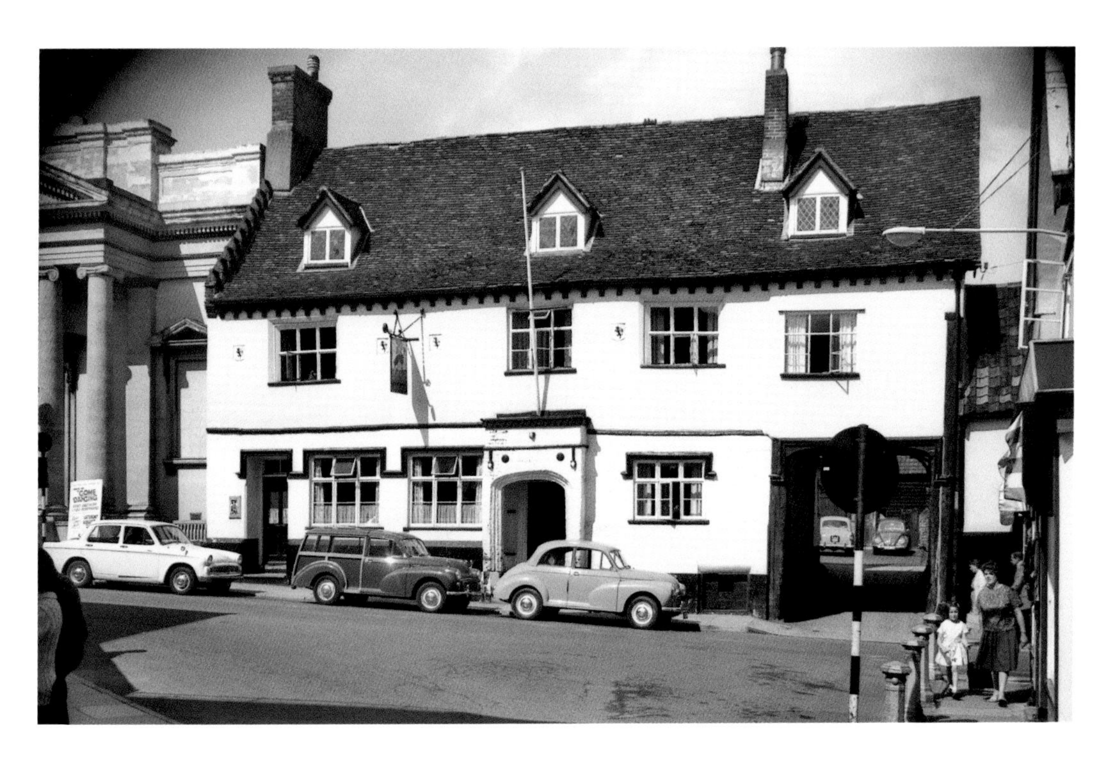

The Greyhound
Rumour has it that James I entertained a 'lady friend' here. Given he was on the throne in the early 1600s, we are talking about another ancient inn (although this building *may* be slightly newer than the one James I supposedly visited on the site). The Greyhound we see today looks smarter than the Victorian pub (*inset*) but all three images obviously show the same place. The Half Moon and Prince of Wales pubs would once also have been serving ale in these parts. (Plunkett/Cleer S Alger Trust; NRO, MS 10824)

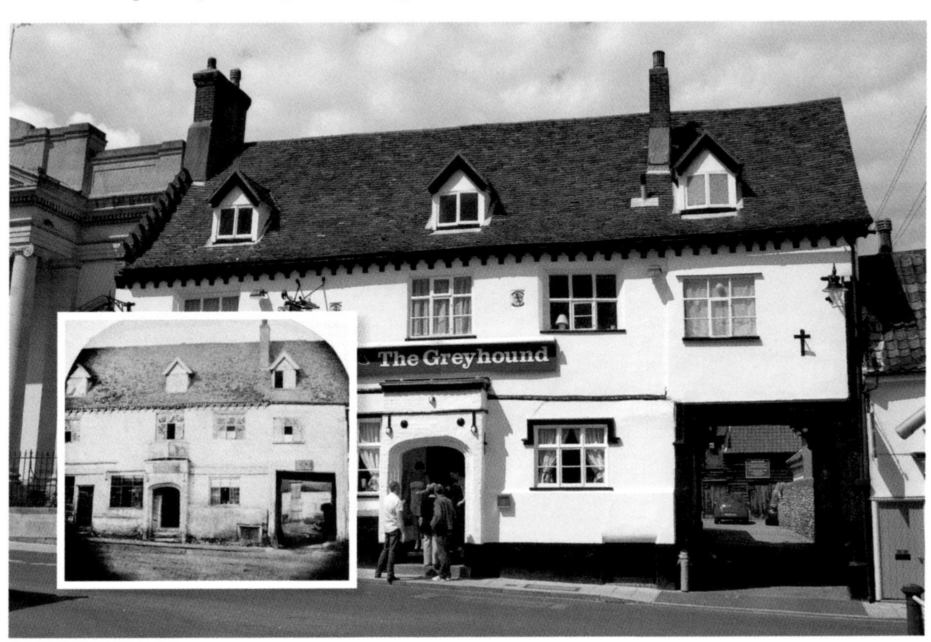

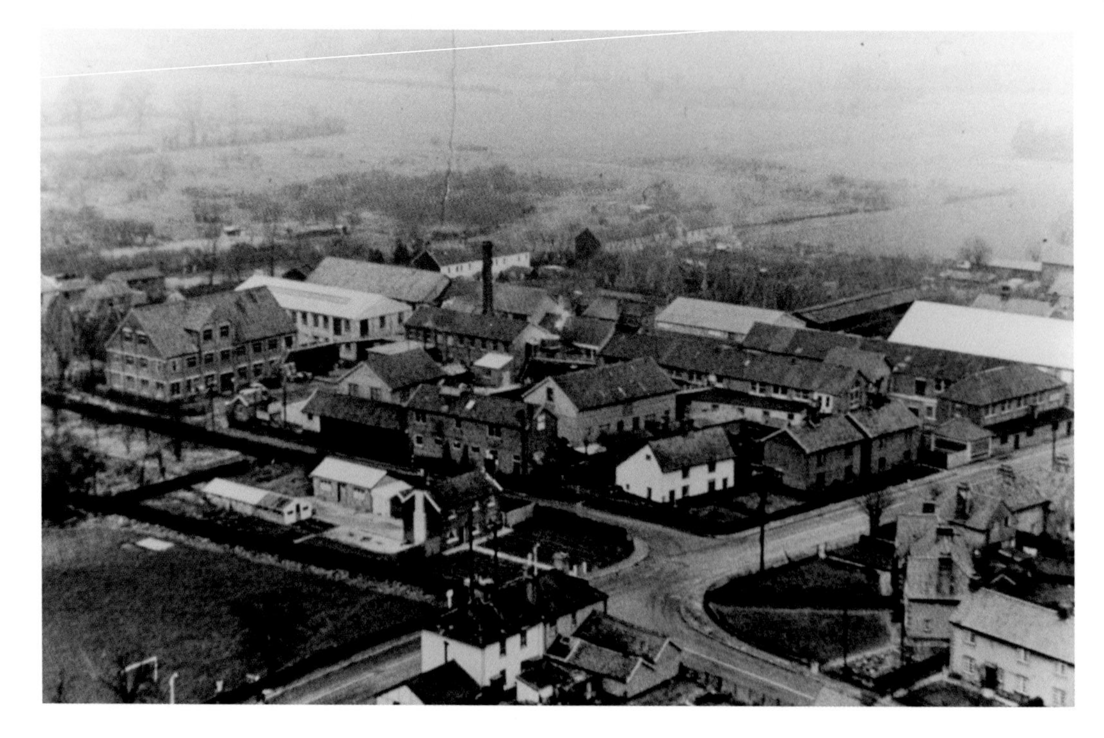

Aldrich's Factory

This is a view that hasn't been seen in Diss since the early 1990s, when Aldrich's brush factory was finally demolished following a decline in trade. Today, the houses on the corner of Shelfanger Road and Factory Lane still exist and can be seen in both images, but the factory has gone, leaving just street-names behind – 'Brushmakers' Way', which winds around the back of the older houses, and further up Factory Lane, 'Aldrich Way'. (Untraced; part of image collection donated to NCC)

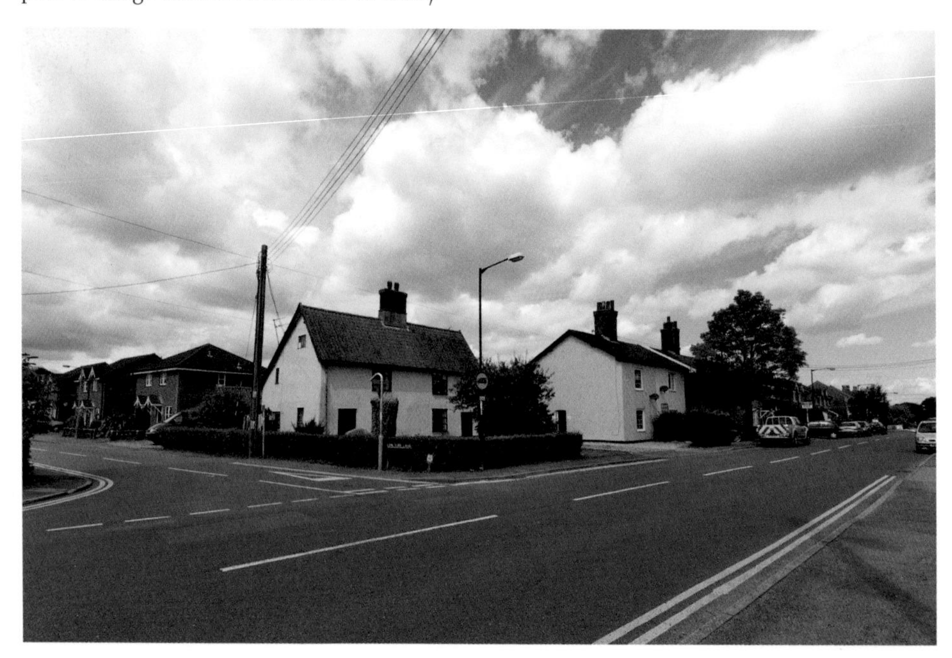

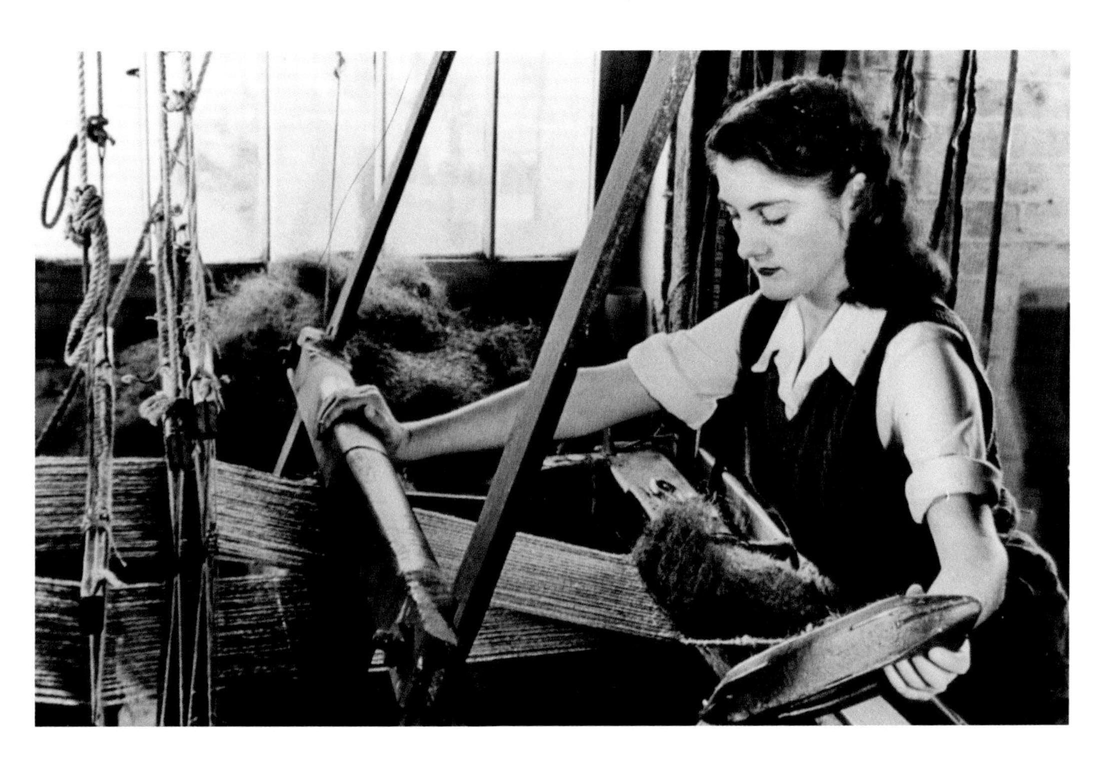

Trade and Industry
This possibly 1940s/50s image shows a beautiful lady weaving coconut matting at Aldrich's factory. A major employer, making several kinds of matting and brushes, Aldrich's was on Crown Street in the 1830s, and moved to Factory Lane before the turn of the century. While some Diss industries may have come and gone, the town now has two industrial estates to the east (pictured), a business centre and many other town-centre employers. (Untraced; part of image collection donated to NCC)

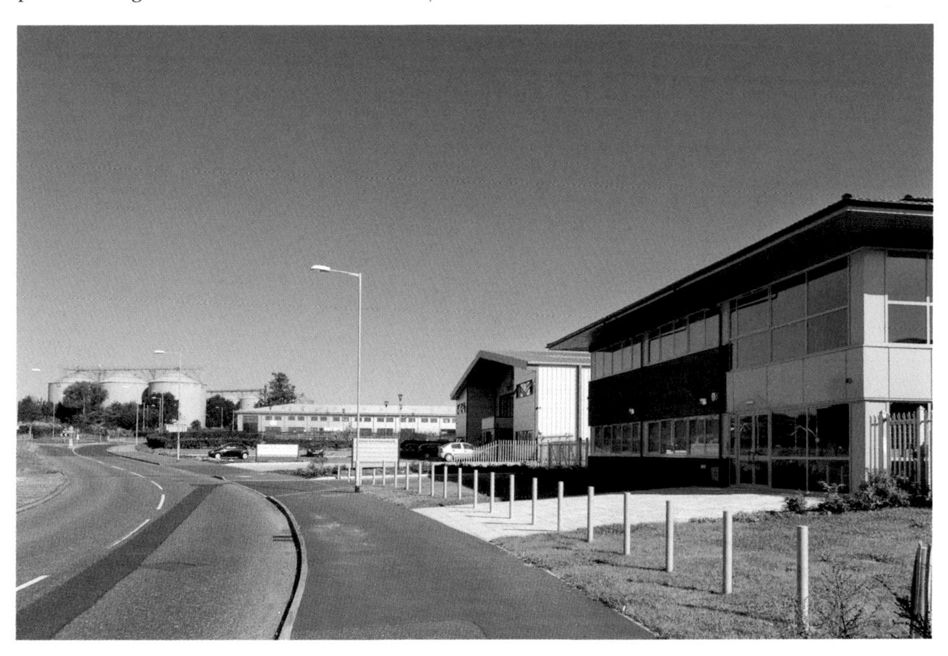

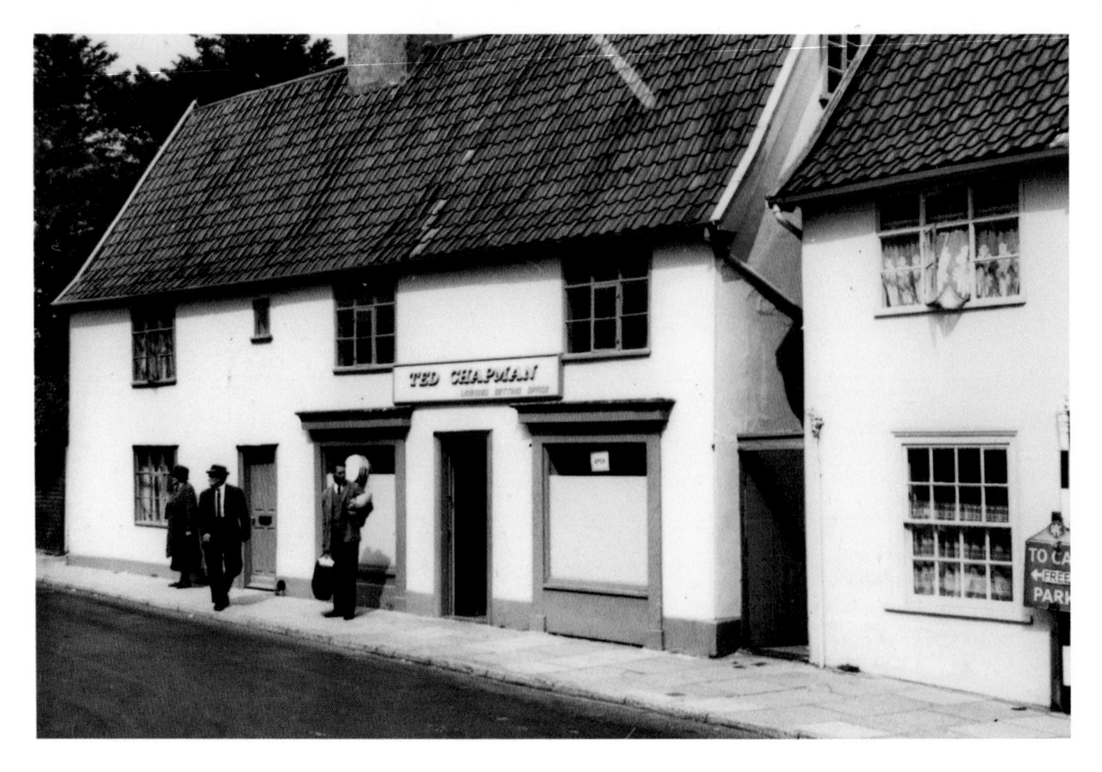

Crossroads

Moving further down the street to the Shelfanger Road/Roydon Road/St Nicholas Street/Denmark Street crossroads, these suave 1950s gentlemen are pictured outside Ted Chapman's licensed betting office. The building is now home to a fabrics shop. Not far from here, on the other side of Shelfanger Road, the car park next to the brewery used to be a 'moat', associated with the brewing process. Another large brewery was sited next to Denmark Green. (NCC)

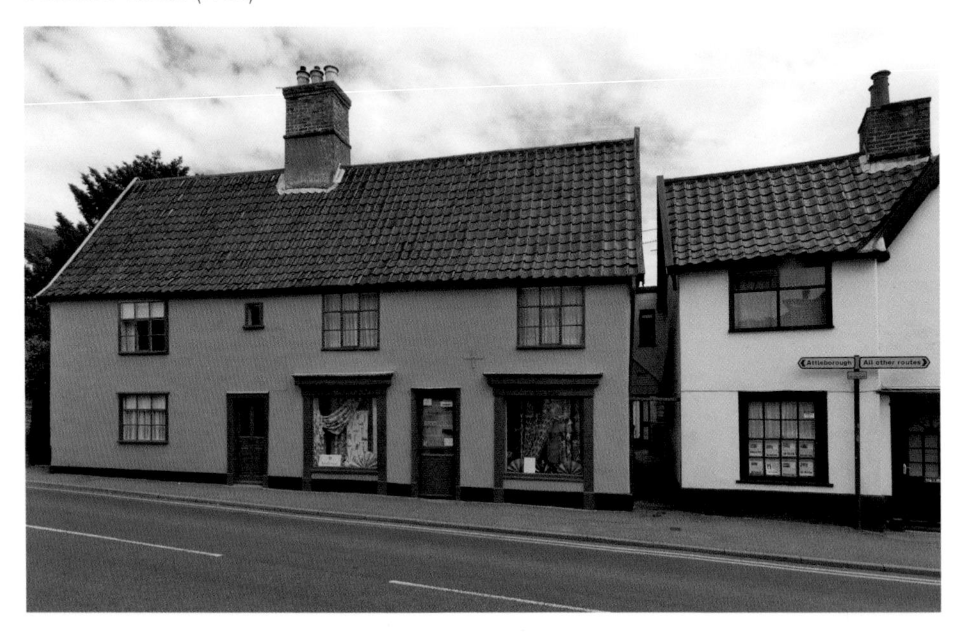

Baptist Church

Diss Baptist church on Denmark Street is one of the most well-known buildings in Diss, enjoying a prominent position on the high side of the Mere. Two Baptist meetings were mentioned in *White's Directory* in 1845, and the current building was erected in 1860 (although the church was founded much earlier, in 1788). Later, in 1926, a lecture hall was added. Older pictures taken from the Mere often show the church on the right of its 'twin' – Grassmere House, sited a little further along. (NCC)

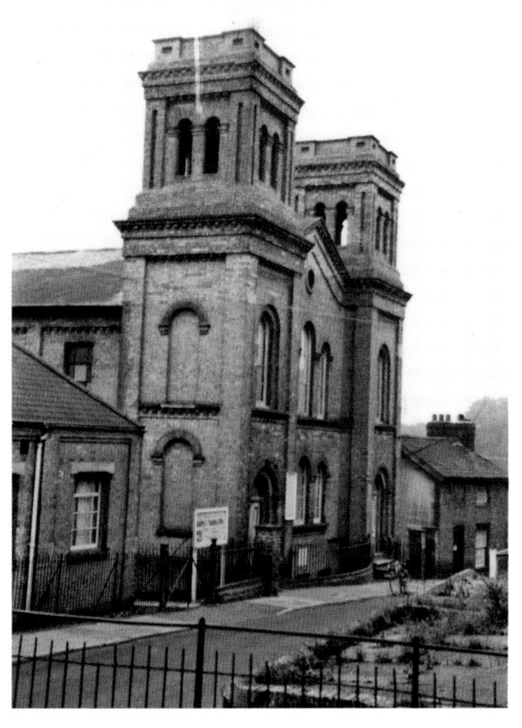

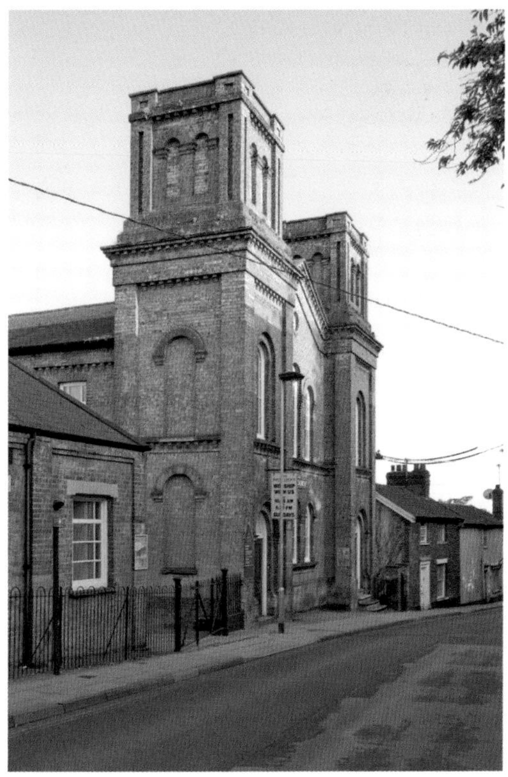

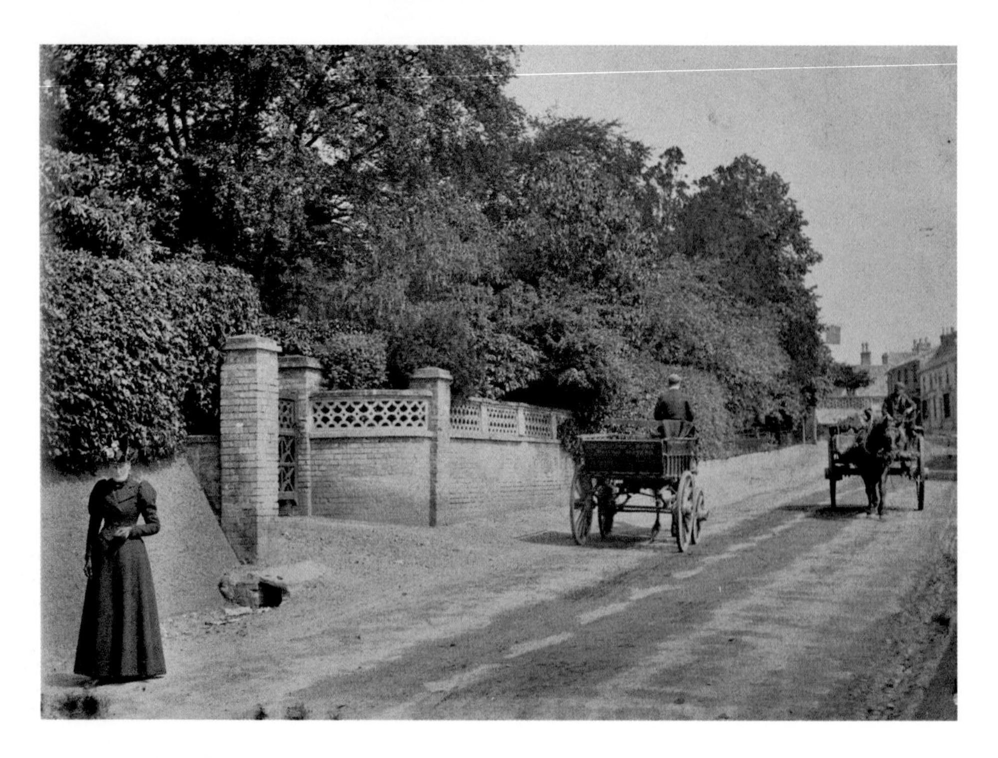

Miss Ward and Mrs Carrick

Labelled as 'Miss Lucy Ward', this Victorian image (*c.* 1885) of Denmark Street depicts a well-dressed woman standing beside a road used by horse-drawn vehicles. Returning to the spot today, I asked my good friend Helen to take the place of Miss Ward to create a modern version of the scene, albeit with a slightly wider aspect. Still a major route through the town, the sign for the Beehive no longer swings above the road at the top of the hill. (Cleer S Alger Trust/NRO, MS 10824)

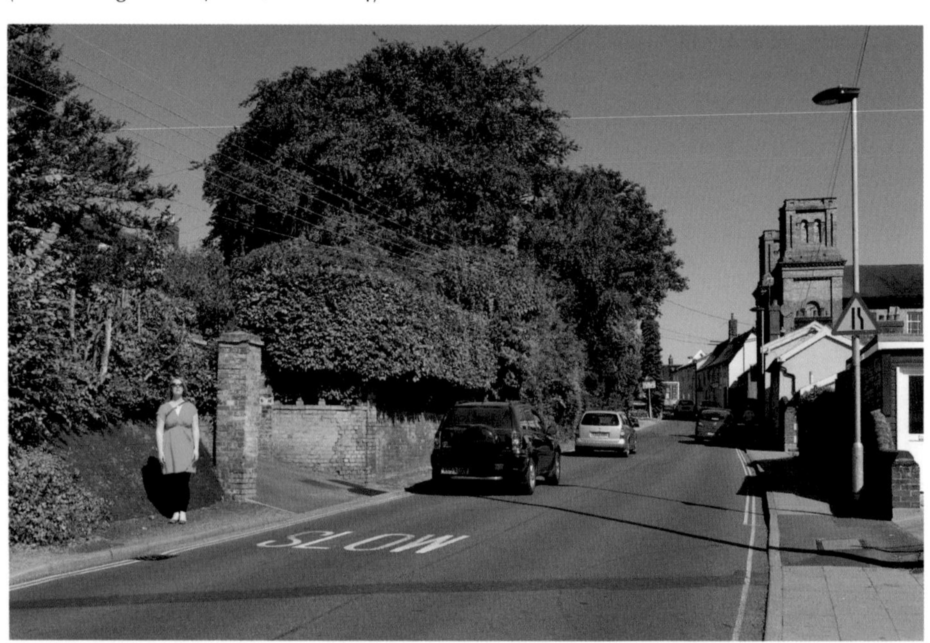

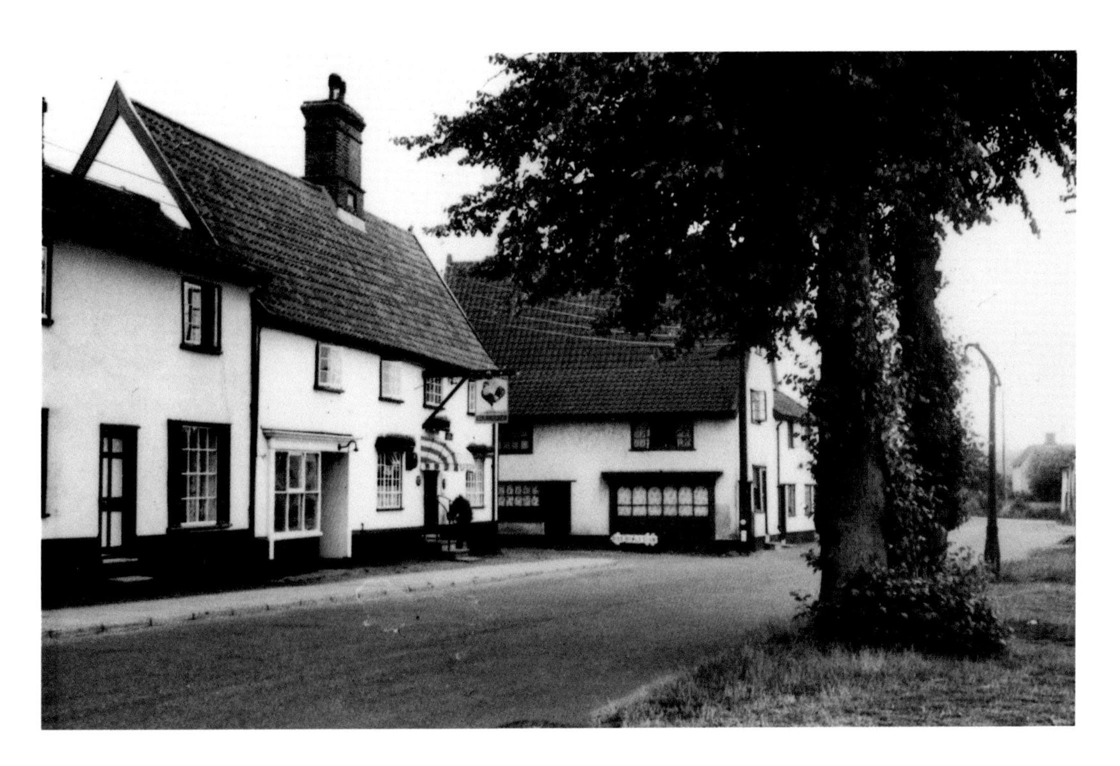

Diss Fair

The Cock Inn is another historic watering hole in Diss. Denmark Street and Fair Green were once Cock Street and Cock [Street] Green, unsurprisingly once famous for cock-fighting. An annual fair had long been a tradition here before *White's Directory* of 1845. The *Directory* says that they were held on 9 November each year. After perhaps 400 years of continual fairs, the Home Secretary abolished them in 1872. Still open, green space today, local events still provide entertainment at regular intervals. (NCC)

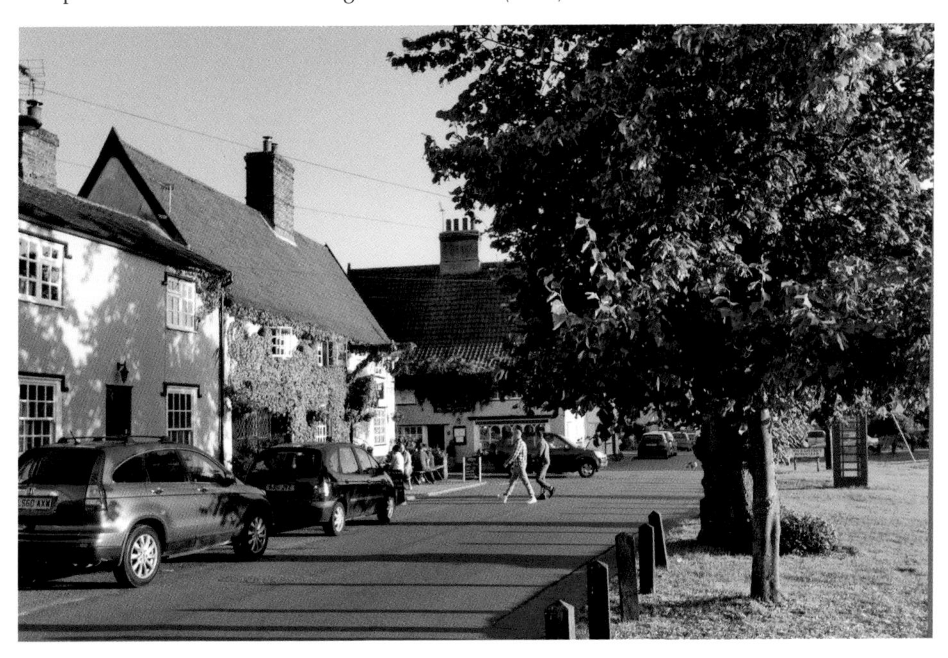

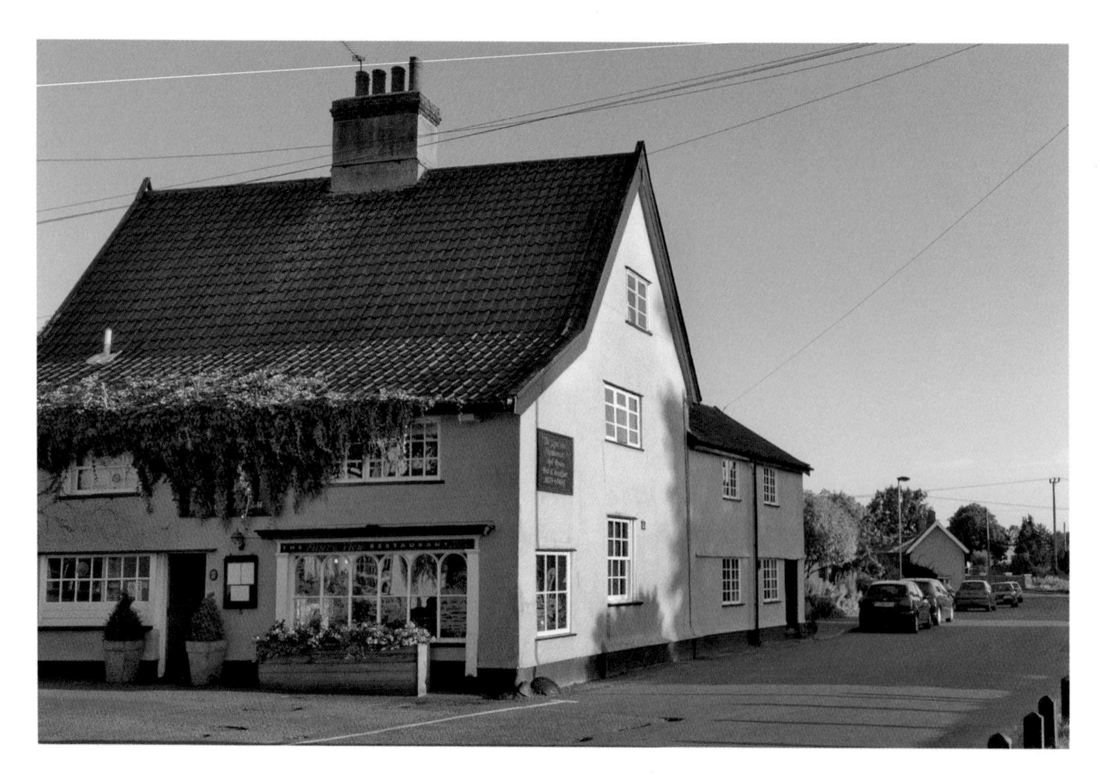

Denmark Street

The building seen here, once a sub-post office, is now the Fayre View Restaurant. Since the older image was taken, the roof of this building has been tiled; only a few thatched buildings now remain in the town where once there would have been many. A row of pretty cottages further down Denmark Street is depicted in the older picture, but pretty as they may have been, they were deemed redundant in the 1960s and demolished. (Untraced; part of image collection donated to NCC)

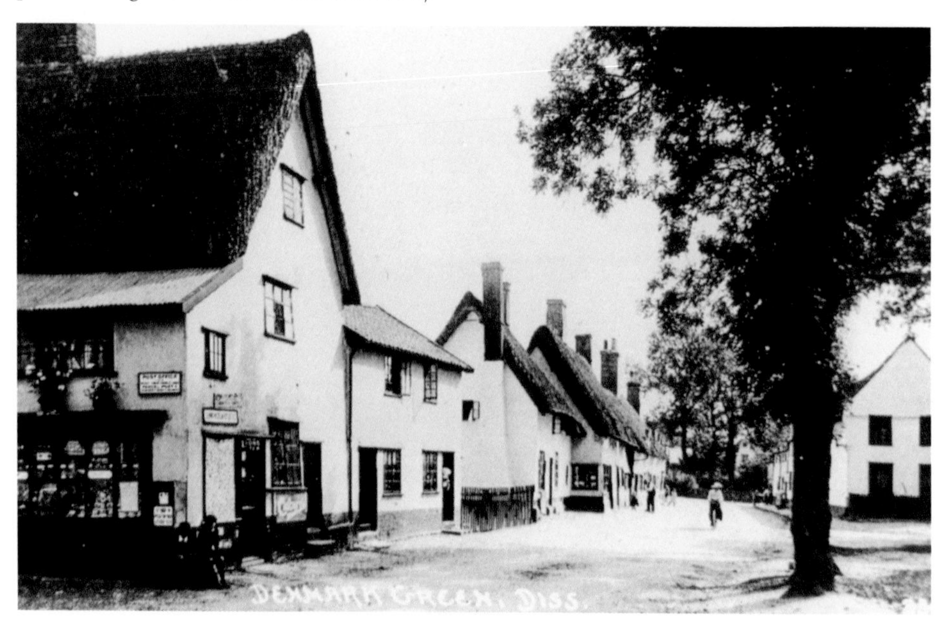

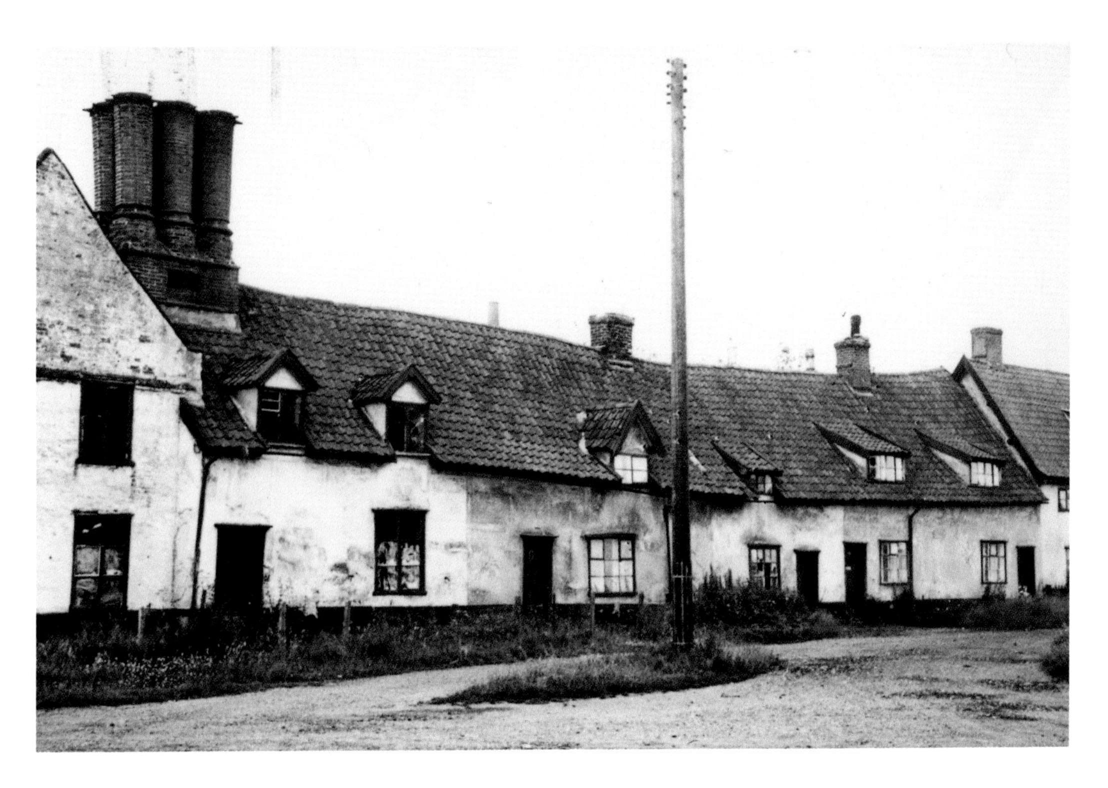

Fair Green Homes

The two older images (*top and inset*) presumably show 'before and after' as again these are 1950s/60s surveyor's shots. The main image shows these homes in a somewhat rambling state. If you look closely, a couple of extra windows are evident in the newer pictures. The modern image allows appreciation of the pretty colours of the houses today, still looking out onto Fair Green under the impressive chimneys so many years after they were built. (NCC)

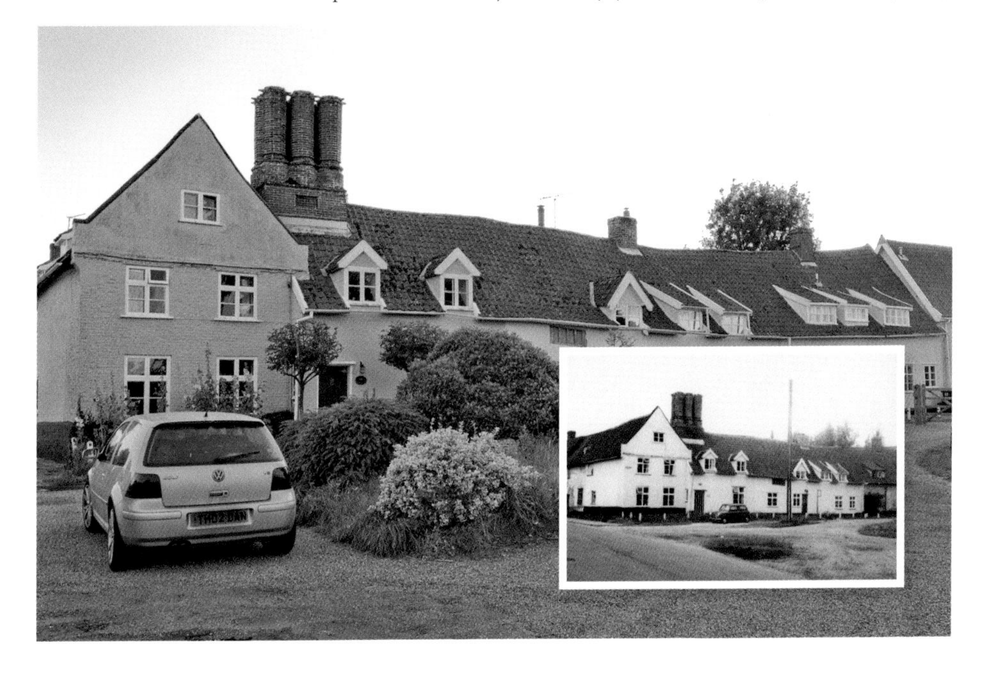

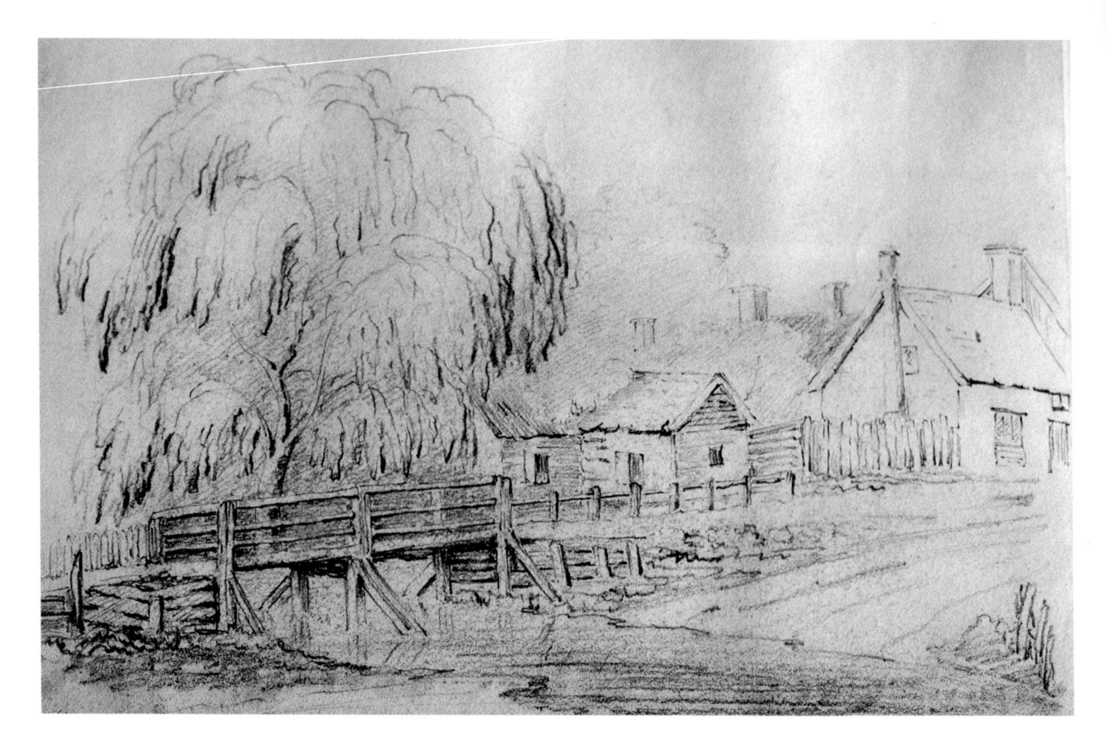

Denmark Bridge

Now we reach the far south of Diss, where Denmark Bridge takes travellers across to Suffolk. This drawing, like the Victorian images, is taken from a scrapbook held at the Norfolk Record Office and shows Cock Bridge (as it then was) drawn by Miss Taylor, a prominent local lady in Victorian Diss. Today the scene isn't quite so picturesque, but the bridge is somewhat sturdier! The River Waveney marks the boundary between Norfolk and Suffolk. (NRO, MS 10825)

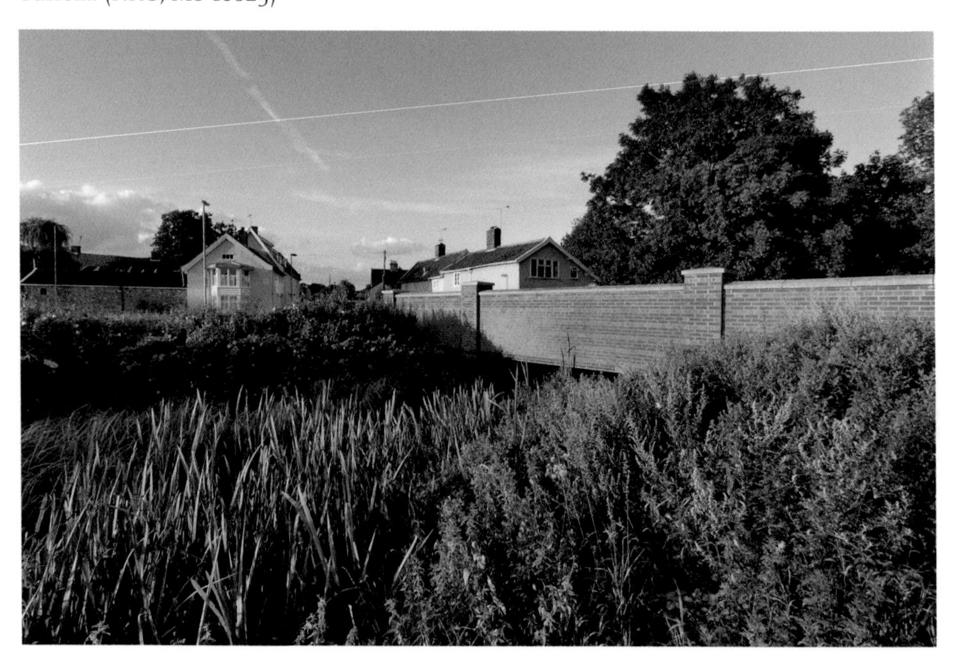

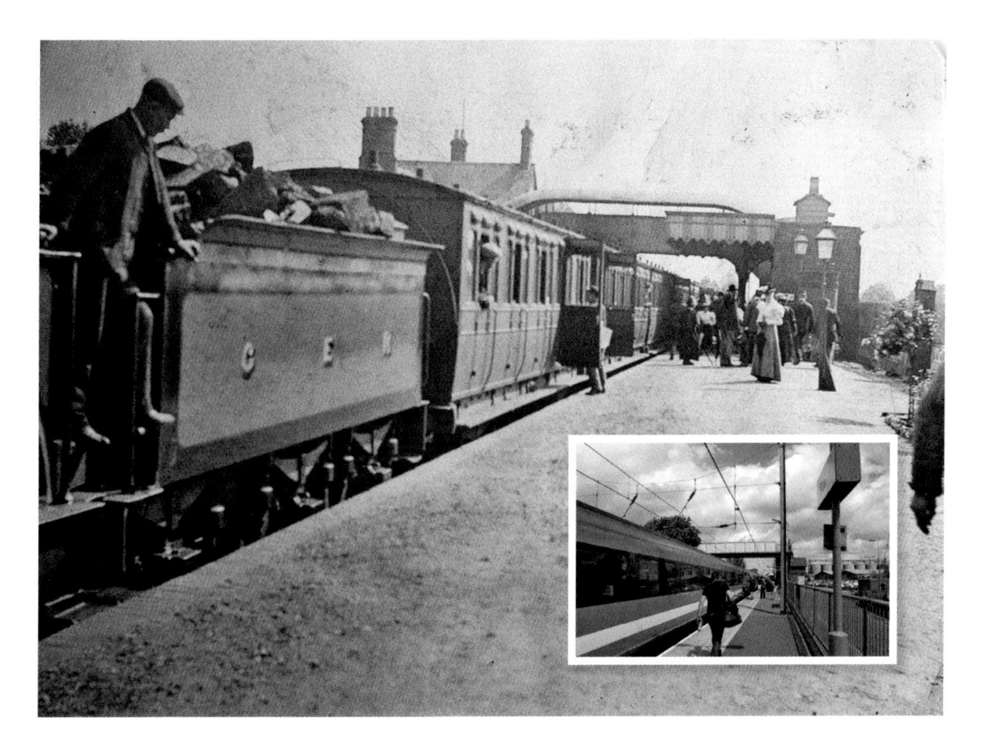

Railway Station

The railway station in Diss was still just a 'projected' one between Ipswich and Norwich in 1845, not being opened until 1849. The first-edition Ordnance Survey map published around 1885 shows open space between what is now the Junior School and the railway station. A later aerial image shows that a similar view across fields could still be had in 1946, and the view was still there even later, into the late '50s and '60s. Now of course, modern development has filled the gap. (NRO, MS 10824)

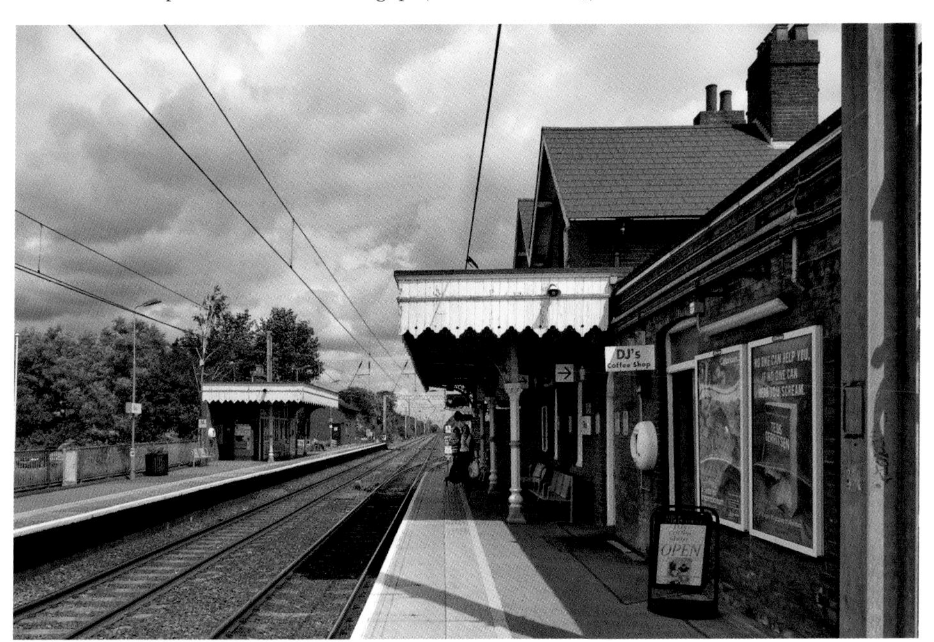

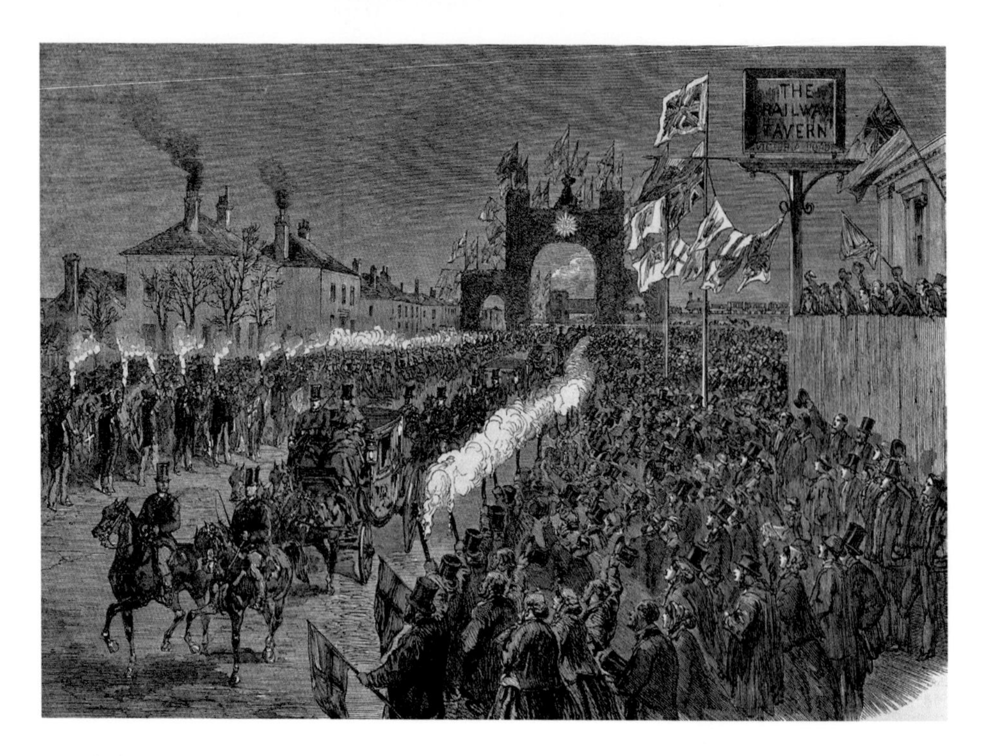

Royal Visit

This *Illustrated London News* picture sees crowds depicted outside the Railway Tavern, now a private home. In honour of the future Edward VII and Queen Alexandra, then Prince and Princess of Wales, the procession passed through Diss in December 1866 on the way from the railway station to Oakley Park in Hoxne. A triumphal arch was erected over Victoria Road for the occasion. After this event, Cock Street was renamed Denmark Street, in honour of Alexandra of Denmark. (*Illustrated London News* image from NRO, MS 10824)

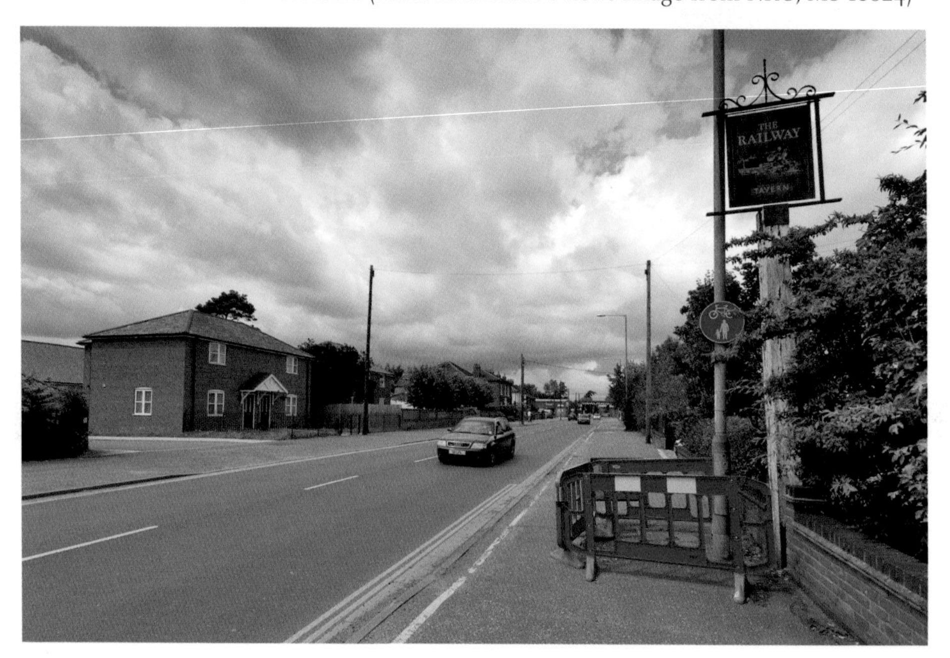

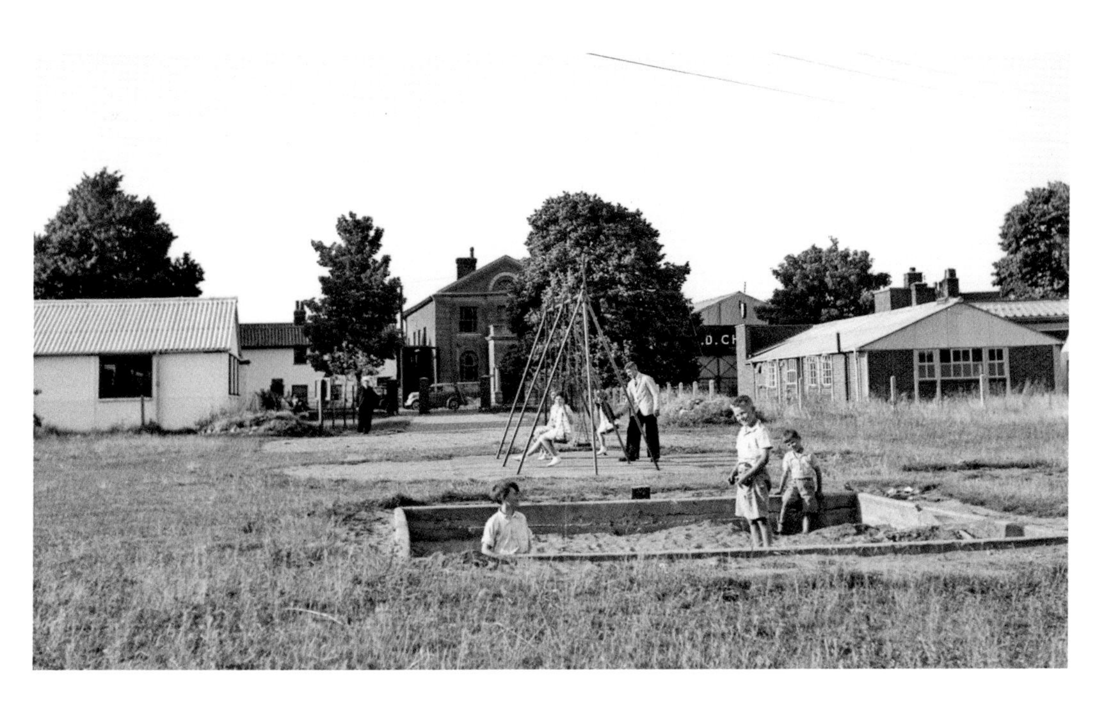

At Play

This play-area image shows traditional favourites off Victoria Road – a sandpit and swings. Today, children have all kinds of outdoor play equipment in the large park next to the Mere. The playground is not far from the Masonic Lodge, formerly the Unitarian chapel. The latter was once fronted by part of the large, open, green area of Park Fields, but the modern-day Diss Park is smaller thanks to a new car park between the old chapel and Park Road. (The Francis Frith Collection)

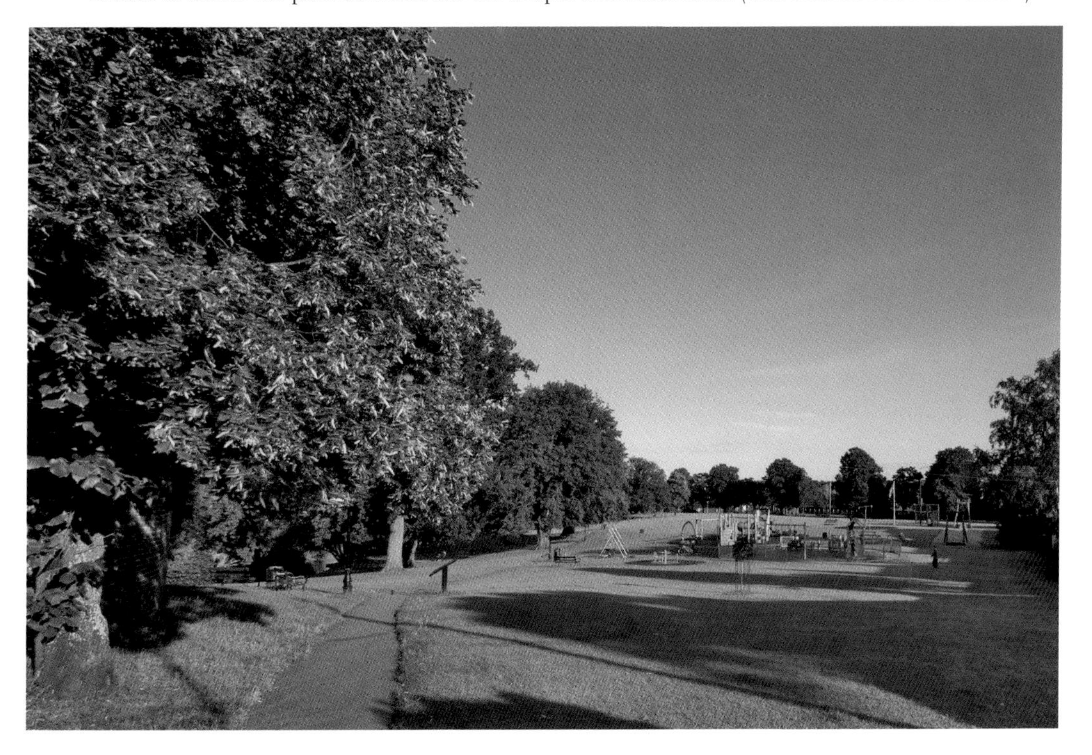

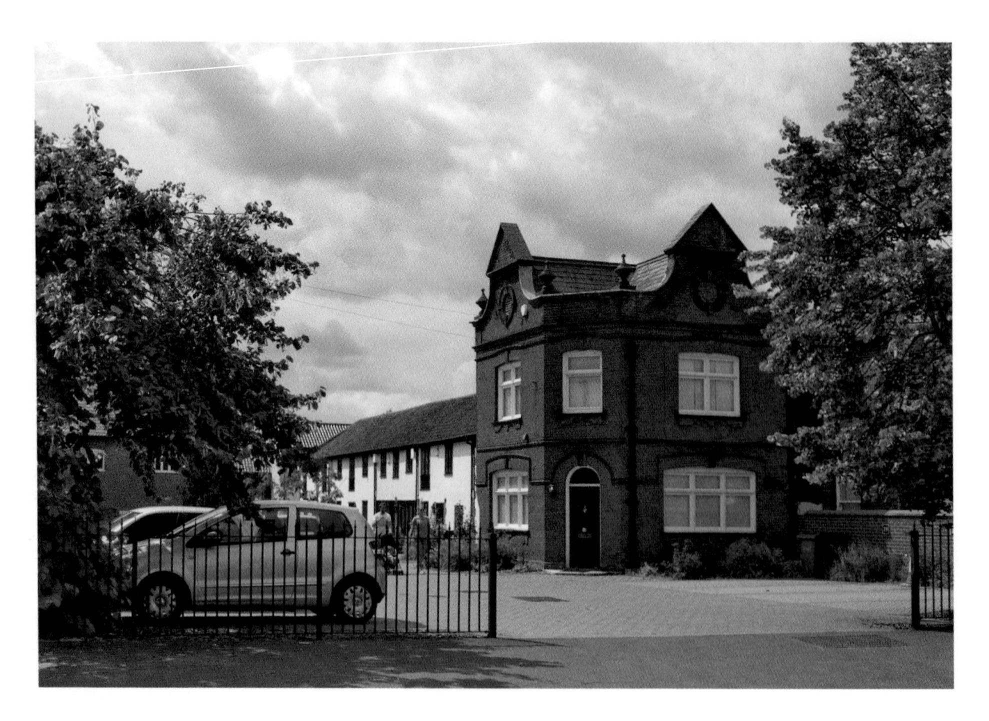

Change of Use

The 1864 *White's Directory* for Norfolk lists five maltsters in Diss alone, including Chaplyn's, Cuthbert's, Farrow's, Leathers' and Taylor's. This one, Cuthbert's Maltings on Victoria Road, has now been redeveloped to housing, by no means the only formerly industrial building in Diss to have been converted in recent years. There were of course brewers in Diss too, including Youngs, Crawshay & Youngs and Taylor, Sons & Dowson. These days, local microbreweries continue the tradition. (NCC)

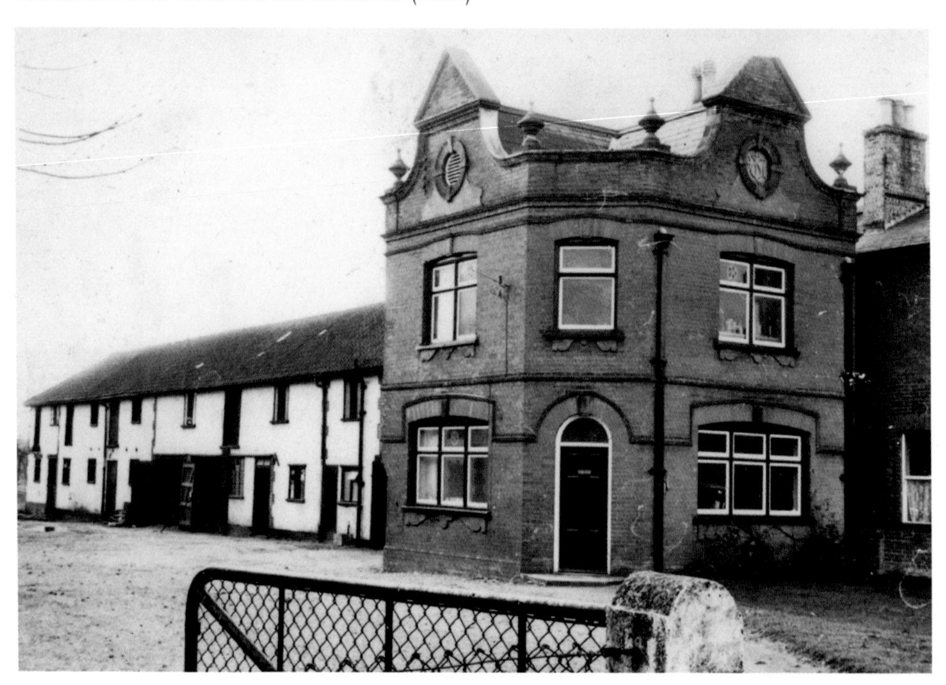

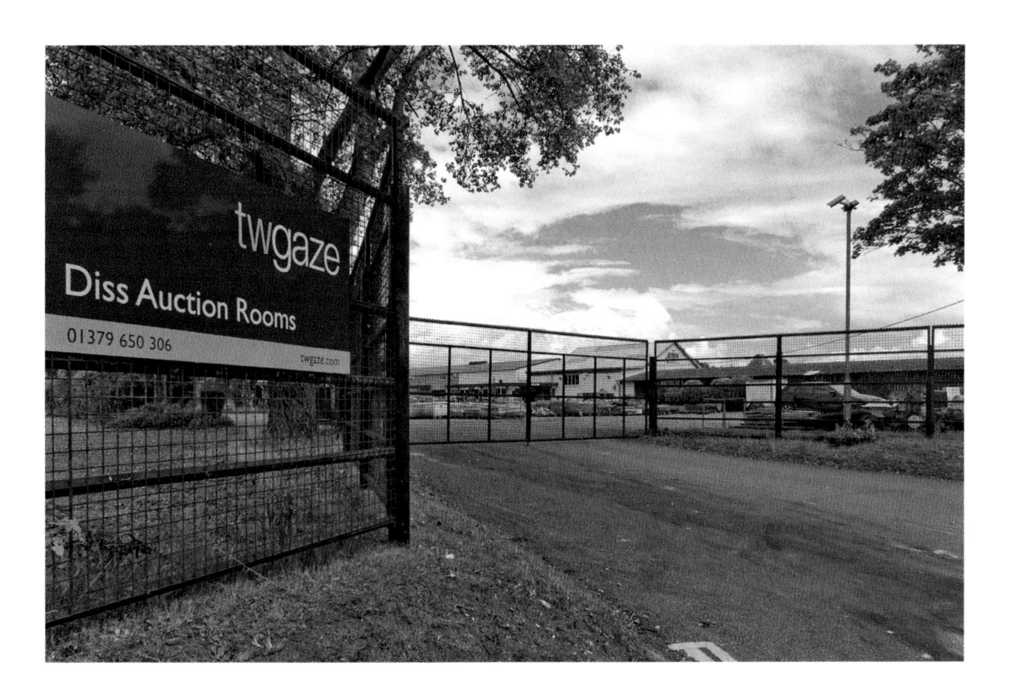

Friday Sales

Like so many others, I remember going to Gaze's auction on a Friday even as a little girl. Established by Thomas William Gaze in 1857, TW Gaze has changed over the years. Where it once held regular livestock markets at its sales ground on Roydon Road, the business now puts on fine art and antique auctions (still on a Friday) at Diss Auction Rooms. The company also has interests in property, and opened a new office in Wymondham only recently. (NCC)

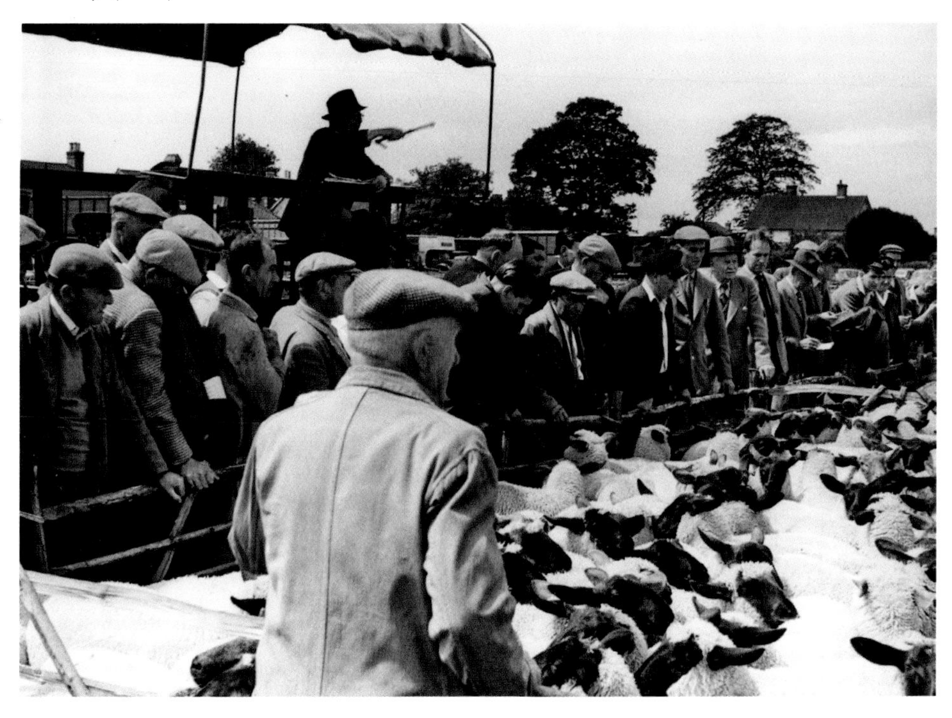

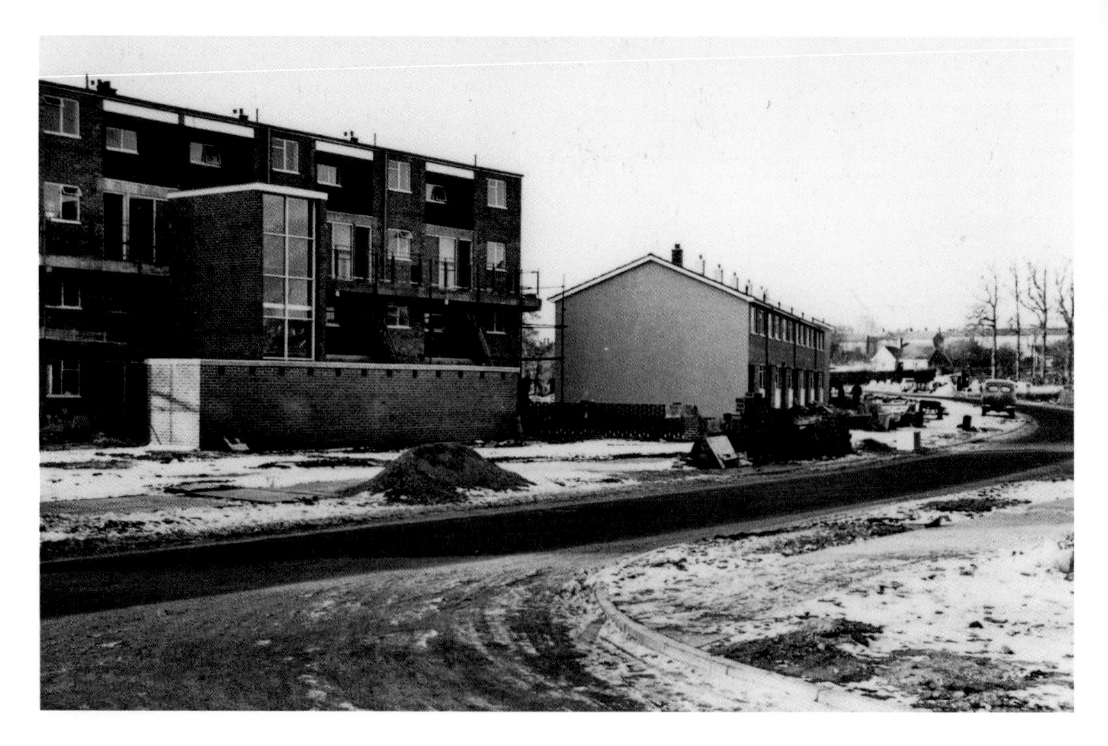

Skelton Road

This old, wintry shot of flats on Skelton Road in the 1950s/60s must have been taken before much of the housing to the east of Diss town centre was built – there are relatively open views to the right of the image. It would be difficult to find a market town in Norfolk that hasn't experienced growth like that shown in these two images. Today, this area is built up and the views from the remaining scattered pre-war buildings are somewhat different than they were. (NCC)

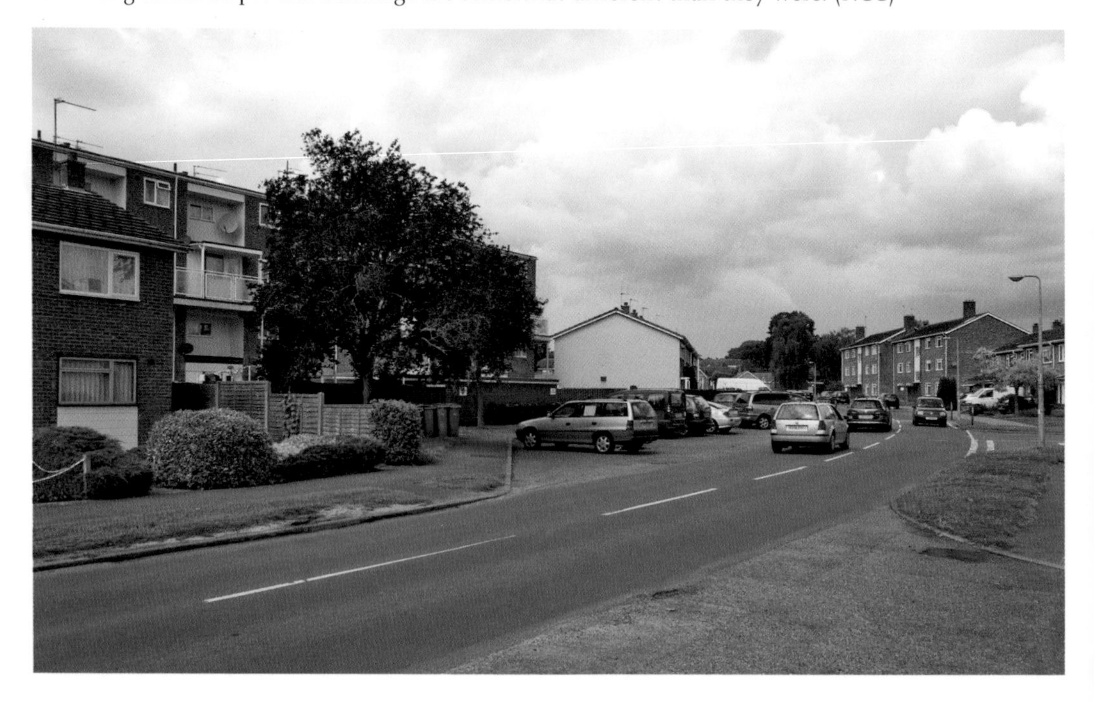

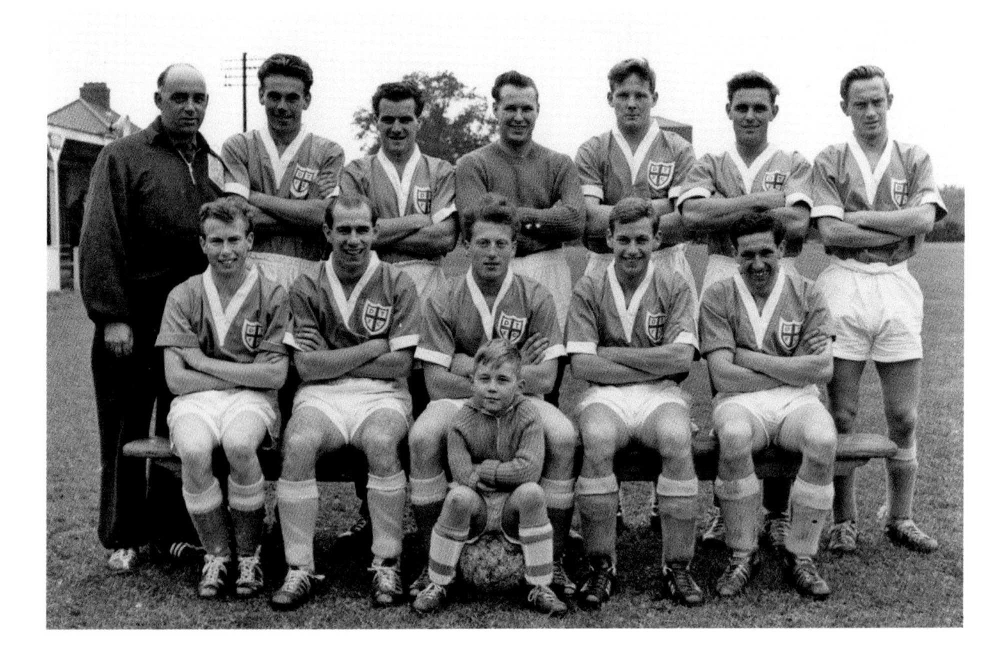

Football Club

Here we have the Diss Town football team of 1973/74, including Ivan 'Pip' Wilby (trainer, back-left) his son Grayham (the mascot) along with Des Tebble (captain, back-middle) who kindly identified everyone in the photograph. Also pictured are, left to right from the back row: Ken Mackeral, Godfrey Chenery, John Eaton, Alan Sheldrake, Derek Hubbard, John Maskel, Ray Button, Roger Parker, Colin Martin and Gordon Cobb. The club is now based on Brewers Green Lane, and the image is twinned with the modern team, who achieved promotion to the Ridgeons Premier League in 2010/11. (NCC, also thanks to John Hutton and DTFC)

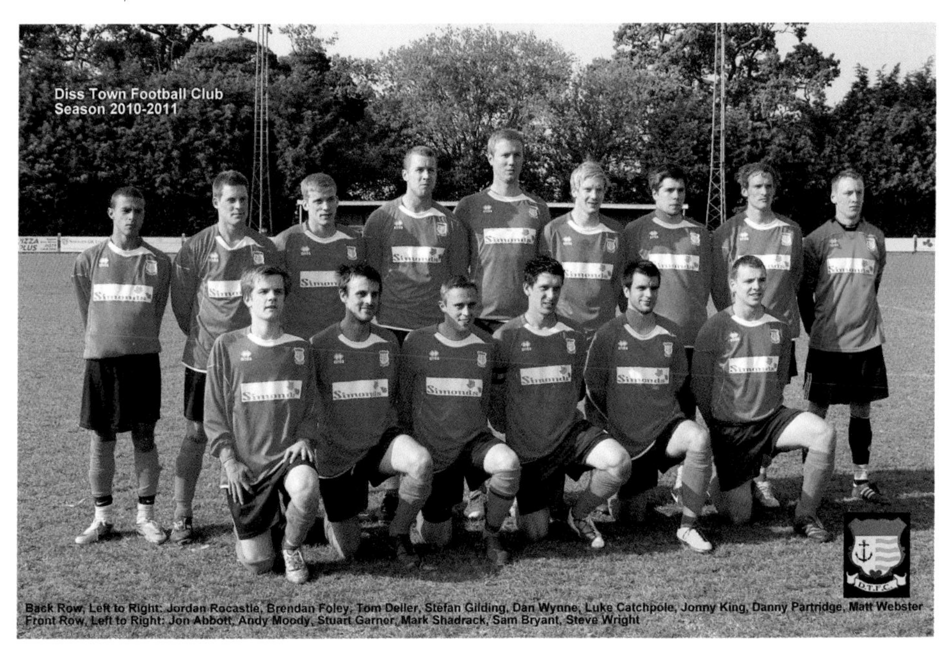

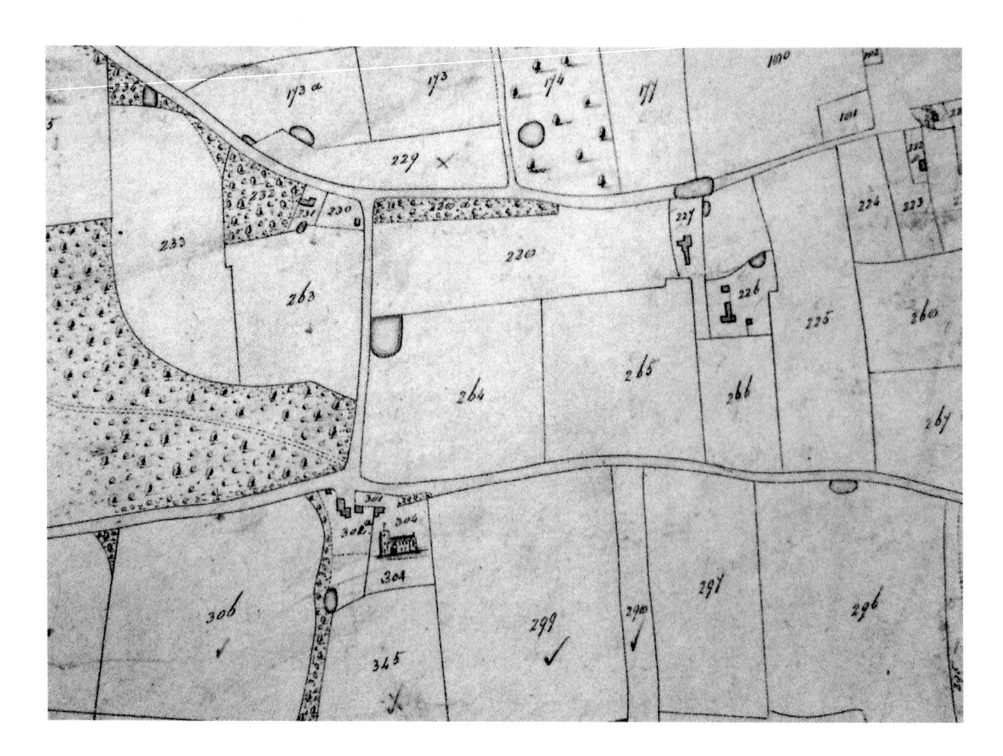

Roydon

Moving on to district, we'll begin in Roydon and work clockwise, encompassing the historic parishes bordering Diss on the Norfolk side of the county divide. Roydon has grown a great deal in the last century; from around 400 in 1801 to 700 in 1911, the population in 2011 was getting on for 2,500. The tithe map image above shows this change wonderfully when compared to a more recent aerial photograph – the church appears in both, but with very different surroundings. (NRO, DN/TA 247/Norfolk Historic Environment Service)

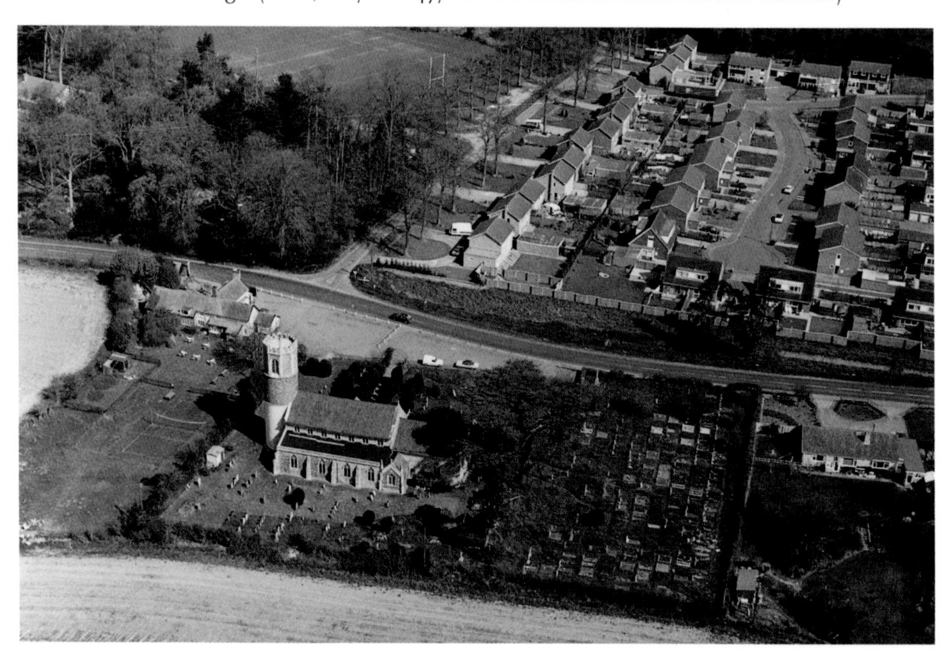

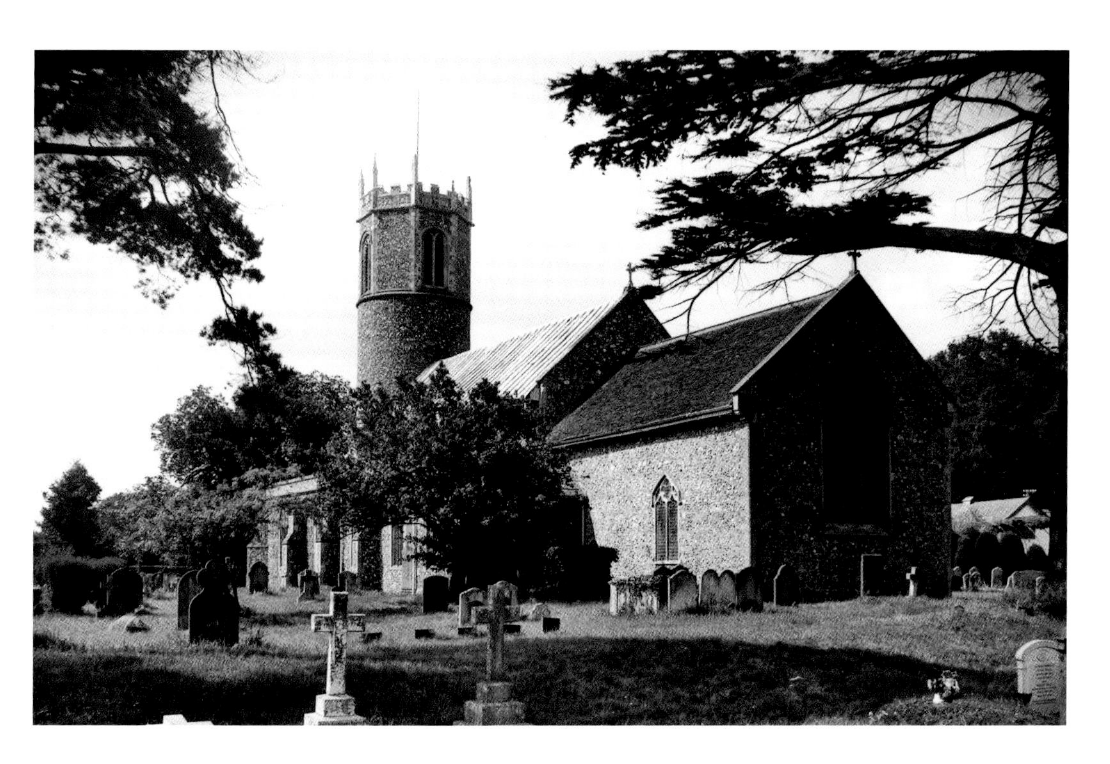

Church of St Remigius
The form of St Remigius will be very familiar to those that regularly travel through Roydon. It is said that four of six known dedications to the saint in England are in Norfolk – the others at Hethersett, Dunstan and Testerton. At one time there was a school in front of the church and pub, but now the car park stretches across the site. A new village school was built in the 1890s and remains the village's primary school today, although it has been extended somewhat since then. (Plunkett)

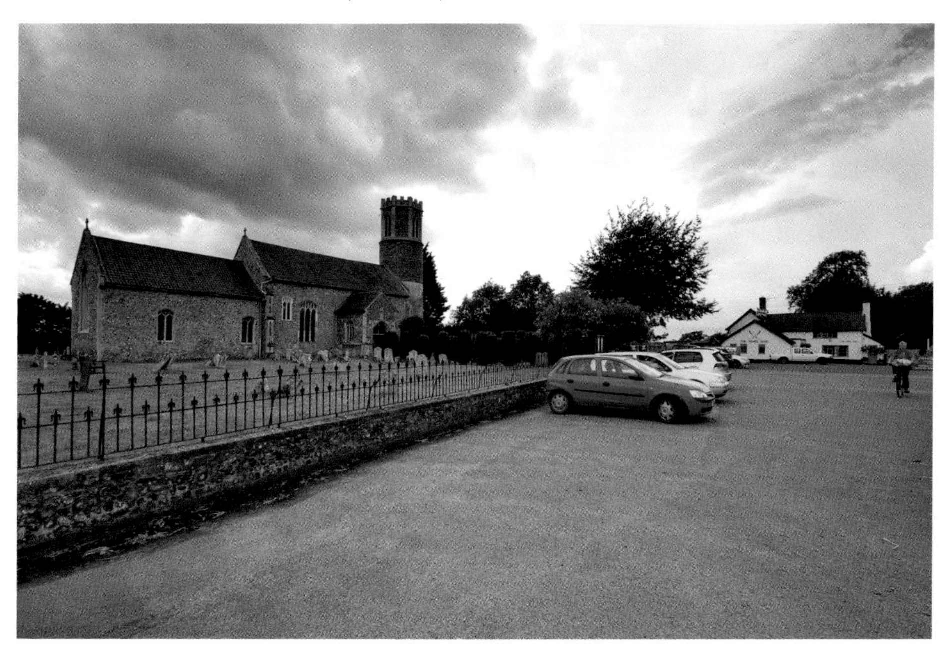

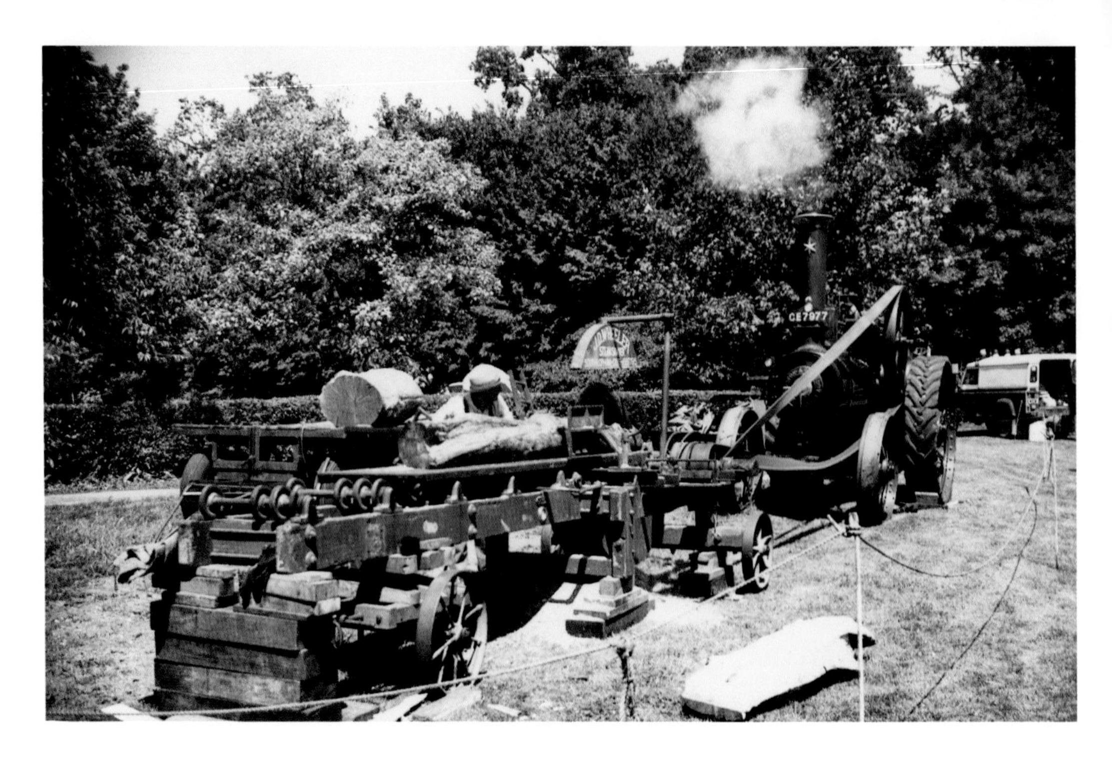

Steam and Gardens

Moving on, locals and visitors alike cannot have failed to notice the Bressingham Steam Museum and Gardens, with steam locomotives, gallopers and traction engines. George Plunkett took this older image on a visit twelve years ago, while the newer image shows one of four railways which today take visitors around gardens and woodland. The gardens pre-date the steam elements, which first arrived in 1961, and today you can also find 'Walmington-on-Sea' High Street in this corner of Norfolk. (Plunkett)

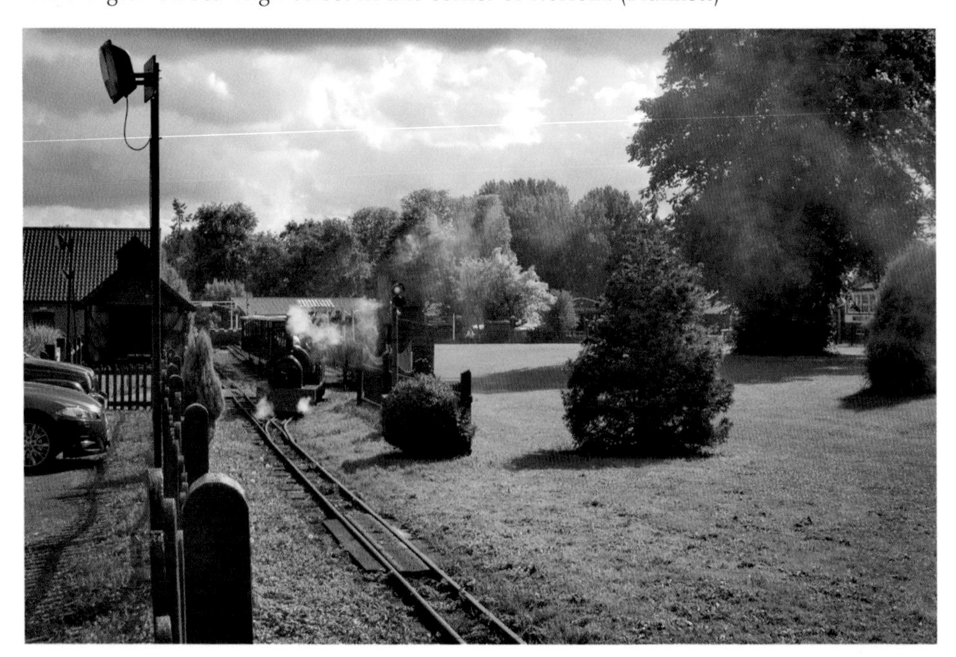

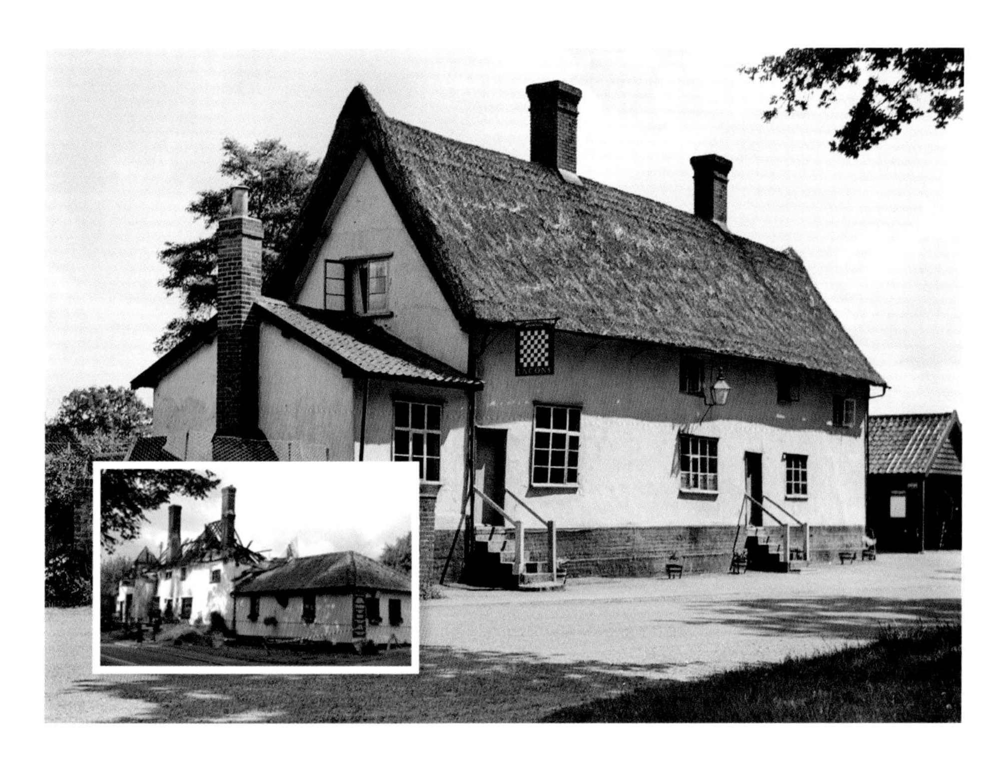

The Chequers Inn

Bressingham Chequers has risen from the flames after a terrible fire in October 2009. During the rebuild a pre-seventeenth-century skeleton was discovered, possibly pre-dating the building, as well as pistols, a rifle and ammunition dating from the Second World War, found buried against an outside wall. The pub was briefly (relative to its whole history) named the Old Garden House before reverting to the Chequers Inn – after a tree of the same name once used in the beer industry, its fruits used to flavour the beer. (English Heritage and inset, Bressingham Chequers)

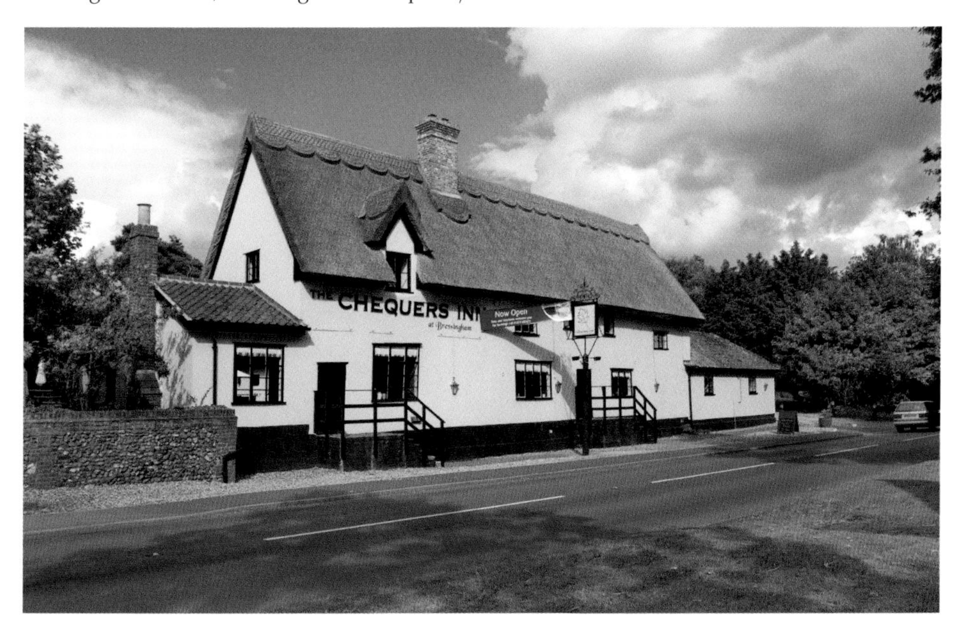

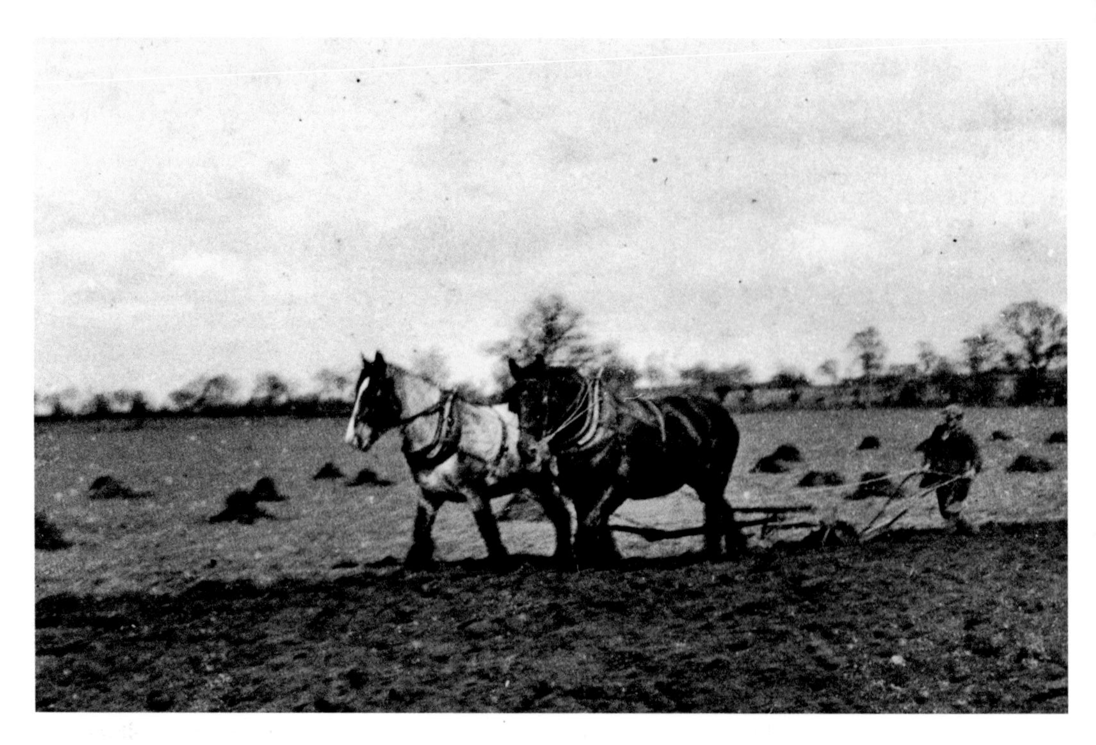

Toiling the Soil

It would be wrong to produce a book about this area without including a nod to agriculture. The older image here was probably taken in Bressingham (perhaps Valley Farm), while the later image was taken one evening from the Diss to Shelfanger Road nearby, looking back down the hill. In 1845, the *Directory* recorded that 'the soil is generally fertile, belongs to a great number of proprietors ... in four Manors ... many of the owners are resident here, some in large and handsome mansions'. (NCC)

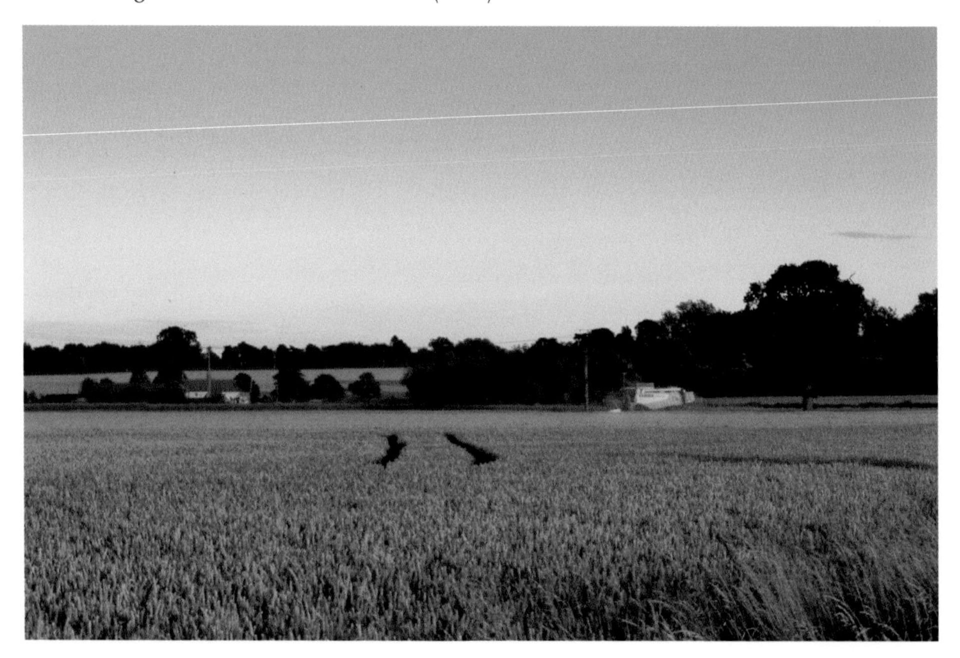

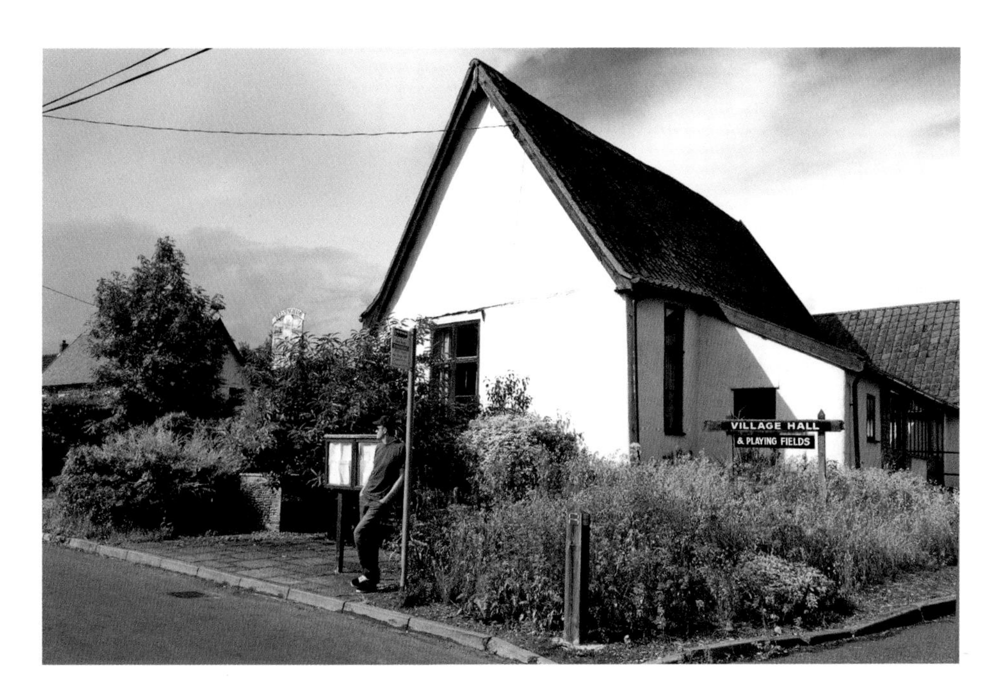

Transport

The previous image, this image and indeed the one after it, come from a marvellous collection of images of Bressingham, one dated 1922, which are part of the Picture Norfolk archive at Norfolk Heritage Centre. This one is entitled 'On the way to the station' – perhaps taken at Valley Farm on the way to Diss. These days, the vehicle is much more likely to be a car or perhaps a bus, as pictured in the new image, taken at the bus stop outside the village hall. (NCC)

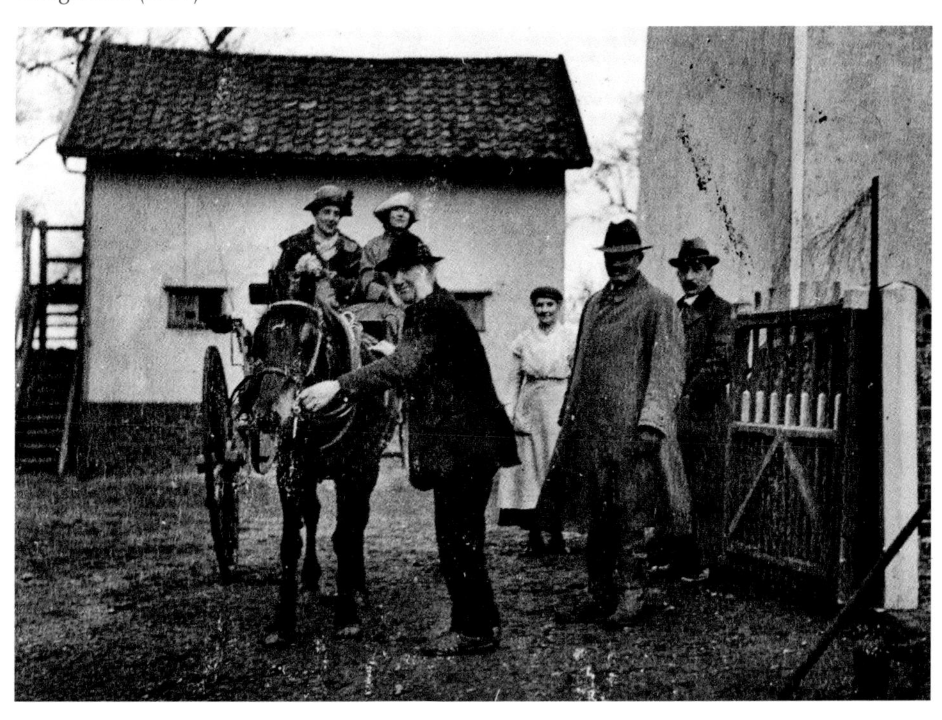

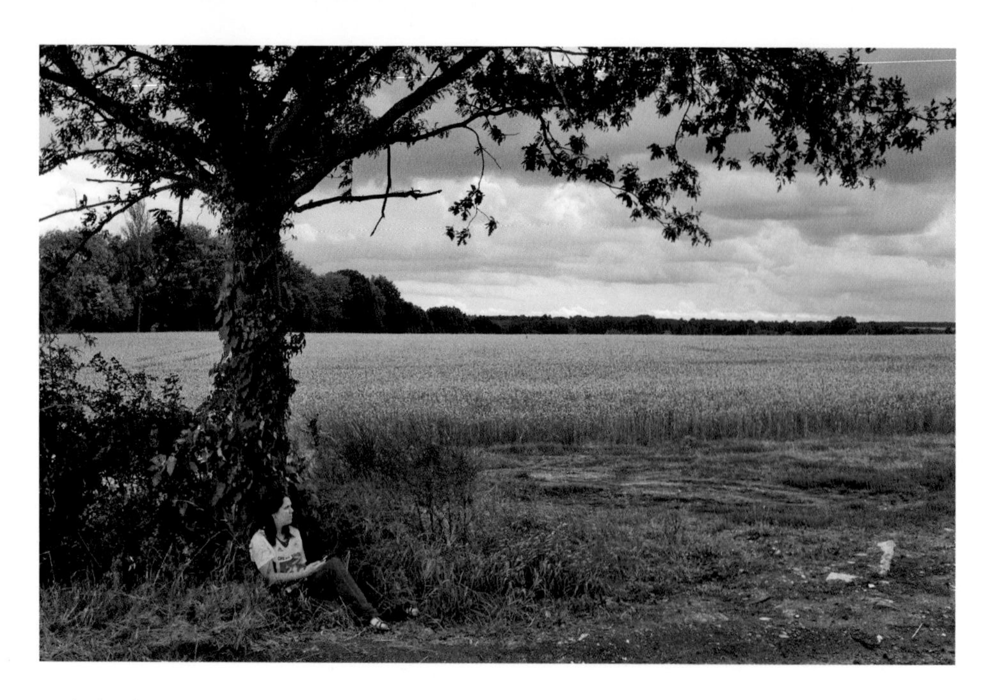

Lady in the Lane

Finally for this trio of Bressingham images, we have this gorgeous image of 'a lady in the lane'. So many years later, I couldn't resist getting my husband to take a modern version of the shot – the only image in this book that features the author – sitting under a different tree in Bressingham as the storm clouds rolled in during our damp 2012 summer. Clutching an iPhone and wearing a London 2012 Olympics teeshirt, the newer image will be easy to date in the future. (NCC)

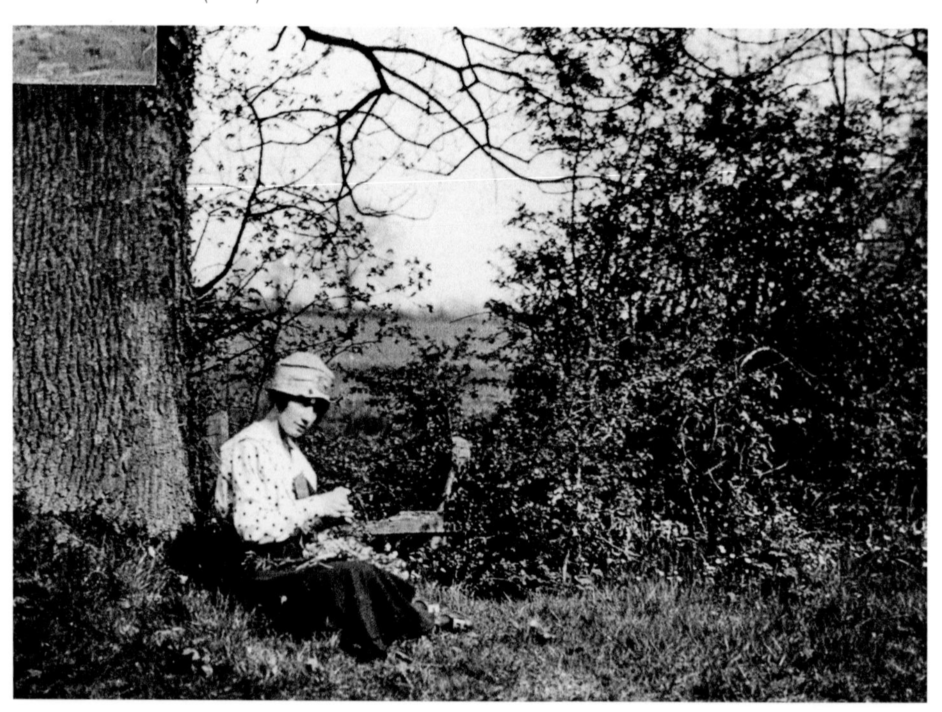

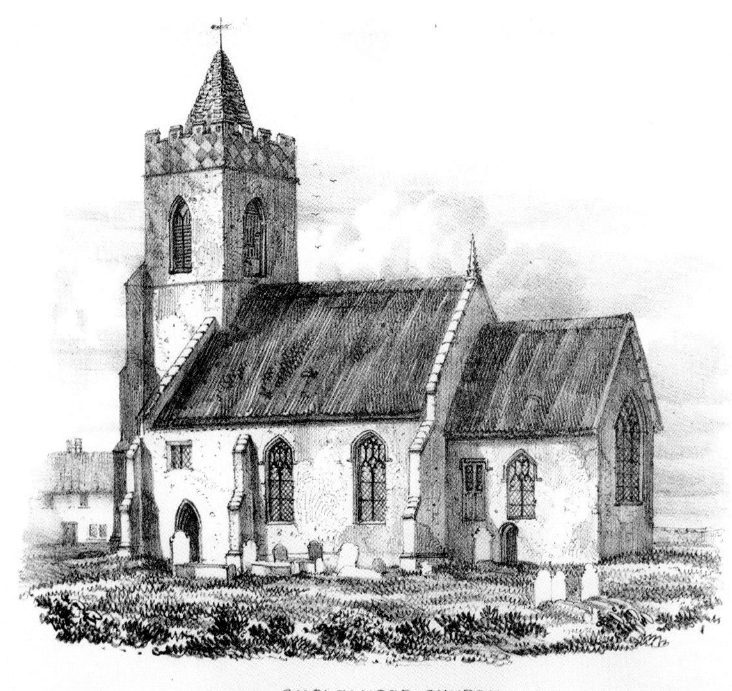

All Saints, Shelfanger

Moving ever northwards, we arrive at Shelfanger. This image of the church is by Robert Ladbrooke (1770–1842), who drew many of Norfolk's churches, creating a fascinating archive for modern comparison. The church is known for its late-thirteenth-century wall-paintings, rediscovered under plaster in 1966. This is a very pretty building, situated above the road through the village. The lovely porch, chequer-work at the top of the tower and red pyramidal roof will be familiar to many. (NCC)

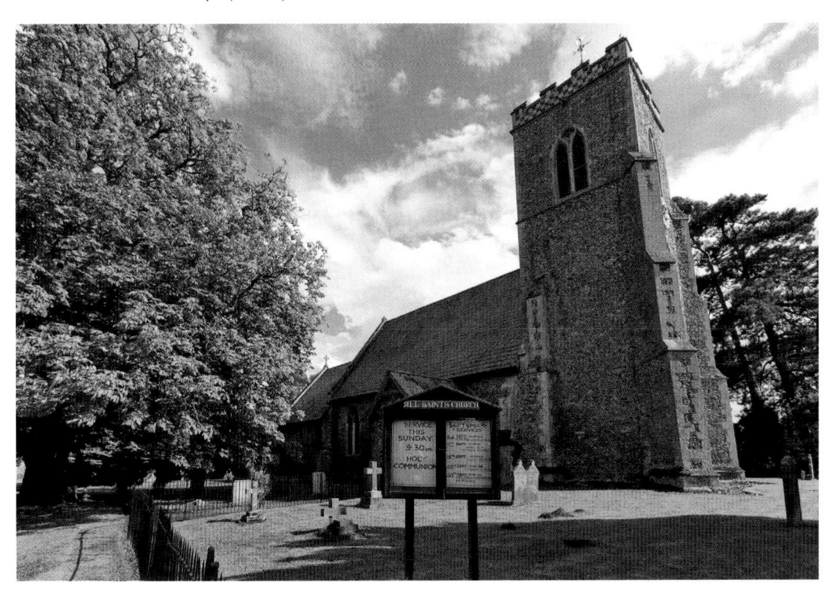

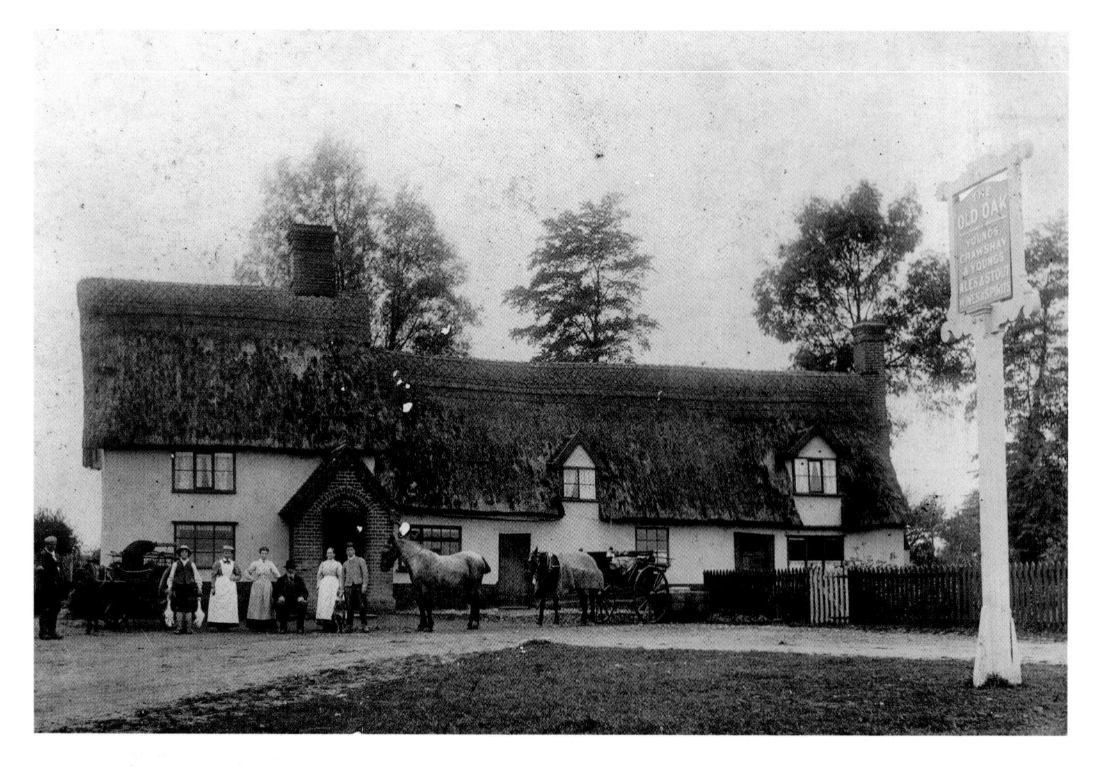

Winfarthing Pubs

Continuing to Winfarthing, this magnificent old image shows the Old Oak inn as it was in around 1900. The pub closed in 1963 and is now a private house. On Short Green, the pub would have once received passing trade between Diss, Old Buckenham and Attleborough. Nearer the centre of the village, the Fighting Cocks (*inset*), these days a pink building, is currently the only pub in the village. (Untraced; part of image collection donated to NCC)

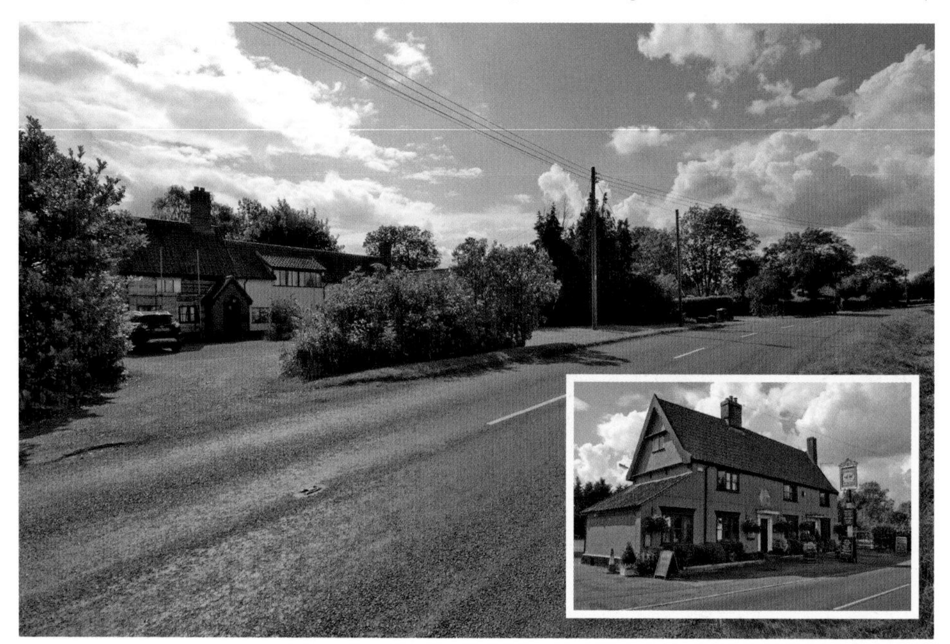

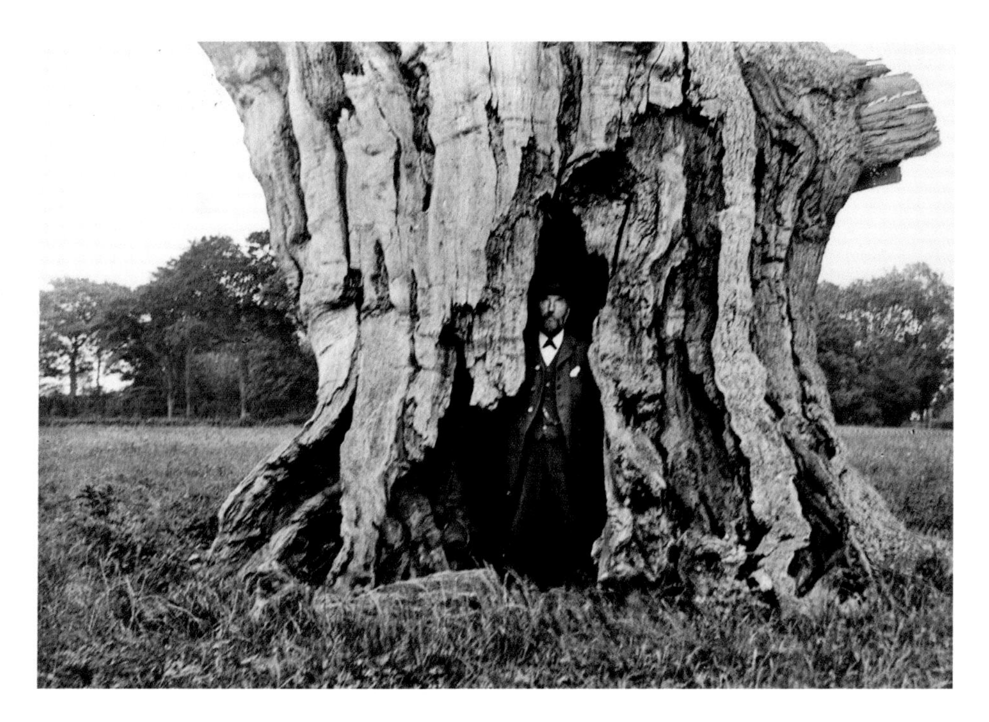

The Old Oak

Here we see the old oak itself, near Lodge Farm, as well as an earlier painting (*inset*). 'A grand and picturesque old ruin ... considered to be more than 1,200 years old. It ... must have been a magnificent spreading tree, with enormous arms ... it is now a mere shell, bleached snowy white' (*White's*, 1864). There are tales of the hollow trunk being used as a cow shelter, and even as a location for parish meetings. Little is left today, but the tree seeded many other oaks all over the village, and lives on in them. (NCC/NRO, MS 10825)

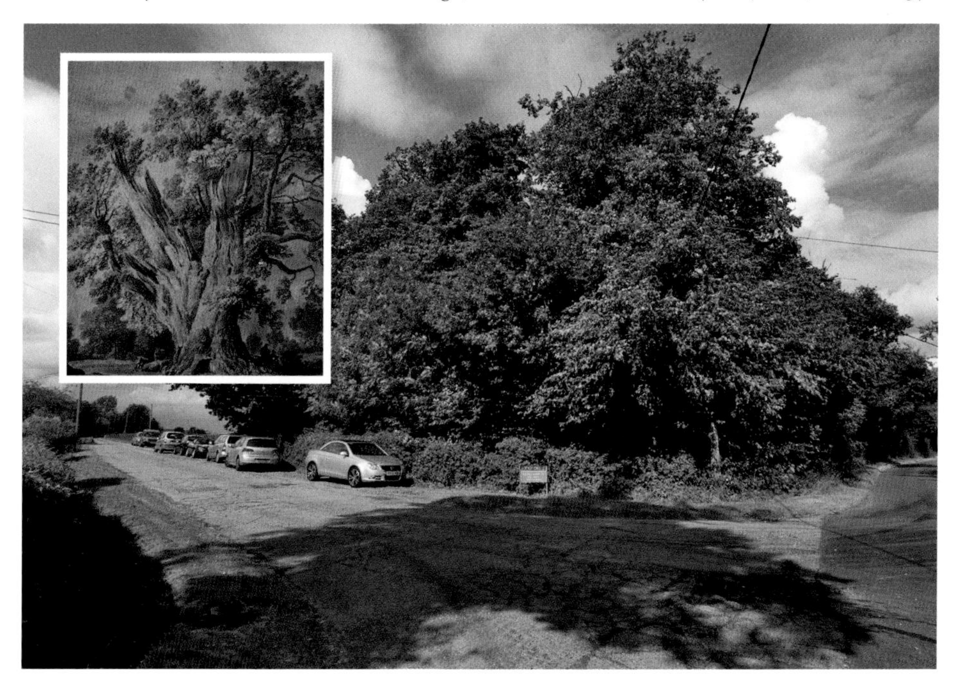

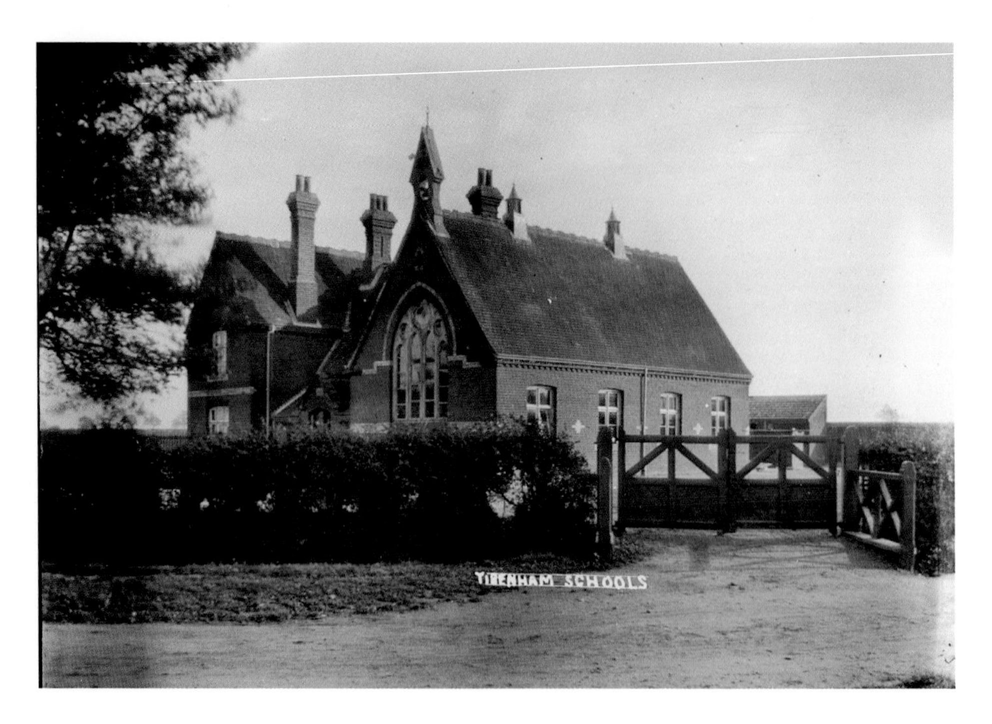

Tibenham School

Moving further north from Winfarthing to Tibenham, these handsome school buildings, erected in 1876, were designed for 120 children. Further extensions came later, so this image must have been taken before 1911 (the whole collection of Tibenham photographs included in this book may have been taken at the same time). When the school closed (deposited records end in 1986), the buildings were demolished and modern houses built on the site. Only a wall behind the houses, with painted hoops on it, hints to its previous use. (NCC)

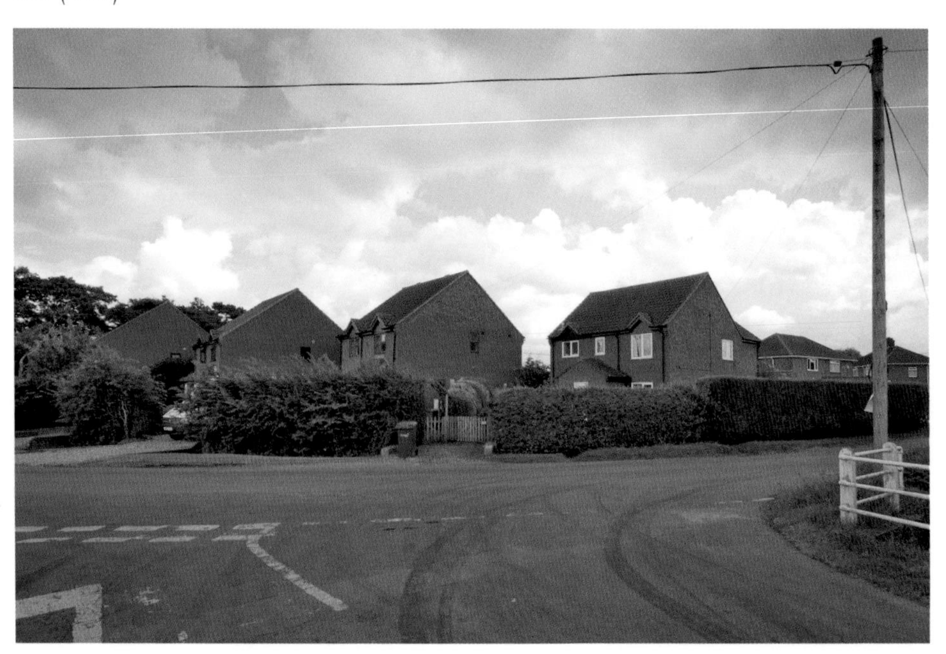

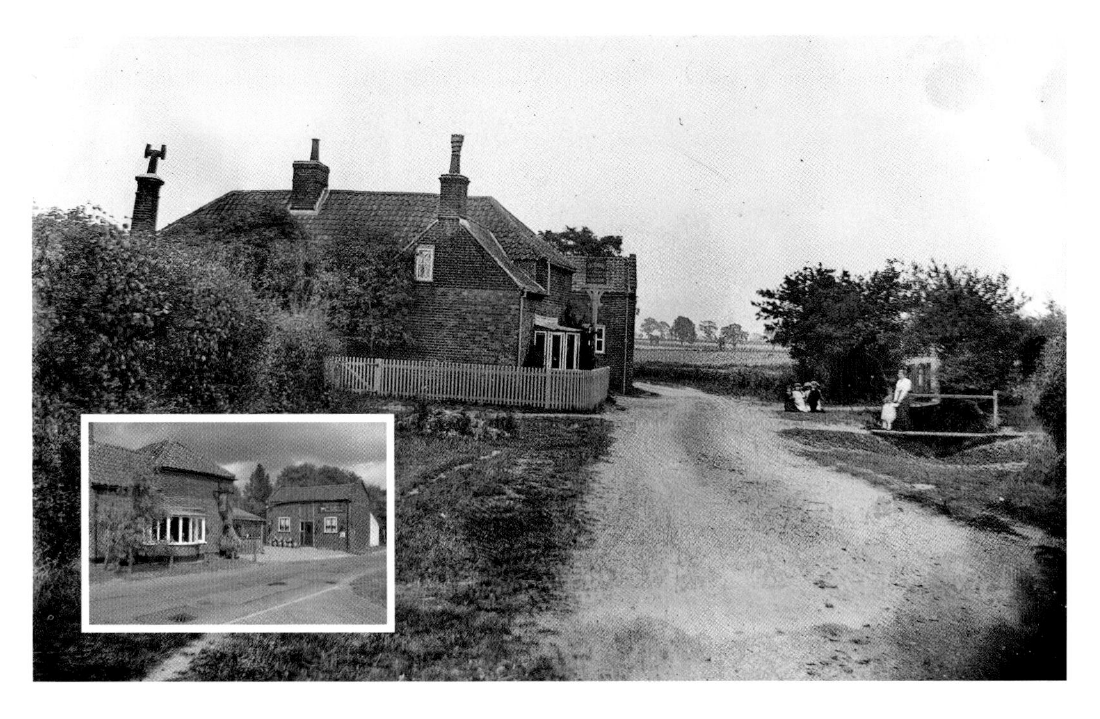

The Greyhound

Travelling along the road to towards the other end of Tibenham, we find another Greyhound public house. This one opened in 1710 and is still thriving, being awarded Community Pub of the Year in 2011 by the local council. The village once also had a public house called the Boot, which closed in the 1970s and is now a private house. The images looking down the street show little change but the addition of telegraph poles and wires. (NCC)

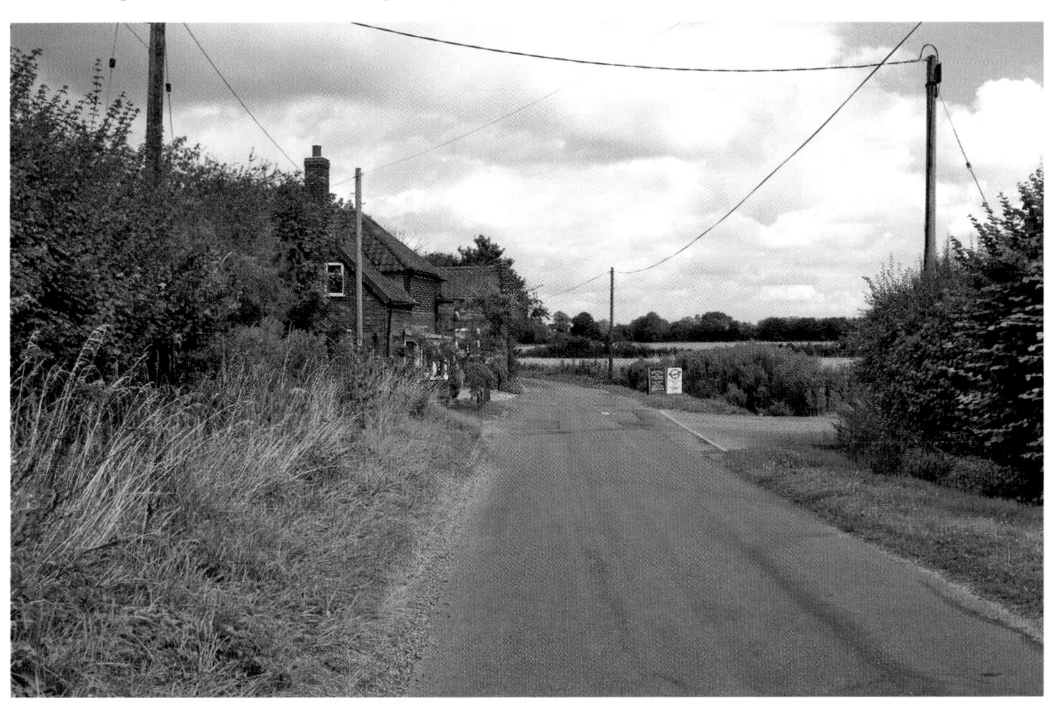

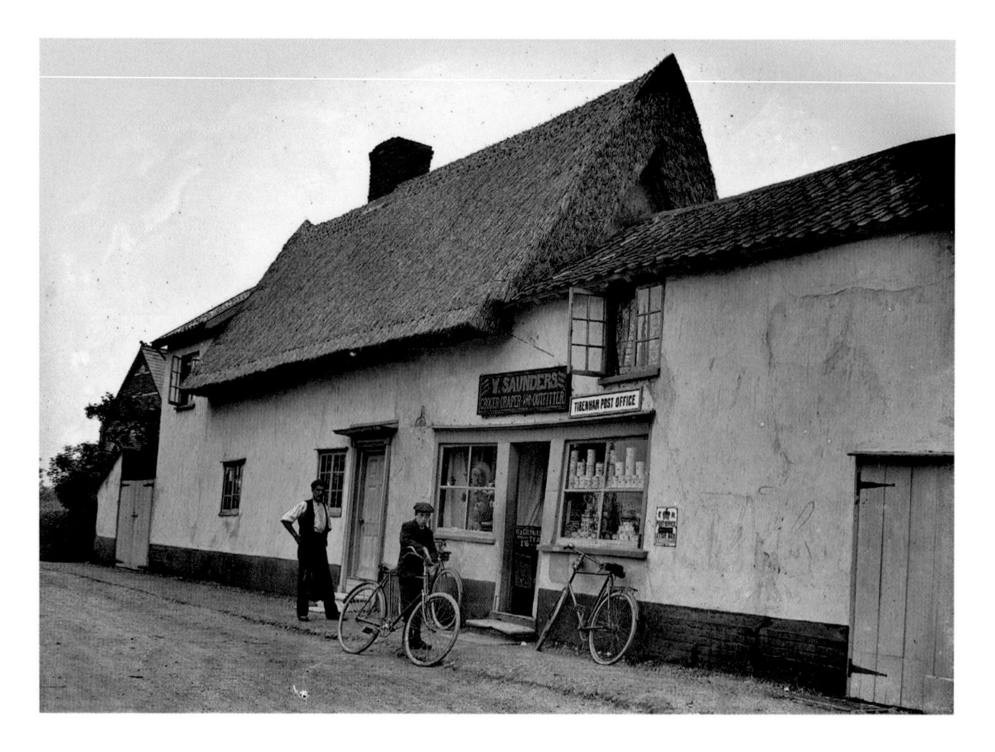

Post Office

This image shows the post office and shop before it became a private home. The window display features 'wonderful' colonial tea, flour, rice and various other essentials. W. Saunders' sign reads 'Grocer Draper and Outfitter, flour and meals, boots and shoes'. The post office stores finally closed in 1994 after at least 150 years (the building, however, is much older than this). Today, changes in the building are evident, but the character of the property and the thatched roof remain. (NCC)

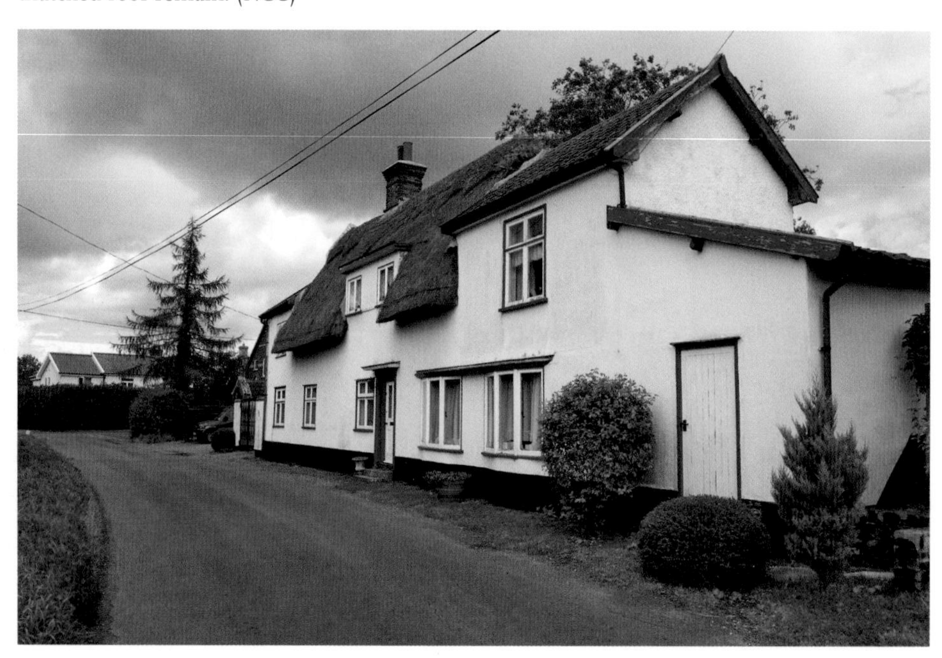

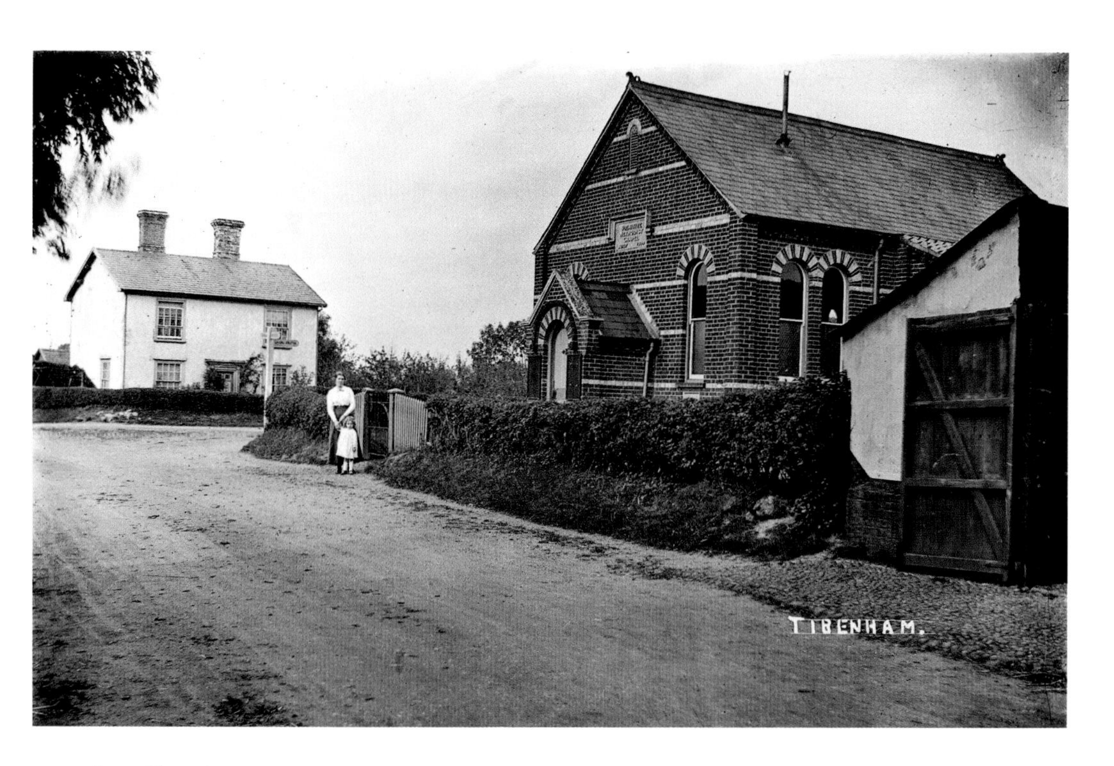

Free Churches

This area had many choices for worship in the Victorian era, and indeed before that. The 1851 religious census recorded that Diss had more Nonconformist meetings than any other Norfolk market town (eight compared to Wymondham's six – although the latter had more *types* of worship). Tibenham, too, had choices outside of the parish church, including the Primitive Methodist chapel pictured here, built in 1848, and now converted for use as a private home. (NCC)

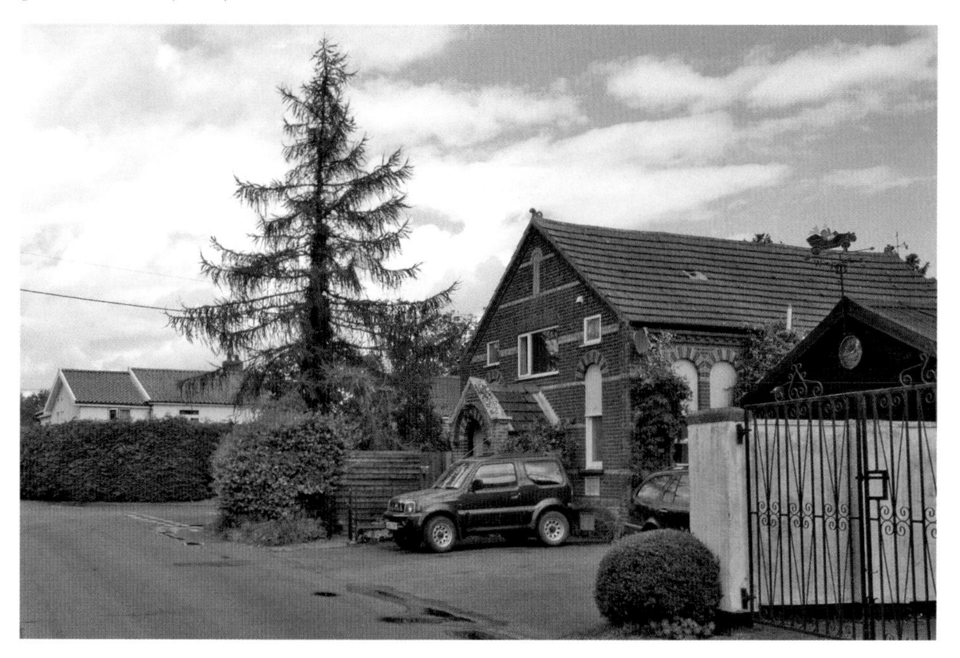

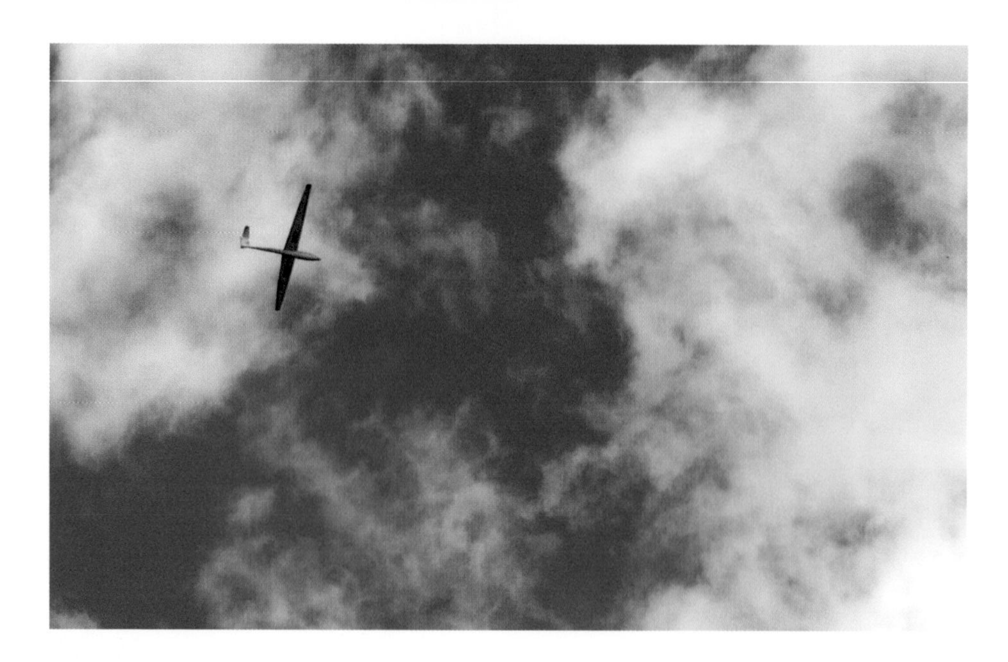

Gliding and Flying

I couldn't resist including this lovely image of a girl with a bird of prey in Tibenham. Again I've used a little bit of artistic license here as the image I've twinned it with is a different kind of glider altogether – Tibenham now being home to the Norfolk Gliding Club, established on the old Second World War airfield in 1959. During the Second World War, the airfield was home to the part of the USAF 2nd Air Division, the 445th Bombardment Group, which flew well over 6,000 sorties from here. (NCC)

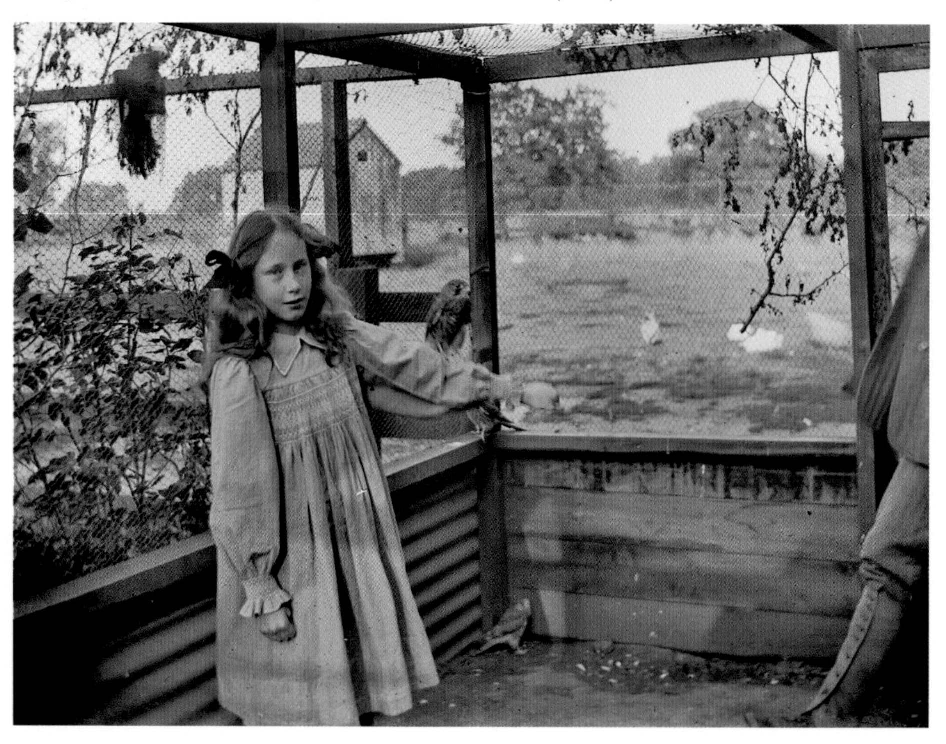

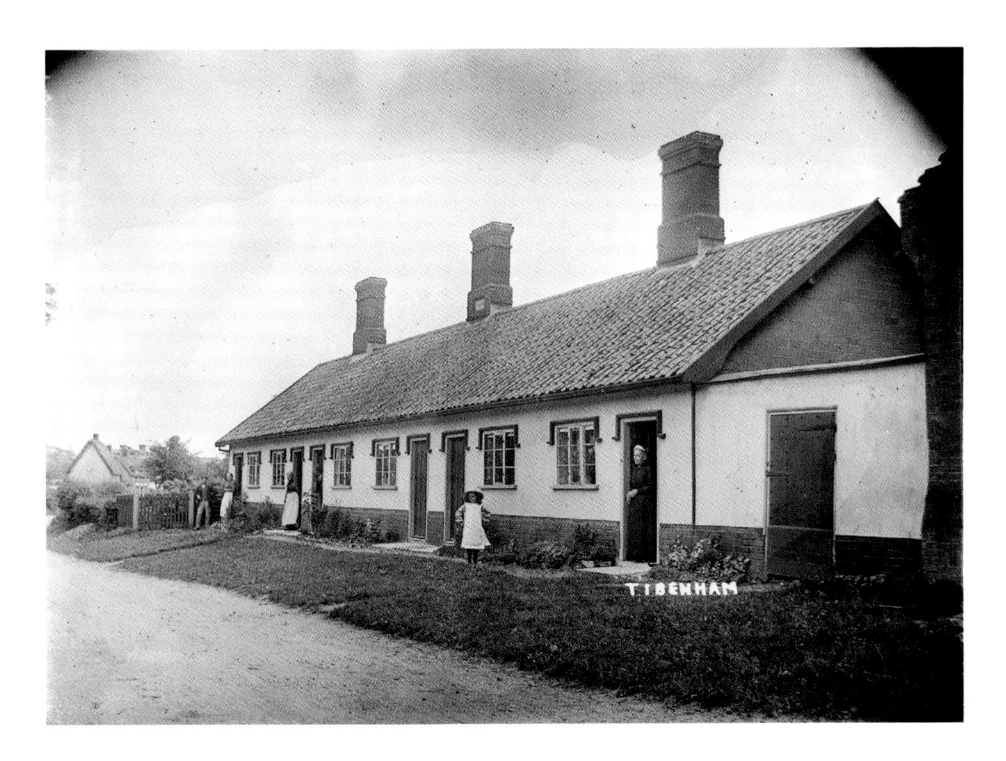

Almshouses

Around 1844, these almshouses were built to house six of the parish poor on the site of the old guildhall. A wall has gone to make way for car parking, but otherwise these homes have changed little, at least on the outside – internally, they now contain three dwellings, not six, so things aren't quite as cramped. The almshouses are around the corner from All Saints' church and next to the Old Parish Schoolroom, the latter dating from 1831. (NCC)

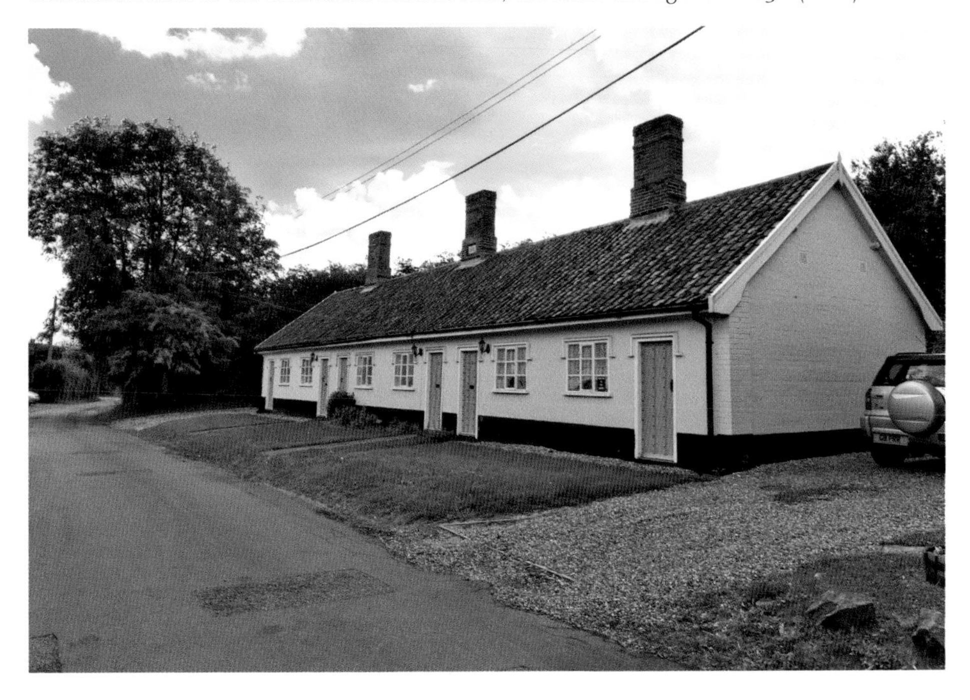

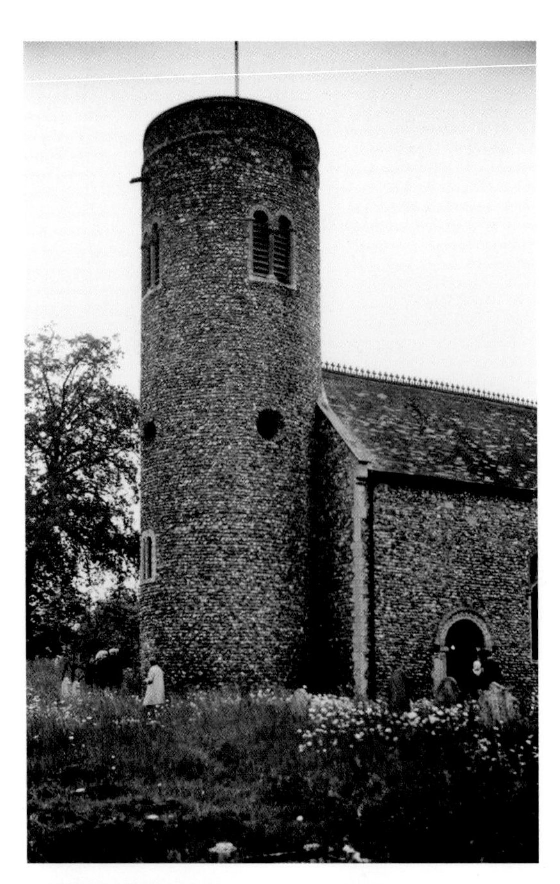

Round Towers
Here we see two wonderful images of Gissing St Mary church, taken forty years apart, almost to the day, but from different viewpoints. Norfolk is very proud of its round-towered churches, and rightly so. The Round Tower Churches Society knows of 185 such churches built in England using traditional techniques, and it says that 126 of these are in this county. Gissing is a very good example of this type of church, providing us with a glimpse of the village's Norman history. (Plunkett)

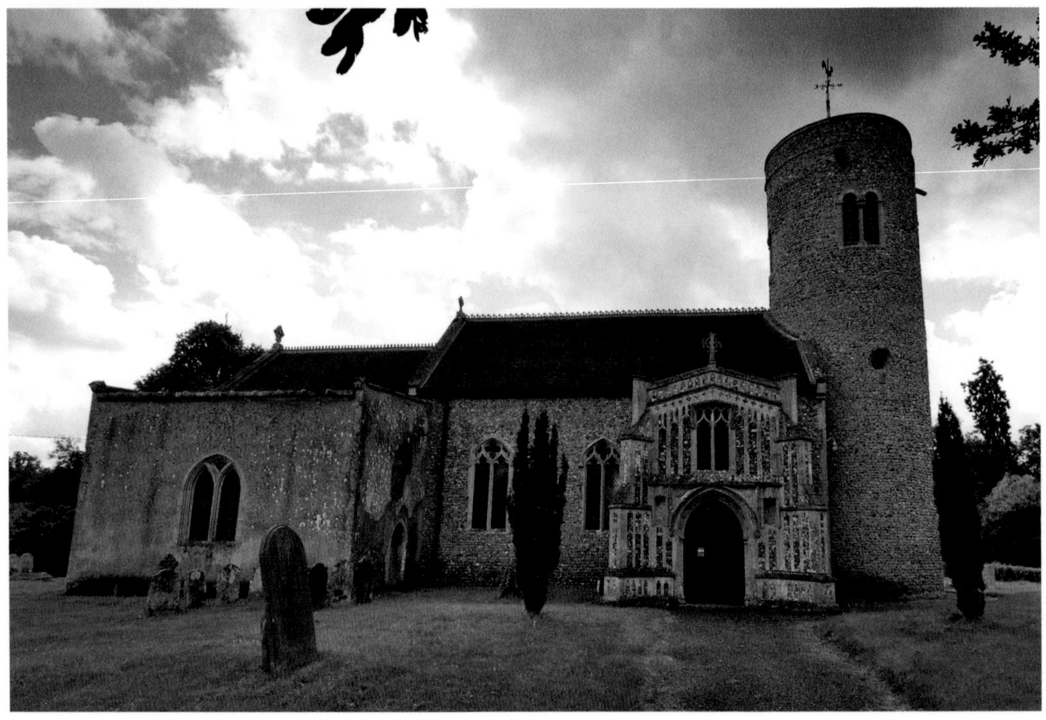

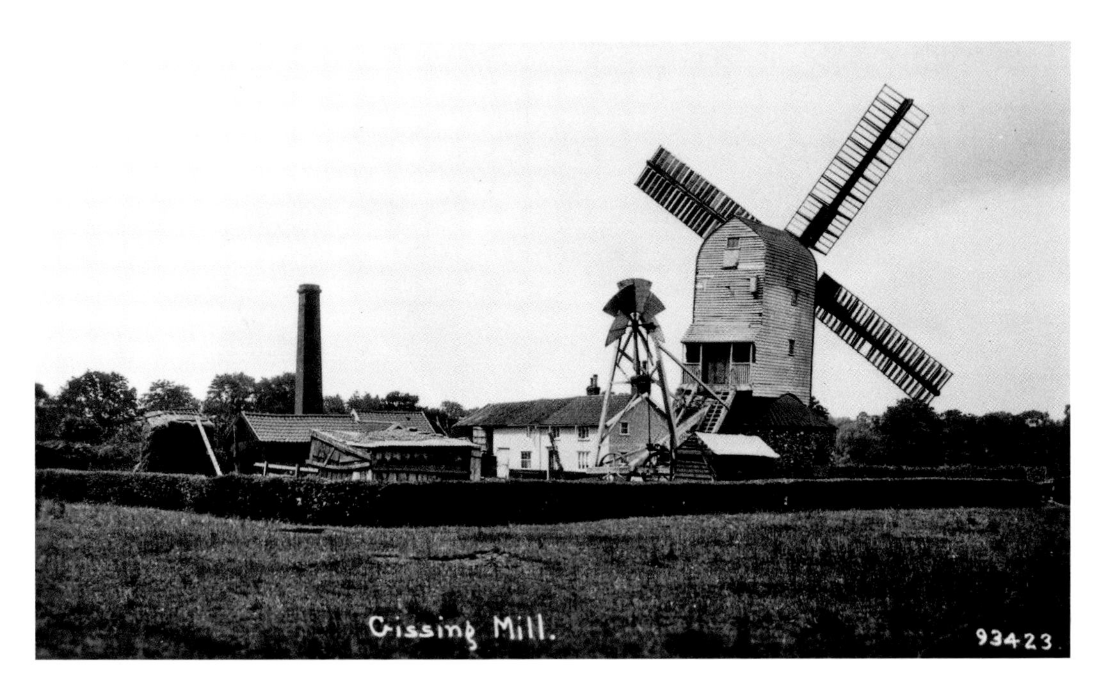

Power of the Wind

The older image of this pair depicts Gissing Mill as it was around 1915. The mill (or a predecessor) was probably originally built in the early 1800s. It operated until 1926. In 1949, much of the mill was demolished and the site is now occupied by the Old Mill House and Millfield. There were once windmills all over this part of Norfolk, including several in Diss and others in Roydon and Burston. (Untraced; part of image collection donated to NCC)

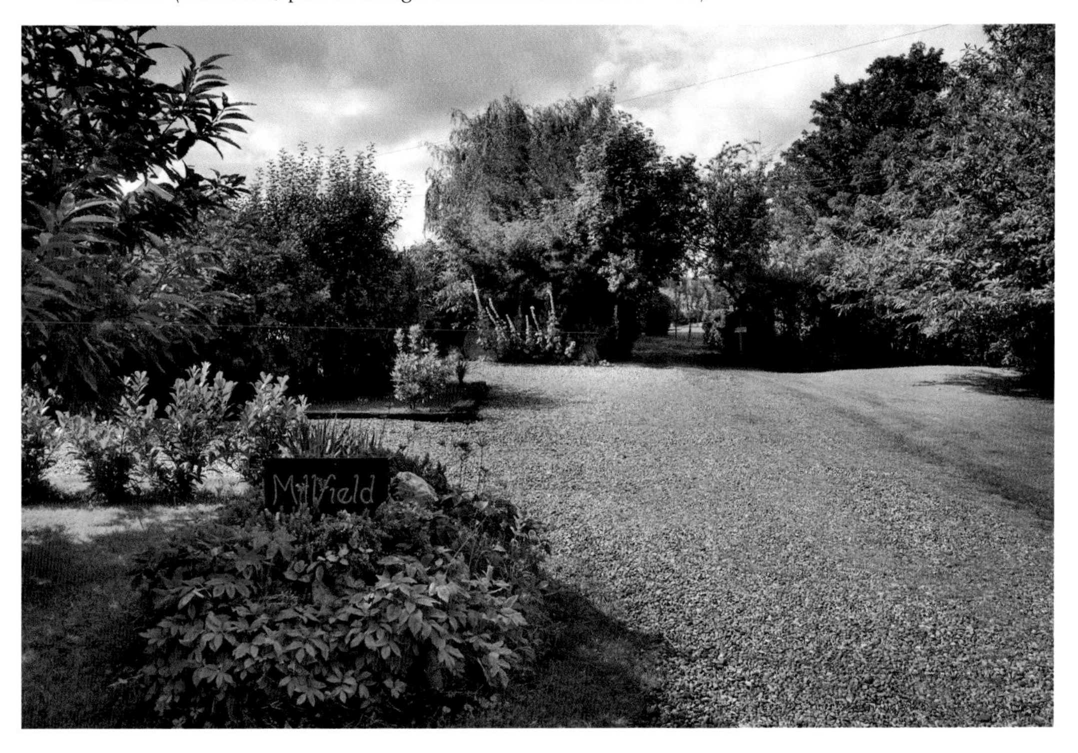

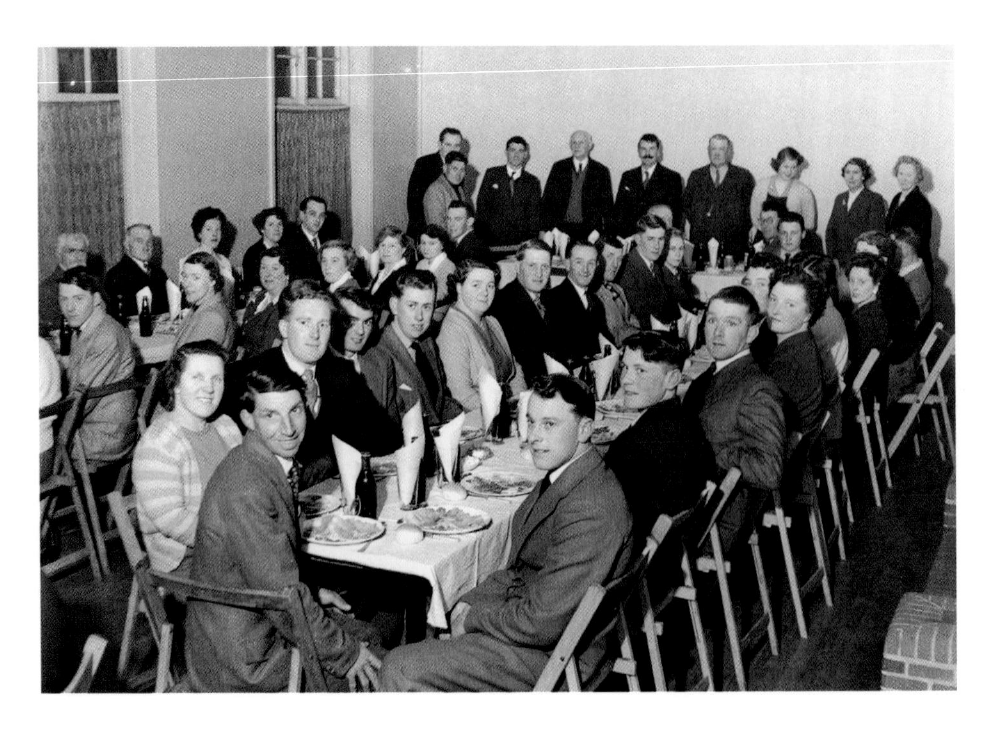

Sport and Leisure

This is the last shot I took for this book. My friends and I celebrated with a pint of local ale at the Gissing Crown. The older picture of Gissing Cricket Club dinner, in 1956, shows a whole different generation enjoying a bottle of ale. As in so many villages, the Crown is the only surviving pub here – the Chequers closed in 1968 and the Three Horse Shoes in 1961. The older part of the building has probably been here since at least the early 1700s (only the extension is dated 1925). (NCC)

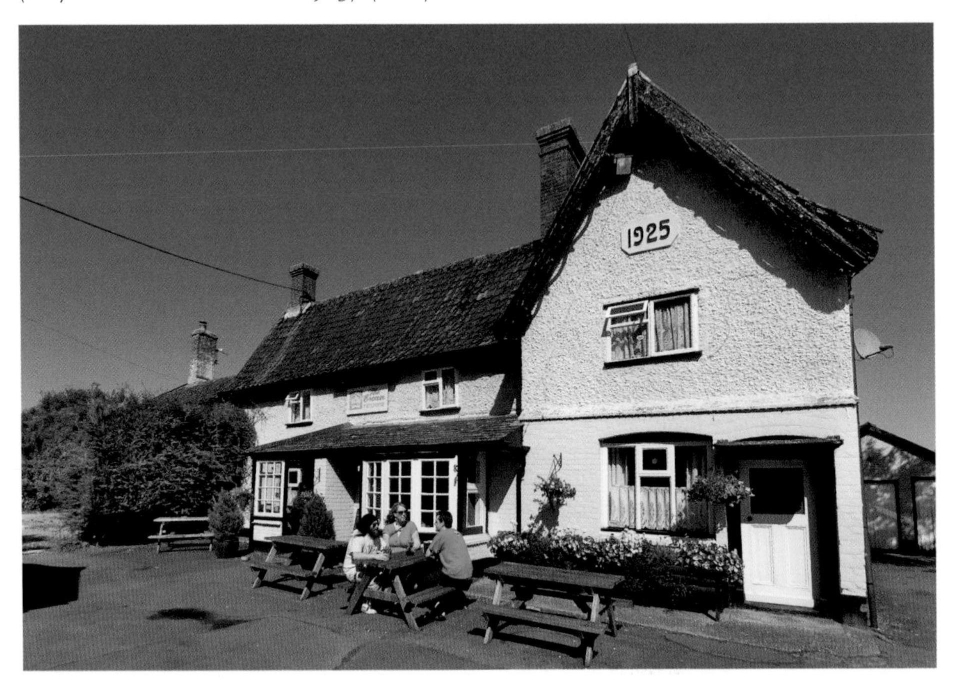

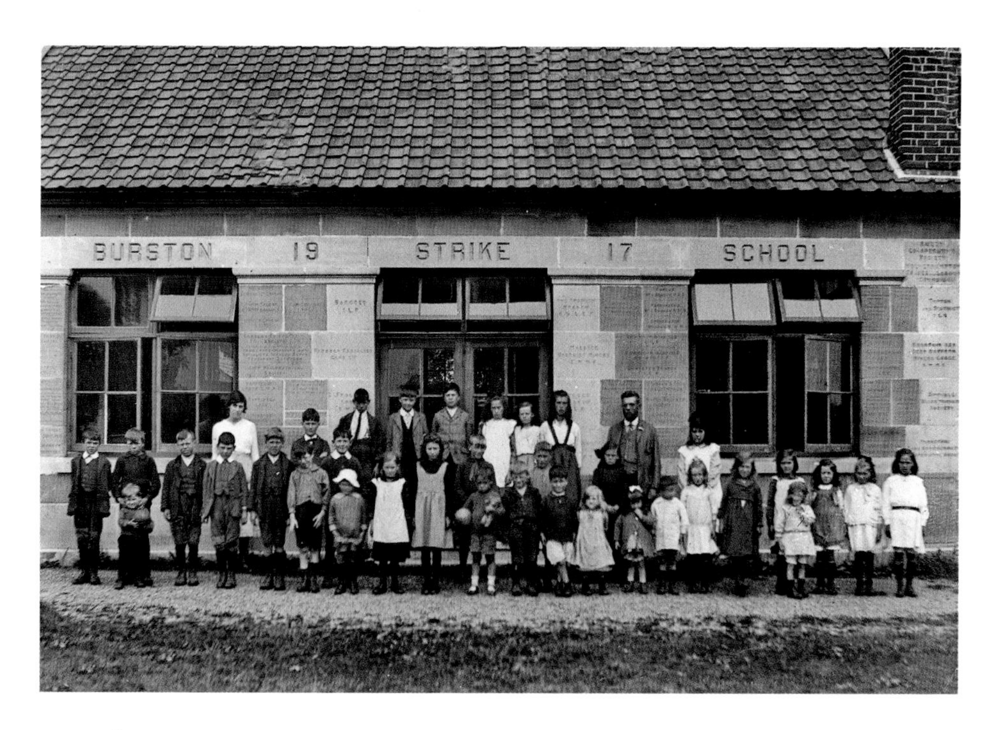

On Strike

The Burston Strike School, pictured here *c.* 1917, hardly needs a caption at all. Now a museum, the school was at the centre of the longest-running strike in British history (1914–39). When teachers Annie and Tom Higdon were sacked, the management team, schoolchildren and families went on strike to support them. They set up an alternative school on the village green, where a permanent building opened on 13 May 1917, funded by donations. Since 1984, an annual rally has been held on the first Sunday in September, attended in 2012 by over 1,000 people. (NCC)

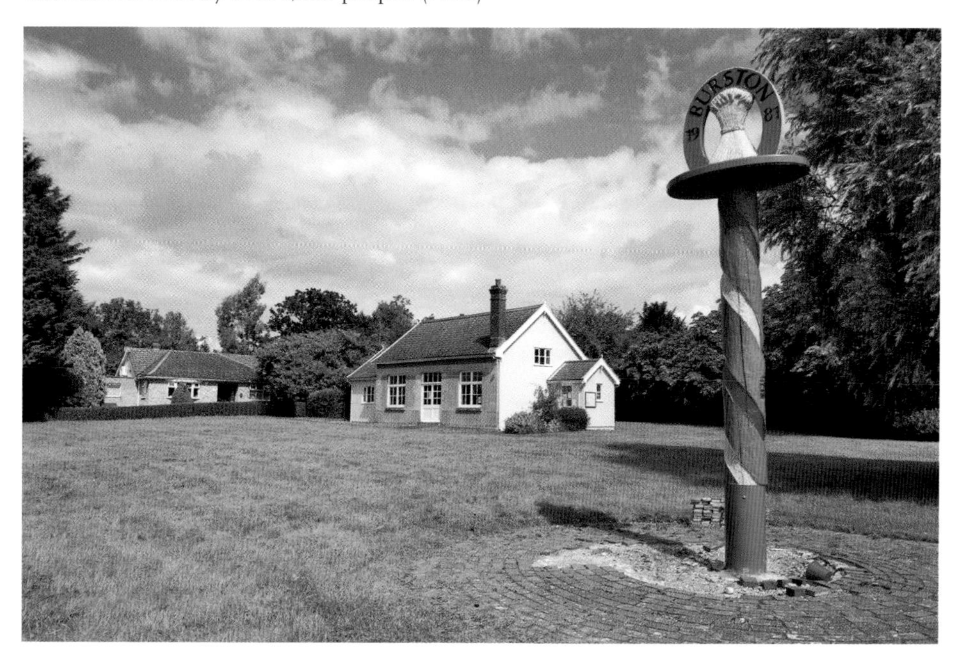

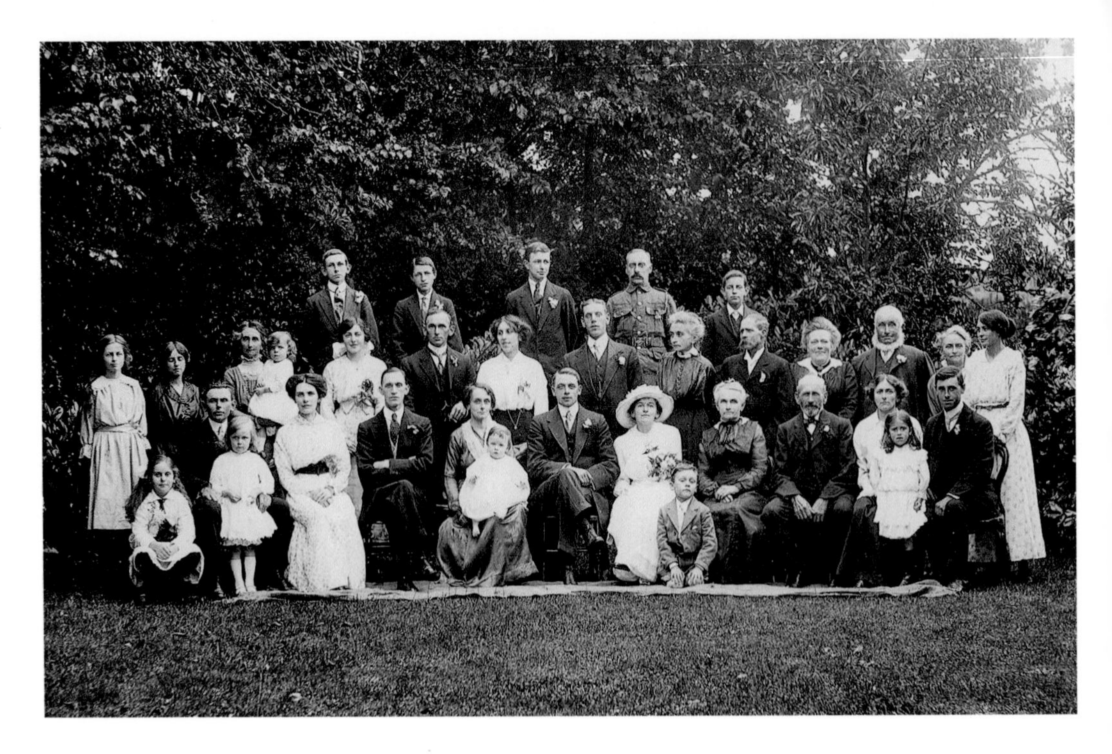

Wedding Bells

On 4 August 1915 at St Mary's church, Burston, Frank Elliott married Olive Grace King Fisher (centre, front row). The groom came from Warwickshire but the bride was a native of Burston, her father, Charles Edward King Fisher, having farmed in the parish for over seventy years by the time he died in 1935. Charles and his wife Elizabeth Ann Norman, pictured to the right of the bride and groom, were also married at Burston church, on 18 October 1876. The church as it looks today is pictured below. (With thanks to the Bolster family)

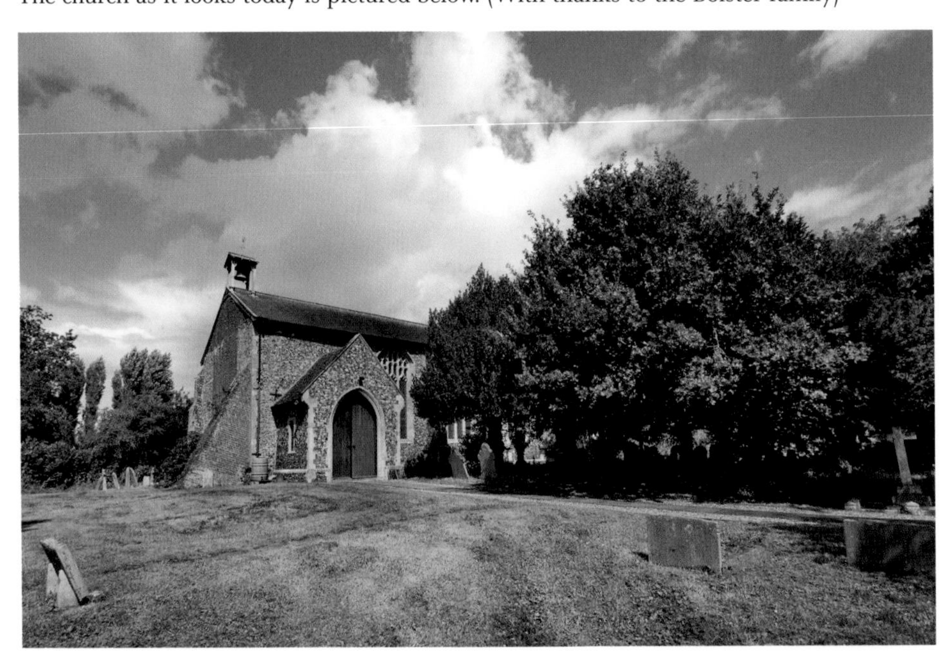

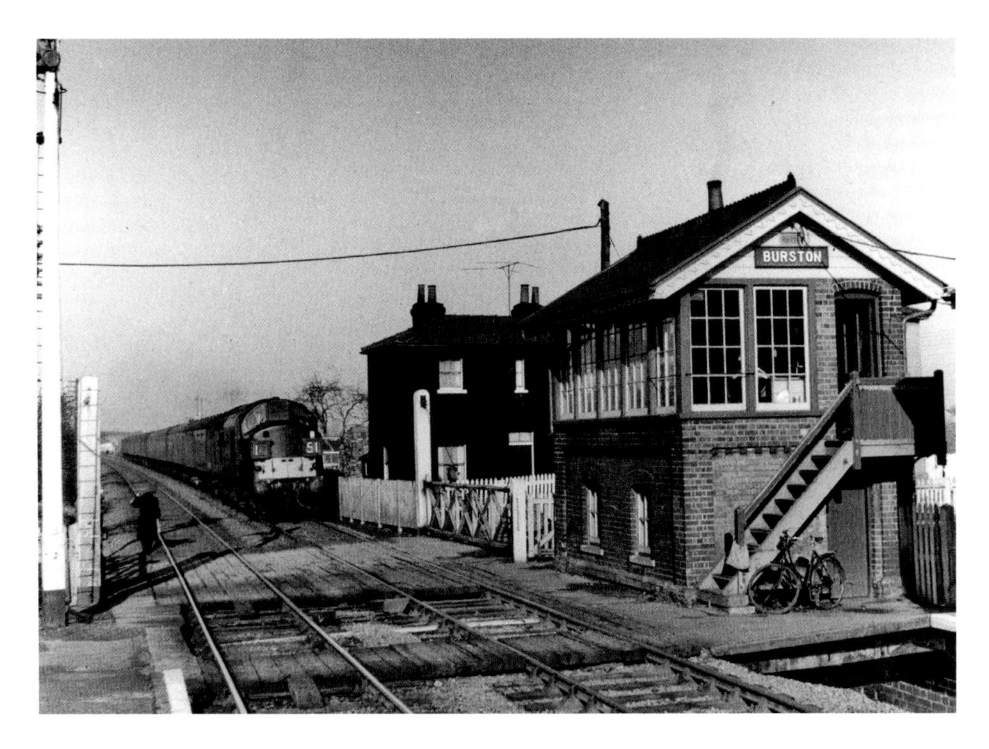

Oh, Mr Beeching

Burston station opened in 1849. For a while it was the terminus of the line that would one day reach all the way to Norwich from London. Like many other Norfolk stations, it was closed in 1966 following the Beeching Report. The images here show that much evidence of the station has now gone. Although the railway line still passes through, the cottage and signal box have disappeared. The house in the new image is just visible behind the signal box in the older image. (Untraced; part of image collection donated to NCC)

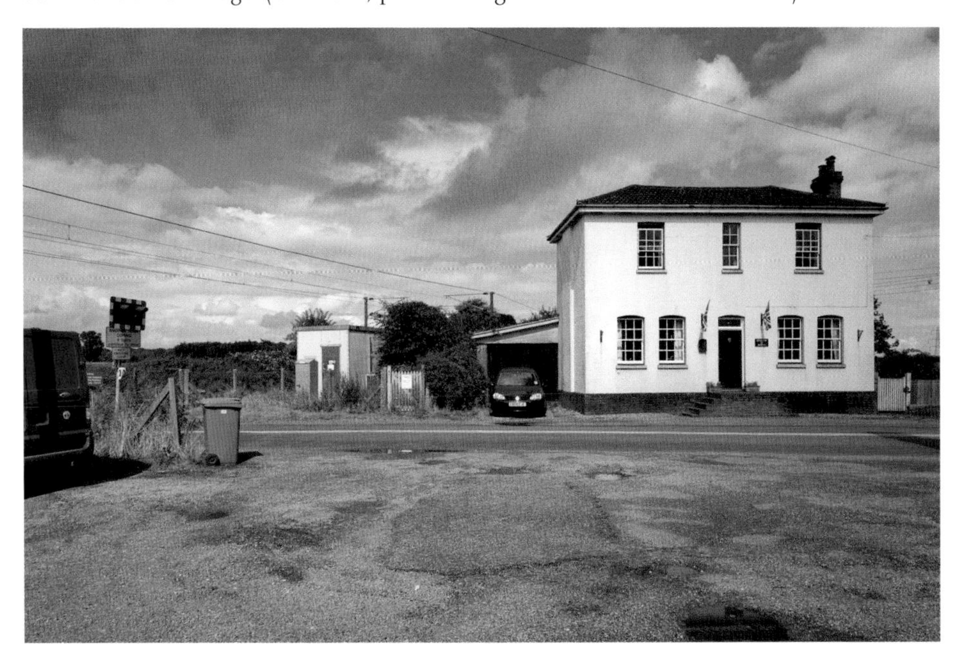

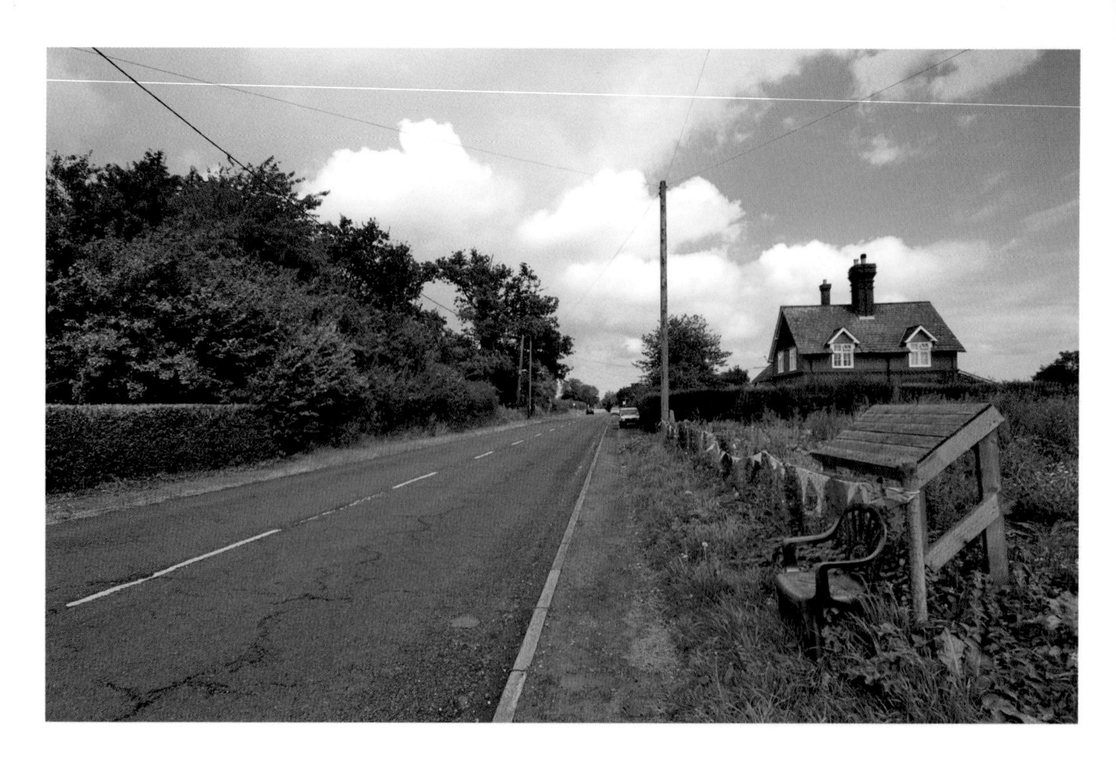

Rural Schooling

The small village of Thelveton (or Thelton) was recorded as having 160 inhabitants in 1864. The school was similarly small, built for fifty children, and had an average attendance of thirty-eight in 1904. At the time, the children were under the tutelage of Mrs Jane Rose, mistress. Deposited records for the school end in 1963 and the building is now a private house. The view down Norwich Road to the old school today, besides power lines, has probably changed little over time. (Untraced; part of image collection donated to NCC)

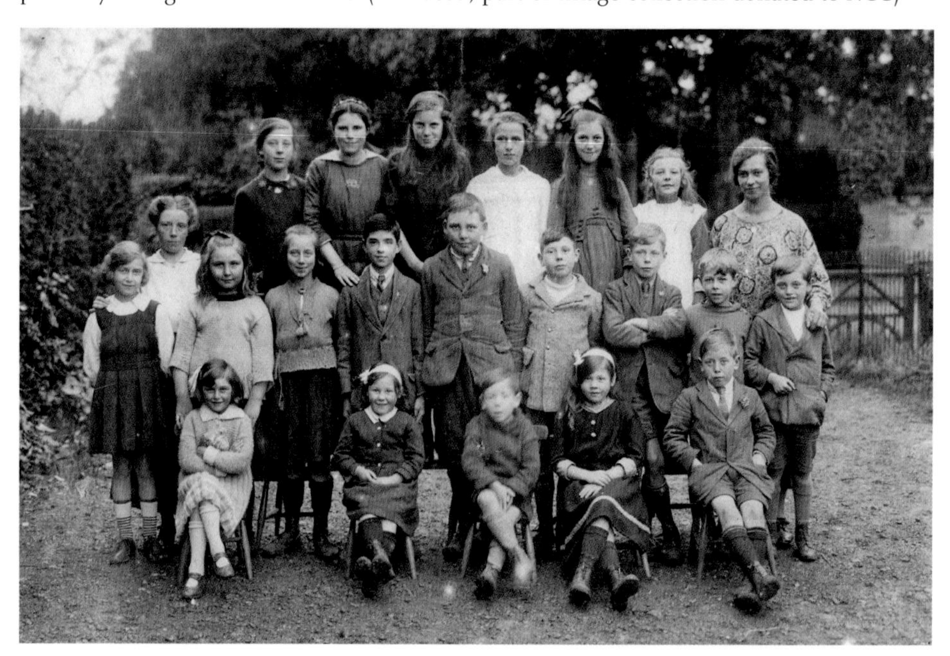

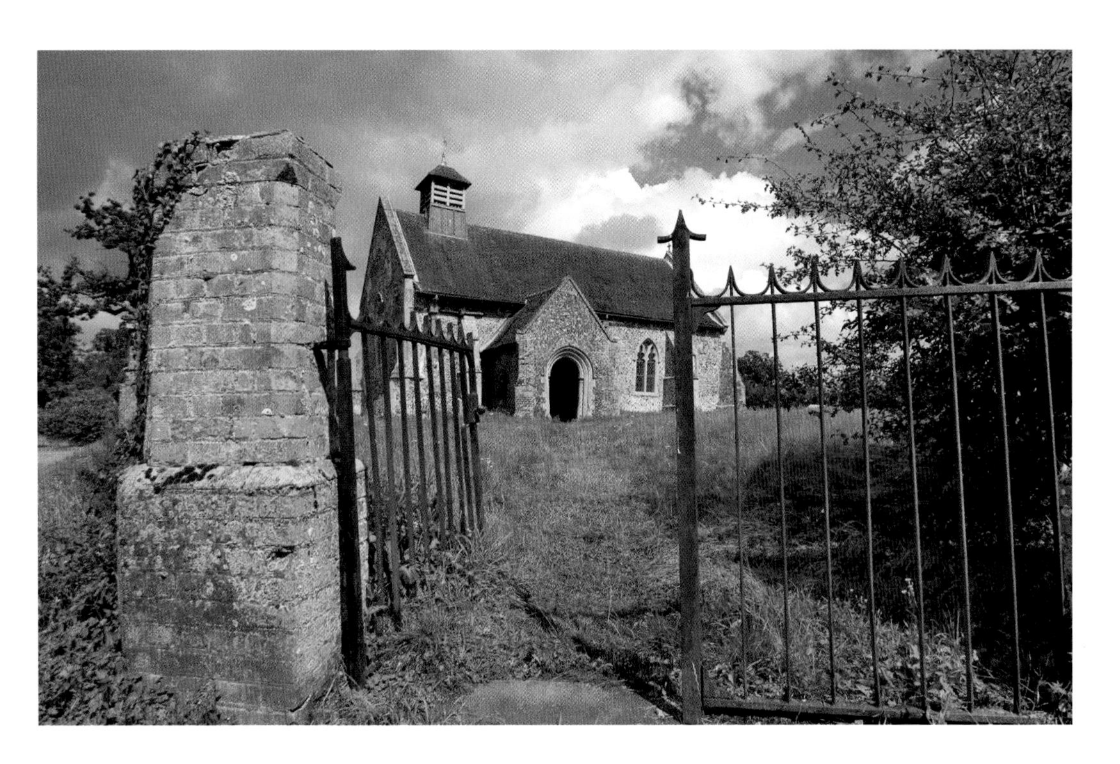

Frenze

This very pretty church (St Andrew's) is tucked away beyond the corner of a farmyard next to Frenze Hall. The painting below has a date of 1845 and appears in one of the beautiful grangerised (extended with images) Blomefield volumes in the local studies collection at Norfolk Heritage Centre. By 1851, the religious census already showed a tiny congregation and the church is now in the care of the Churches Conservation Trust. Special services are still held here now and then, though. (NCC)

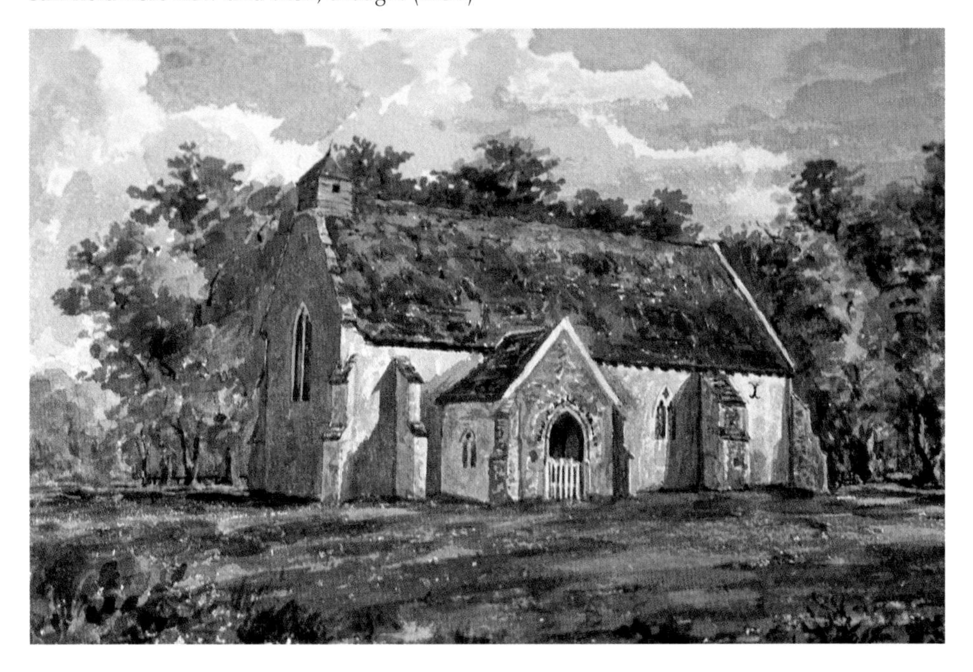

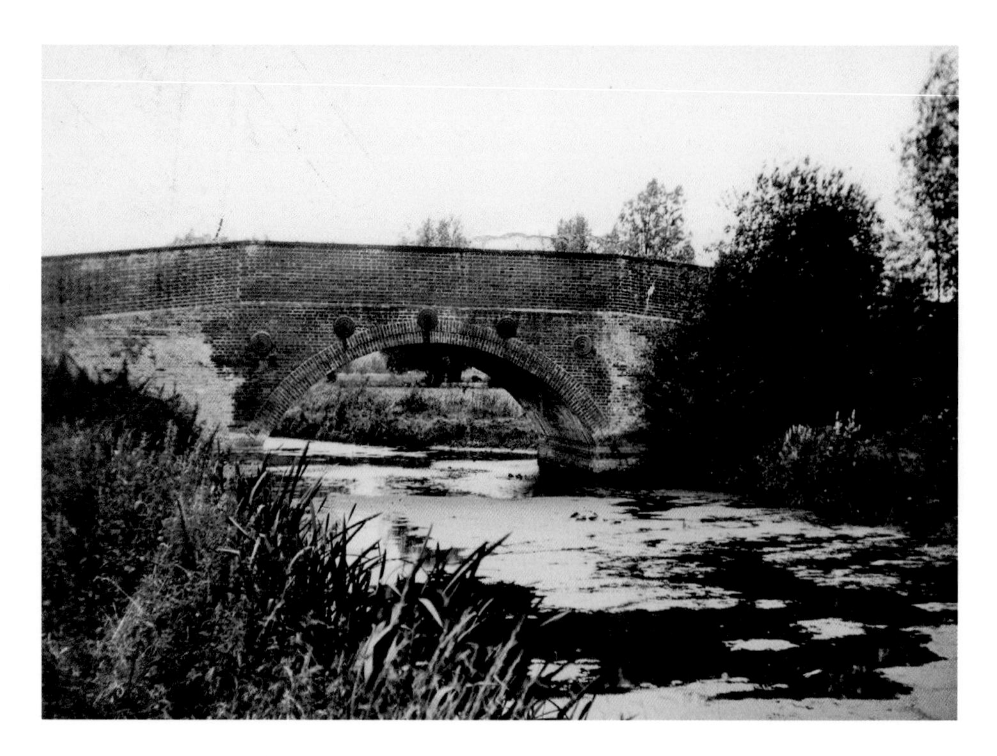

Water, Water Everywhere

Water is a common theme in this part of the world. The Waveney Valley area is understandably popular with walkers of all ages due to the wonderful scenery and close links to the Angles Way long-distance footpath. Where there is water there are bridges, and Scole is no exception. Here we see two bridges, the newer one accessed from the now-closed south end of Bridge Road. Before the days of the A140, this took traffic south over Scole Bridge and into Suffolk. (Untraced; part of image collection donated to NCC)

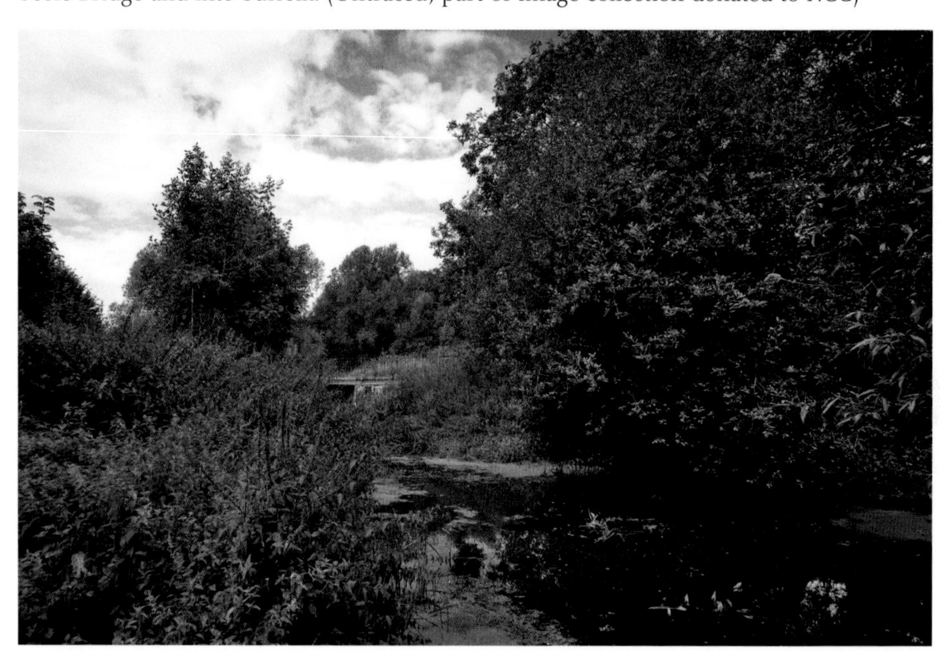

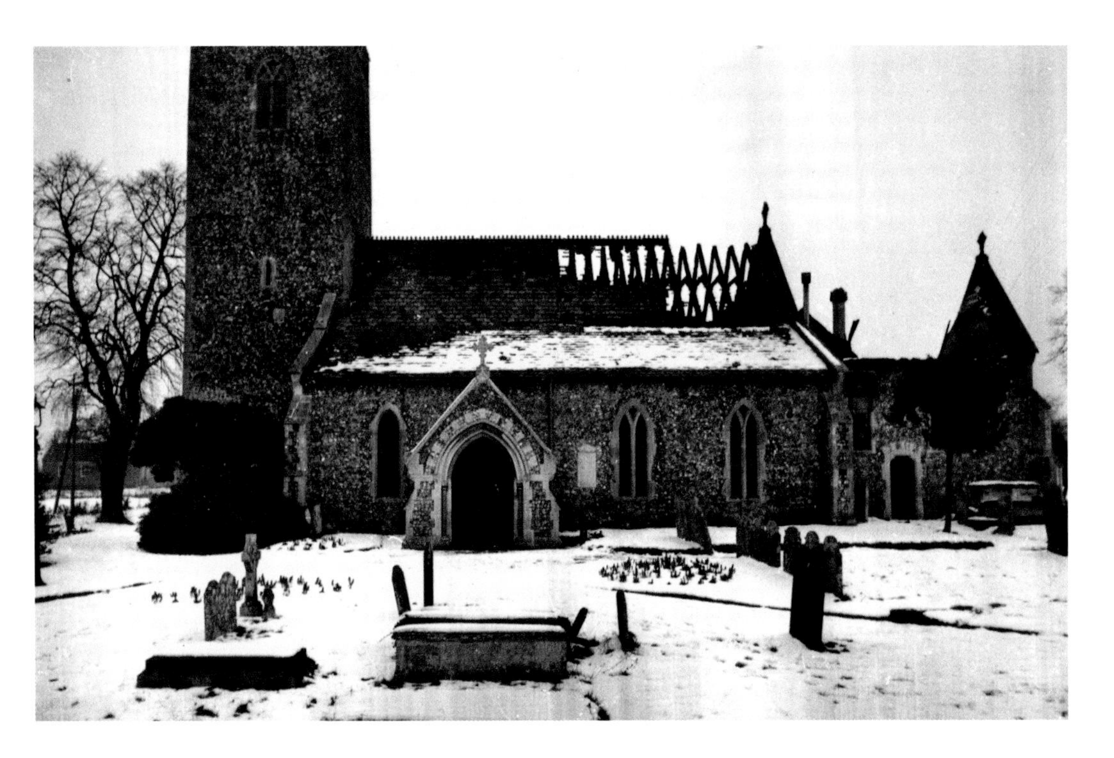

Phoenix from the Flames
Another St Andrew's church can be found in Scole. A familiar sight to commuters between Ipswich and Norwich, in 1963 an enormous amount of damage was done by a terrible fire, the aftermath of which is shown in these two older images. The subsequent refurbishment included a new East Window which floods the restored church with light. Despite the fire, some older features remain – even graffiti left behind by worshippers, perhaps from as long ago as the 1600s. (Courtesy of Fielden and Mason)

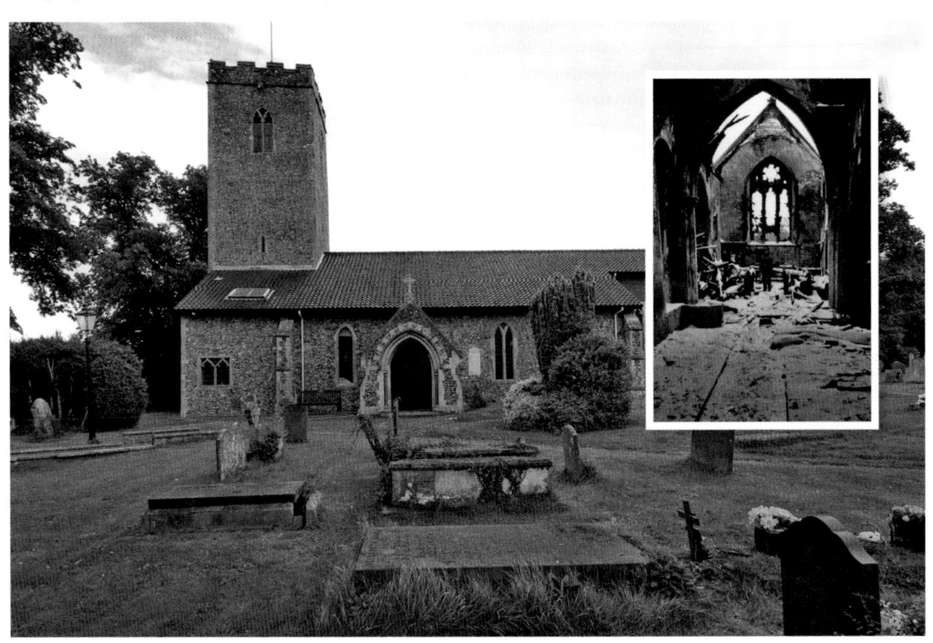

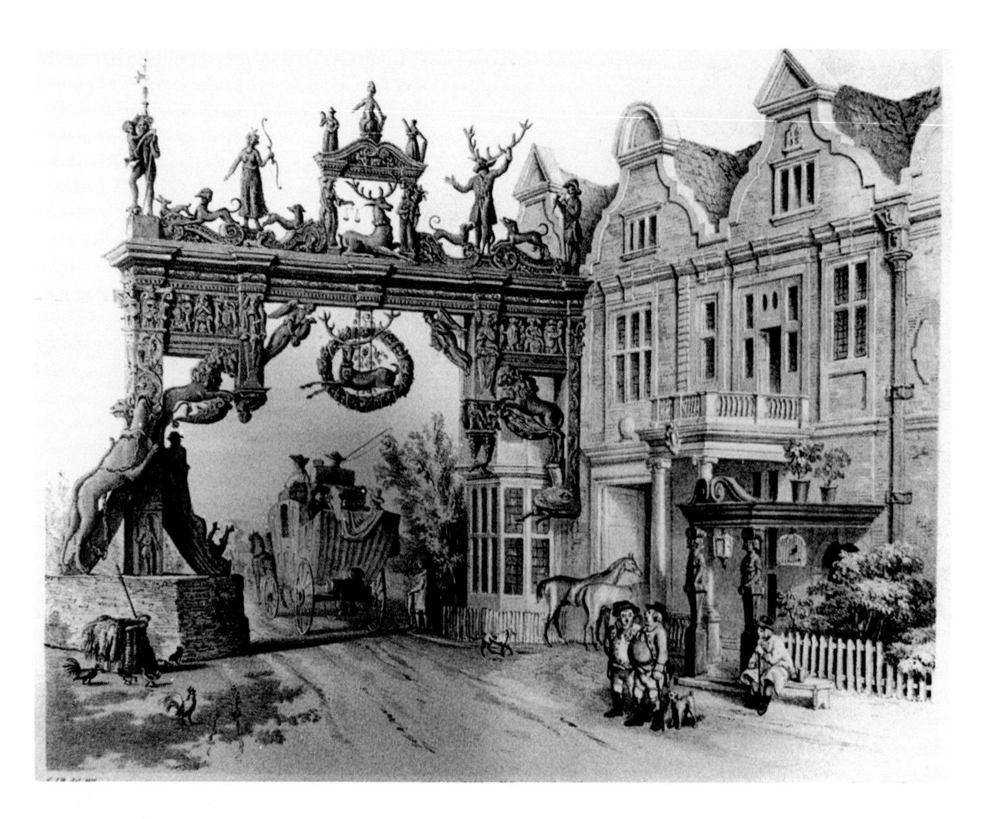

London to Norwich

The impressive form of the White Hart (or Scole Inn) has long been a feature of the old road to Norwich. This print shows the inn as it was when an elaborate sign extended across the road here. Built around 1655 for John Peck, a Norwich wool merchant, the sumptuous building inspired others in surrounding villages and once received up to forty mail coaches a day on the way from London to Norwich. Once a busy route, the village has now been bypassed by the A140. (NCC prints collection; Picture Norfolk)

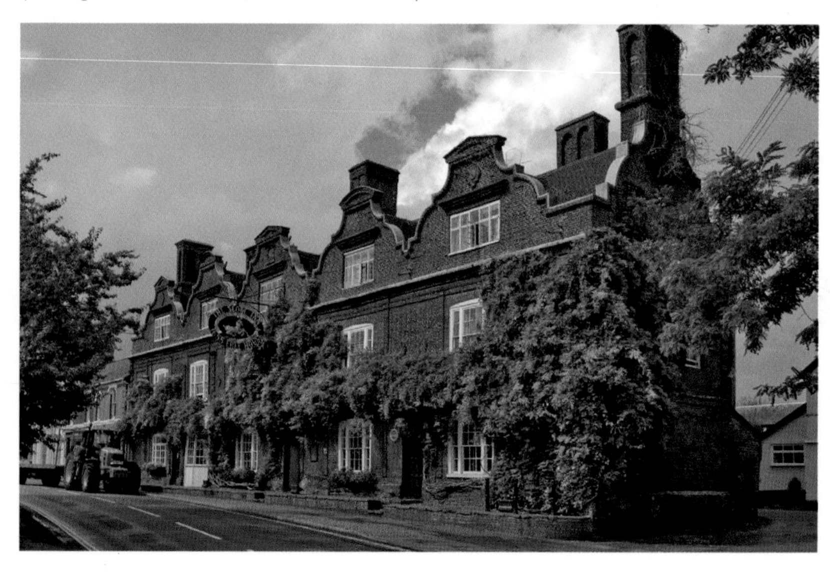

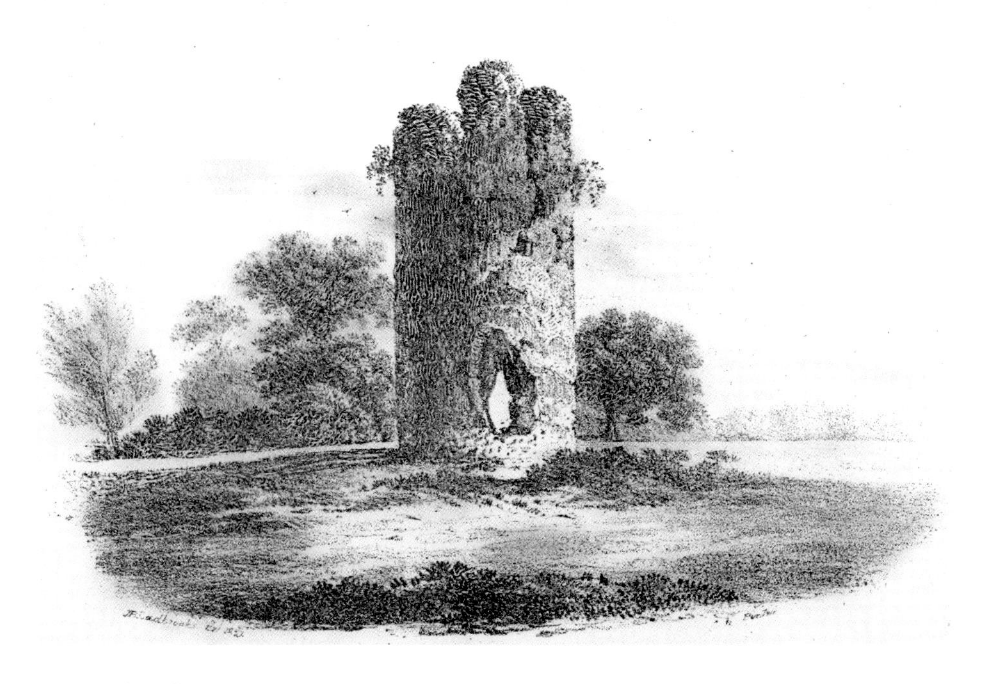

A Lost Church

The church of St Mary the Virgin in Thorpe Parva (or Little Thorp) was, even in Blomefield's time, 'quite demolished', having possibly been abandoned during the reign of Elizabeth I. The ruin has changed little since Plunkett's image of 1965, but was more substantial when Robert Ladbrooke drew it in the late 1700s or early 1800s. Nearby Scole was recorded as Osmondeston in the Domesday Book, suggesting a derivation from 'Osmond's enclosure' or 'Osmond's farm'. (NCC, Plunkett)

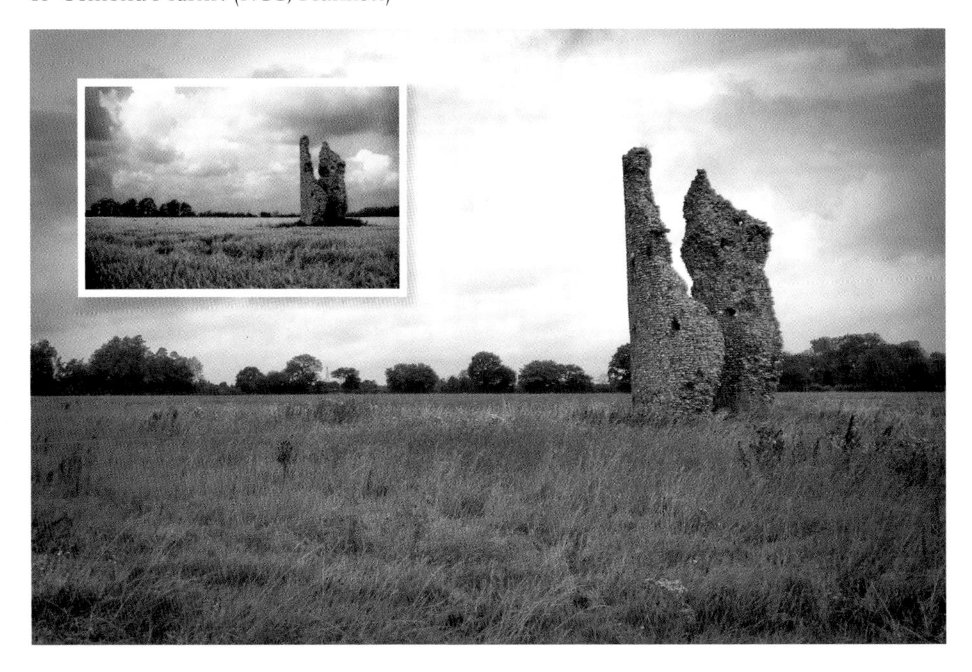

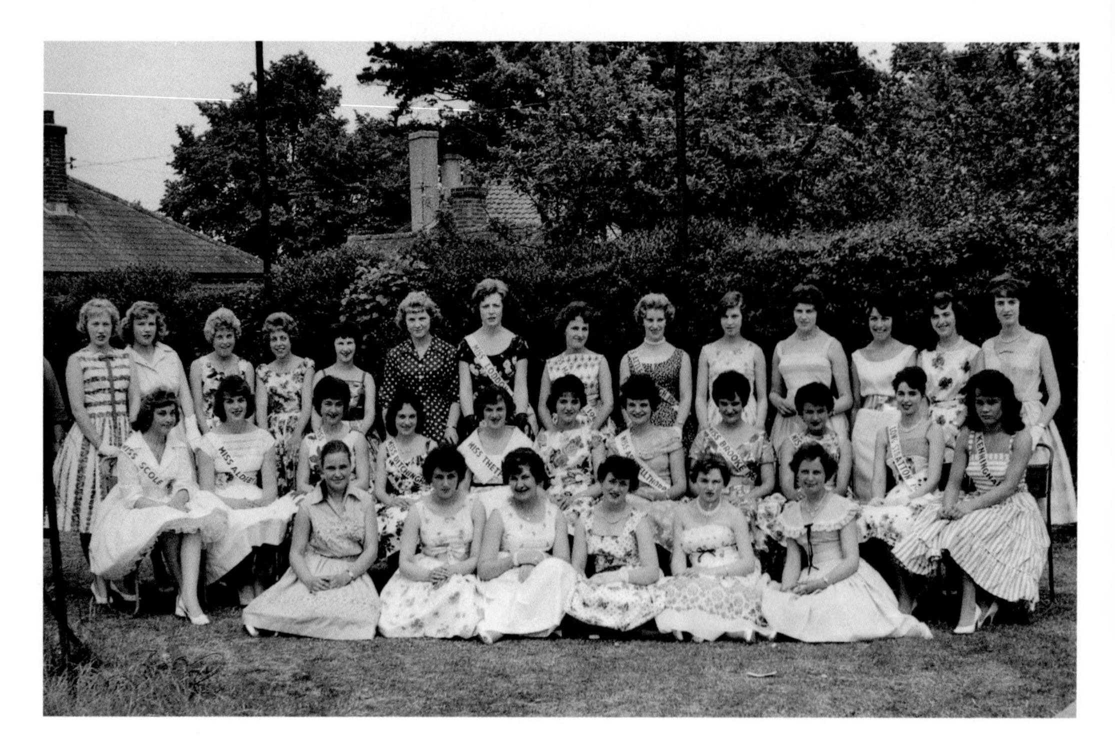

Miss Scole and Friends

Finishing with a fabulous image of the county's women, here we see a photograph taken during the heyday of beauty contests in the 1950s and 1960s, Norfolk being no exception to the rise in their popularity after the Second World War. Look closely at this image and you can see 'Miss Scole' on the far left of the middle row, as well as representatives from other local villages. The inset showing a view of Scole village was taken at a similar time, and the new image shows that the view has changed little today. (NCC)

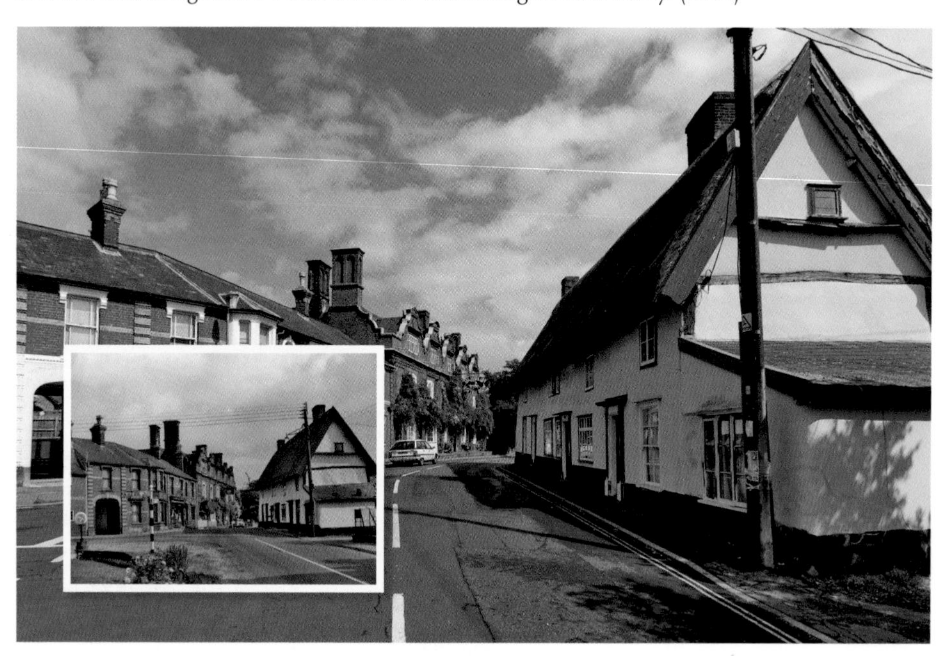